William Cowper, William Benham

**Letters**

William Cowper, William Benham

**Letters**

ISBN/EAN: 9783337105617

Printed in Europe, USA, Canada, Australia, Japan

Cover: Foto ©ninafisch / pixelio.de

More available books at **www.hansebooks.com**

# LETTERS

OF

# WILLIAM COWPER

EDITED, WITH INTRODUCTION, BY THE

REV. W. BENHAM, B.D., F.S.A.,
RECTOR OF ST. EDMUND THE KING, LOMBARD STREET

London
MACMILLAN AND CO.
1884

# TABLE OF CONTENTS.

|  |  | PAGE |
|---|---|---|
| Introduction | | xi |

### LETTERS FROM LONDON.

| 1762. | To Clotworthy Rowley | *Sept.* 2 | 1 |
| 1763. | To Lady Hesketh. | *Aug.* 9 | 3 |

### LETTERS FROM HUNTINGDON.

| 1765. | To Joseph Hill | *June* 24 | 5 |
| ,, | To Lady Hesketh. | *July* 1 | 6 |
| ,, | To the Same. | *July* 4 | 7 |
| ,, | To the Same. | *Sept.* 14 | 9 |
| ,, | To Joseph Hill | *July* 3 | 11 |
| ,, | To the Same. | *Aug.* 14 | 13 |
| ,, | To the Same. | *Oct.* 25 | 14 |
| 1766. | To Mrs. Cowper | *Oct.* 20 | 15 |
| 1767. | To Joseph Hill | *May* 14 | 17 |
| ,, | To the Same. | *July* 16 | 18 |

### LETTERS FROM OLNEY.

| 1767. | To Joseph Hill | *Oct.* 10 | 20 |
| 1769. | To Mrs. Cowper | *Aug.* 31 | 21 |
| 1770. | To Mrs. Madan | *March* 24 | 22 |
| ,, | To Joseph Hill | *Sept.* 25 | 23 |
| 1776. | To the Same. | *Nov.* 12 | 24 |

## TABLE OF CONTENTS.

| | | | PAGE |
|---|---|---|---|
| 1778. To the Rev. W. Unwin | . . . | July 18 | 25 |
| 1779. To the Same . . . | . . . | May 26 | 26 |
| ,, To the Same . . . | . . . | July | 27 |
| ,, To the Same . . . | . . . | July 17 | 29 |
| ,, To the Same . . . | . . . | Sept. 21 | 31 |
| ,, To Joseph Hill . | . . . | Oct. 2 | 32 |
| ,, To the Rev. W. Unwin | . . . | Oct. 31 | 33 |
| 1780. To the Same . . . | . . . | Feb. 27 | 35 |
| ,, To the Rev. J. Newton | . . . | May 3 | 37 |
| ,, To the Rev. W. Unwin | . . . | July 27 | 39 |
| ,, To the Rev. J. Newton | . . . | Aug. 21 | 40 |
| 1781. To the Same . . . | . . . | Jan. 21 | 42 |
| ,, To the Rev. W. Unwin | . . . | Feb. 6 | 43 |
| ,, To Joseph Hill . | . . . | Feb. 3 | 46 |
| ,, To the Rev. J. Newton | . . . | Feb. 18 | 47 |
| ,, To the Rev. W. Unwin | . . . | Feb. 27 | 48 |
| ,, To the Same . . . | . . . | May 1 | 50 |
| ,, To Joseph Hill . | . . . | May 9 | 52 |
| ,, To the Rev. W. Unwin | . . . | May 10 | 53 |
| ,, To the Same . . . | . . . | May 23 | 55 |
| ,, To the Rev. J. Newton | . . . | July 12 | 59 |
| ,, To the Same . . . | . . . | Aug. 16 | 61 |
| ,, To the Same . . . | . . . | Aug. 21 | 63 |
| ,, To the Same . . . | . . . | Sept. 9 | 66 |
| ,, To the Same . . . | . . . | Sept. 18 | 68 |
| ,, To the Same . . . | . . . | Nov. 7 | 70 |
| ,, To Joseph Hill . | . . . | Nov. 30 | 72 |
| 1782. To the Rev. W. Unwin | . . . | Jan. 5 | 72 |
| ,, To the Same . . . | . . . | April 1 | 75 |
| ,, To the Same . . . | . . . | Aug. 3 | 76 |
| ,, To Mrs. Newton . | . . . | Nov. 23 | 79 |
| ,, To Joseph Hill . | . . . | Dec. 7 | 82 |
| 1783. To the Rev. J. Newton | . . . | Jan. 26 | 83 |
| ,, To the Rev. W. Unwin | . . . | May 12 | 85 |
| ,, To the Rev. William Bull | . . . | June 3 | 87 |
| ,, To the Rev. W. Unwin | . . . | June 8 | 88 |
| ,, To the Same . . . | . . . | Aug. 4 | 90 |
| ,, To the Same . . . | . . . | | 93 |
| ,, To the Rev. J. Newton | . . . | Nov. 30 | 95 |
| 1784. To the Rev. W. Unwin | . . . | March 21 | 98 |
| ,, To the Rev. J. Newton | . . . | March 29 | 100 |
| ,, To the Same . . . | . . . | April 26 | 103 |
| ,, To the Rev. W. Unwin | . . . | July 3 | 106 |

## TABLE OF CONTENTS.

|  |  |  | PAGE |
|---|---|---|---|
| 1784. | To the Rev. J. Newton | Sept. 18 | 108 |
| ,, | To the Rev. W. Unwin | Oct. 20 | 110 |
| ,, | To the Same | Nov. 1 | 113 |
| ,, | To the Rev. J. Newton | Nov. 27 | 115 |
| ,, | To the Same | Dec. 13 | 117 |
| ,, | To Mr. Johnson (Printer) |  | 120 |
| ,, | To the Rev. W. Unwin | Dec. 18 | 121 |
| 1785. | To the Same | April 30 | 123 |
| ,, | To the Rev. J. Newton | Sept. 24 | 126 |
| ,, | To Lady Hesketh | Oct. 12 | 130 |
| ,, | To the Same | Nov. 9 | 132 |
| 1786. | To the Same | Feb. 9 | 136 |
| ,, | To the Same | April 10 | 138 |
| ,, | To the Rev. J. Newton | May 20 | 144 |
| ,, | To Lady Hesketh | May 25 | 147 |
| ,, | To the Same | May 29 | 150 |
| ,, | To Joseph Hill | June 9 | 152 |
| ,, | To Lady Hesketh | June 12 | 153 |
| ,, | To the Rev. W. Unwin |  | 159 |
| ,, | To the Same | Sept. 24 | 161 |

### LETTERS FROM WESTON UNDERWOOD.

|  |  |  |  |
|---|---|---|---|
| 1786. | To Lady Hesketh | Nov. 26 | 164 |
| ,, | To the Same | Dec. 4 | 166 |
| ,, | To Joseph Hill | Dec. 9 | 168 |
| ,, | To Lady Hesketh | Dec. 11 | 168 |
| ,, | To the Same | Dec. 21 | 172 |
| ,, | To the Same | Dec. 24 | 173 |
| 1787. | To Samuel Rose | July 24 | 177 |
| ,, | To Lady Hesketh | Sept. 15 | 178 |
| ,, | To the Same | Oct. 5 | 178 |
| ,, | To the Same | Nov. 27 | 181 |
| ,, | To the Rev. W. Bagot | Dec. 6 | 183 |
| ,, | To Lady Hesketh | Dec. 10 | 185 |
| ,, | To the Same | Dec. 19 | 186 |
| 1788. | To the Same | Feb. 7 | 189 |
| ,, | To the Same | March 3 | 192 |
| ,, | To the Same | July 28 | 194 |
| ,, | To Mrs. King | Aug. 28 | 196 |
| ,, | To the Same | Oct. 11 | 198 |
| ,, | To the Rev. W. Bagot | Oct. 30 | 200 |

## TABLE OF CONTENTS.

| | | | PAGE |
|---|---|---|---|
| 1789. | To Samuel Rose | Jan. 19 | 202 |
| ,, | To the Same | Jan. 24 | 203 |
| ,, | To the Rev. W. Bagot | Jan. 29 | 203 |
| ,, | To Samuel Rose | June 5 | 204 |
| ,, | To Mrs. Throckmorton | July 18 | 205 |
| ,, | To Samuel Rose | Aug. 8 | 206 |
| ,, | To Joseph Hill | Aug. 12 | 207 |
| 1790. | To Mrs. Bodham | Feb. 27 | 208 |
| ,, | To John Johnson | Feb. 28 | 210 |
| ,, | To Lady Hesketh | March 22 | 212 |
| ,, | To John Johnson | March 23 | 214 |
| ,, | To the Same | April 17 | 216 |
| ,, | To Mrs. Throckmorton | May 10 | 217 |
| ,, | To Lady Hesketh | May 28 | 219 |
| ,, | To the Same | June 3 | 219 |
| ,, | To the Rev. W. Bagot | June 22 | 220 |
| ,, | To John Johnson | July 31 | 220 |
| ,, | To Mrs. Bodham | Sept. 9 | 222 |
| ,, | To Samuel Rose | Sept. 13 | 223 |
| ,, | To Joseph Hill | Sept. 17 | 224 |
| 1791. | To John Johnson | Jan. 21 | 225 |
| ,, | To the Same | Feb. 27 | 226 |
| ,, | To the Rev. Mr. Hurdis | March 6 | 227 |
| ,, | To Joseph Hill | March 10 | 228 |
| ,, | To the Rev. W. Bagot | March 18 | 229 |
| ,, | To Mrs. Throckmorton | April 1 | 231 |
| ,, | To the Rev. Mr. Buchanan | May 11 | 231 |
| ,, | To John Johnson | June 1 | 232 |
| ,, | To Lady Hesketh | June 23 | 232 |
| ,, | To the Same | July 11 | 234 |
| ,, | To the Rev. William Bull | July 27 | 237 |
| ,, | To John Johnson | Aug. 9 | 238 |
| ,, | To Lady Hesketh | Aug. 30 | 238 |
| ,, | To Samuel Rose | Sept. 14 | 241 |
| ,, | To Mrs. King | Oct. 21 | 242 |
| ,, | To Joseph Hill | Nov. 14 | 243 |
| ,, | To Samuel Rose | Dec. 21 | 244 |
| 1792. | To the Rev. J. Newton | Feb. 20 | 245 |
| ,, | To John Johnson | March 11 | 247 |
| ,, | To the Rev. J. Newton | March 18 | 248 |
| ,, | To the Rev. Mr. Hurdis | March 23 | 251 |
| ,, | To Lady Hesketh | March 25 | 252 |
| ,, | To William Hayley | April 6 | 253 |

## TABLE OF CONTENTS.

| | | | PAGE |
|---|---|---|---|
| 1792. | To the Same . . . . . . | *June* 5 | 255 |
| ,, | To Lady Hesketh . . . . . | *June* 11 | 256 |
| ,, | To William Hayley . . . . | *June* 19 | 258 |
| ,, | To the Same . . . . . . | *July* 15 | 259 |
| ,, | To the Same . . . . . . | *July* 22 | 261 |
| ,, | To the Rev. William Bull . . . | *July* 25 | 262 |
| ,, | To William Hayley . . . . | *July* 29 | 264 |

### LETTERS FROM EARTHAM.

| | | | |
|---|---|---|---|
| 1792. | To the Rev. Mr. Greatheed . . . | *Aug.* 6 | 266 |
| ,, | To Mrs. Courtenay . . . . | *Aug.* 12 | 267 |
| ,, | To Lady Hesketh . . . . . | *Aug.* 26 | 269 |
| ,, | To the Rev. Mr. Hurdis . . . | *Aug.* 26 | 271 |
| ,, | To Lady Hesketh . . . . . | *Sept.* 9 | 272 |
| ,, | To Mrs. Courtenay . . . . | *Sept.* 10 | 274 |

### LETTERS FROM WESTON UNDERWOOD.

| | | | |
|---|---|---|---|
| 1792. | To William Hayley . . . . | *Sept.* 21 | 277 |
| ,, | To the Same . . . . . . | *Oct.* 2 | 278 |
| ,, | To John Johnson . . . . . | *Nov.* 5 | 280 |
| ,, | To Samuel Rose . . . . . | *Nov.* 9 | 281 |
| ,, | To the Rev. J. Newton . . . | *Nov.* 11 | 282 |
| ,, | To John Johnson . . . . . | *Nov.* 20 | 284 |
| ,, | To Lady Hesketh . . . . . | *Dec.* 1 | 285 |
| 1793. | To John Johnson . . . . . | *Jan.* 31 | 288 |
| ,, | To Lady Hesketh . . . . . | *Feb.* 10 | 289 |
| ,, | To the Rev. Mr. Hurdis . . . | *Feb.* 23 | 290 |
| ,, | To the Rev. John Johnson . . . | *April* 11 | 291 |
| ,, | To the Rev. W. Bagot . . . | *May* 4 | 293 |
| ,, | To Thomas Park . . . . . | *May* 17 | 293 |
| ,, | To the Rev. J. Newton . . . | *June* 12 | 295 |
| ,, | To Thomas Park . . . . . | *July* 15 | 296 |
| ,, | To Mrs. Charlotte Smith . . . | *July* 25 | 298 |
| ,, | To the Rev. John Johnson . . . | *Aug.* 2 | 299 |
| ,, | To Mrs. Courtenay . . . . | *Aug.* 20 | 300 |
| ,, | To William Hayley . . . . | *Oct.* 5 | 301 |
| ,, | To Mrs. Courtenay . . . . | *Nov.* 4 | 302 |
| ,, | To Samuel Rose . . . . . | *Dec.* 8 | 304 |

## TABLE OF CONTENTS.

### LETTERS FROM NORFOLK.

|       |                                  |           | PAGE |
|-------|----------------------------------|-----------|------|
| 1795. | To the Rev. Mr. Buchanan         | *Sept.* 5 | 305  |
| ,,    | To Lady Hesketh, Cheltenham      |           | 306  |
| ,,    | To the Same, Cheltenham          | *Sept.* 26| 308  |
| 1796. | To the Same, at Bath             | *Jan.* 22 | 310  |
| ,.    | To the Same                      | *Feb.* 19 | 311  |
| 1797. | To the Same                      | *May* 15  | 312  |
| 1798. | To the Same                      | *June* 1  | 313  |
| ,,    | To the Rev. J. Newton            | *July* 29 | 313  |
| ,,    | To Lady Hesketh                  | *Oct.* 13 | 314  |
| 1799. | To the Rev. J. Newton            | *April* 11| 315  |

# INTRODUCTION.

Two men of mark in English Literature, Southey and Alexander Smith, have called Cowper "the best of English letter-writers," and few will be found to challenge this opinion.

The charm of Cowper's letters, like that of his poetry, lies first of all in his naturalness and sincerity. He writes simply because he has something to say, or because he loves his correspondent, and has no idea of posing for effect. He never dreamt of his letters being published when he wrote them. It was so with his first poems. He wrote to drive away melancholy, or to amuse his friends, and carelessly sent the last piece written to whatever friend he happened to be addressing, and was nearly fifty years old before the idea of publishing any of these pieces was suggested to him.

His letters, then, are the simple statement of whatever he has in his mind; written in pure and beautiful English; full of the information and refined taste of a well-read man; overflowing now with humour, now with deep religious feeling, for both were natural to him. It follows, as a matter of course, that they are deeply interesting as materials for the biography of the poet, though here one caution is needed. The letters will not unfrequently give us a wrong impression if we forget his peculiar circumstances. We may read one couched in terms of the deepest melancholy, and imagine that there was no sunshine in his life. That was not so. He set down on paper truly enough the sad thoughts of the moment, but he was also able, at all events for many years, to put such thoughts away by an effort, and to be quietly and tranquilly content and cheerful when the fit was over. His correspondence with Mr. Newton, for example, is nearly all of a gloomy character; not so that with his cousins, Lady Hesketh and John Johnson. I have elsewhere, I think, shown that Mr. Newton's influence upon his life, though incontestably well-intentioned, was most disastrous. Cowper always writes as though talking personally to whomsoever he is addressing, and the imaginary presence of Newton before him is sure to depress him at once, and to bring thunderclouds into his sky. And as years went on, Newton, with a perversity that angers one all the more because of his good intentions, seemed to take care that the gloom should not be dispelled, by writing from time to time to scold the poor, delicate-nerved, timid poet for seeking to cast away his cares.

But Cowper's letters are far more than contributions towards his biography. The graceful affectionateness, the shrewd estimate of men and things, the genuine love of fun and appreciation of it in others, all contribute to make his correspondence delightful. In fact, to many readers his prose will be more agreeable than his poetry, though, as in many like cases, his letters were only published because his poetry had made him famous.

Cowper's letters have been preserved from a date much earlier than that of his appearance before the world as a poet. His friends cherished them, feeling that there was a peculiar charm about them, and after his death in 1800 they were published in a piecemeal fashion by several rival editors, each of whom had some portions, and no one the whole. In consequence of which no edition to this day has all the letters complete, or in chronological sequence. Thus some of the most interesting of them were out of Southey's reach until he had finished his edition of the poet's life and works, and these he had therefore to place in a supplementary volume. This is not the only drawback to the multiform character of the editions. One of the editors, Grimshawe, took upon him to judge on religious grounds what portions of the letters were edifying and what not, and he has in consequence frequently cut out paragraphs, apparently only because they are amusing. Then again, not improperly, it was judged well to leave blanks in many cases for the names of people who were living at the time of publication. There is no such necessity now, and in the present selection I have collated the letters with the original manuscripts where they have been within my reach, and restored much which had been suppressed.

The arrangement followed is the simplest, namely, the chronological order. To the Globe Edition of his poems I have prefixed a full biography of Cowper, and therefore refer to that for the details; but for purposes of convenient reference, I have set down the main heads of the poet's life, and given short notices of the friends to whom letters are addressed.

I. He was born at Berkhamstead Rectory in 1731; educated first at a village school in Hertfordshire, then at Westminster; entered of the Middle Temple, 1748; called to the Bar, 1754; lived in London some years, holding a Commissionership worth £60 a year, and writing a few magazine papers; was appointed to a clerkship of the Journals of the House of Lords, but prevented from entering on the office by an attack of insanity, and was sent in December 1763 to Dr. Cotton's Asylum at St. Albans.

*Clotworthy Rowley,* of Tendring Hall, near Stoke-by-Nayland, was a friend and fellow-Templar. The two first of Cowper's extant letters are addressed to him. The first is in Latin; the second is given in the present volume. As in the case of so many of his friends, Cowper ceased all correspondence with him for many years. It was renewed through Rowley's returning some books which Cowper had lent him twenty-five years previously.

*Harriet, Lady Hesketh,* the wife of Sir Thomas Hesketh, was the daughter of Ashley Cowper, the poet's uncle, and the sister of Theodora, his youthful love. On his first leaving London he wrote several letters to Lady Hesketh, chiefly on religious subjects. The tone of them found no sympathy with her, and all correspondence between them ceased for twenty years. Then to the poet's overflowing delight she began it again (see pp. 9 and 130, and *Globe,* p. lix).

II. He remained at Dr. Cotton's until his recovery in June 1765, when he removed to Huntingdon, feeling that London was not a fitting place for him to live in, and desiring also to be within reach of his brother John at Cambridge. Here he began his acquaintance with the Unwin family, consisting of the Rev. Morley Unwin, Mary, his wife, and William and Mary, their children. They lived together at Huntingdon until Mr. Unwin was killed in 1767, then Cowper and Mrs. Unwin removed to Olney. The son took orders, and was soon appointed to a country living; the daughter married Mr. Powley of Dewsbury.

III. The third division of his life is that of his residence at Olney, lasting from Michaelmas 1767 until 1786. His first letters from Olney are some of the most delightful of all, amusing notes of what he has been reading, and accounts of his out-door occupations. They are addressed to Lady Hesketh, Hill, Mrs. Cowper, and Unwin.

*Joseph Hill* was a school-fellow at Westminster, "no otherwise known," says Southey, "than as having been Cowper's correspondent and constant friend through life, but this is to be well known." He proved one of the most valuable friends that the poet had, for he was a man of sound sense and good business habits, as well as of playful wit; and at a time when Cowper would otherwise have come to ruin through straitened means, joined to want of management, Hill took charge of his finances. He was a successful lawyer, residing in George Street, Westminster, and became secretary to Thurlow when the latter became Lord Chancellor. To Hill Cowper addressed some of the brightest of his letters. Many of them are on business affairs, yet it will be seen that he is able to combine with business rich playful humour. As was the case with most of his friends, he nicknames him. Sometimes it is plain "Joe," but it is frequently "Sephus," short for "Josephus." He rarely writes to him without a broad hint that he would like a parcel of fish, for which he had always an extraordinary fondness.

*General and Mrs. Cowper* were both of them the poet's first cousins, for the latter, Frances Maria Madan, was the daughter of John Cowper's sister, and she married her cousin. Her brother, Martin Madan, finds much mention in the poet's life, as being the author of *Thelyphthora* (*Globe*, xliii). Mrs. Cowper's religious views were more in harmony with Cowper's than Lady Hesketh's were. It may be remembered that the General and Lady Hesketh joined in making him an allowance when he came out of Dr. Cotton's asylum. The General, however, died in 1769.

*William Cawthorne Unwin* was the son of the Rev. Morley and Mary Unwin. Readers of the life will remember how, when a young man, he made Cowper's acquaintance at Huntingdon, how he introduced him to his parents and sister, and how the acquaintance ripened into a lifelong friendship. William Unwin in course of time became rector of Stock in Essex, and it is hither that most of Cowper's letters to him are addressed. He died at Winchester, at the early age of forty-one, in December 1786.

But the Olney life is broken into two distinct portions by a fresh interval of insanity. Threatenings of this appeared the year following his move to Olney, which developed into an acute attack in 1772, and lasted for many months. He wrote no letters between 1772 and 1776.

The curate in charge of Olney when Cowper began to reside there was the *Rev. John Newton*, who died in 1807. For the main incidents of his life see the *Globe Cowper*, p. xxxv. He left Olney in September 1779 for the rectory of St. Mary Woolnoth, and then Cowper's correspondence with him begins (see p. 37). The reference in this letter to Lord Bute's gardener is explained by the fact that Lord Bute lived at Luton, not far from Olney. In the first portion of the Olney life Cowper began the Olney Hymns in conjunction with Mr. Newton, but it was in the second that his fame as a poet begins. He had been in the habit of writing short poems and sending them to his friends, but in 1780 Mrs. Unwin urged him to try his hand at some larger work. Hence grew his first published volume, which appeared in 1782. Three years later he published *The Task*, a work which placed him by the common consent of his contemporaries at the head of the poets of his age. A curious illustration of his reserve with his intimate friends will be found in his correspondence with Newton and Unwin about these two volumes of poetry. In the case of the first volume he arranged with Newton for the publication, and said not a word to Unwin of what he was doing. At p. 50 will be found the letter in which he at length told him, and the awkwardness he feels is quite apparent. Evidently Mrs. Unwin has urged him to tell, and he is conscious that he has not treated a tried friend with frankness. Then on p. 110 we find him reversing his former proceeding by secretly negotiating with Unwin for the publication of his second volume, *The Task*, and excluding Newton from his confidence. Both friends in turn were hurt, but Unwin shows to advantage in the course which each of them took, though in both cases peace was restored after a little while.

The other correspondents of the Olney period were the four following :—

The *Rev. William Bull* was an Independent minister of Newport Pagnell, about five miles from Olney. To his care Newton had commended Cowper on leaving for St. Mary Woolnoth. It was he who gave the poet Madame Guyon's poems, which he has translated so gracefully.

*Samuel Rose*, the son of Dr. William Rose, a schoolmaster at Chiswick, coming up from Glasgow University to London, turned aside for the express purpose of seeing the poet of Olney, and bringing to him the thanks of some Scotch professors. The poet took warmly to him, and wrote him several judicious letters of advice about his studies. Rose gave him a copy of the newly published poems of Burns, which he read through twice to his great delight. The friendship between them became so cordial that he stood godfather to one of Rose's children ;

and when a pension of £300 a year was conferred upon him by the Crown, Rose was appointed his trustee.

*John*, the son of Sir Robert Throckmorton, lived at Weston Underwood. The family, being Roman Catholics, were regarded with great suspicion by their neighbours, and some even insulted them. Cowper, however, having received civilities from them, was very grateful, and, to Newton's disgust, became very intimate with the family. Several of his smaller poems are on incidents connected with them. He used playfully to call Mr. Throckmorton and his wife "Mr. and Mrs. Frog." Sir Robert died at the age of eighty-seven in 1791, and his son, on succeeding to the baronetcy, went to live at his father's old house in Oxfordshire.

*George Courtenay* was the younger brother of Sir John Throckmorton, but had changed his name. He came to live at Weston when his brother left it. His wife is the "Catharina" of the poet. They were both as kind to him as their predecessors had been. Mrs. Courtenay had proved for some time one of his most ardent helpers by making a fair copy of his Homer, and he named her "my lady of the ink-bottle."

IV. The renewal of correspondence with Lady Hesketh led to her visiting him at Olney, and this again to the removal of the poet and Mrs. Unwin in November 1787 from Olney to Weston Underwood. The change was partly owing to the inconvenience and unhealthiness of their Olney abode, partly to their desire to be near their friends, the Throckmortons. But the remove had hardly been made when the poet and his faithful companion were shocked by the sudden death of Unwin. The last letter to him will be found at p. 161, and it has a painful interest independently of this. The "young gentleman" referred to is Henry Thornton, with whom Unwin was travelling as tutor when he caught fever and died at Winchester. But the main subject of the letter is the gentle poet's anger at Newton's cruel and unprovoked conduct in directly charging him with "leading a life unbecoming the gospel" because he had been intimate with the Throckmortons, had invited the priest—"the Padre," as Cowper generally calls him—to dinner, and had walked out with his cousin on a Sunday evening. The death of Unwin had an unfavourable effect on Cowper's health, though he had a remarkable power of shaking off depression. He had another fit of fierce insanity for six months in 1787. He recovered from that, but remained in a state of melancholy, which, however, he still more or less shook off when writing to most of his friends, though never to Newton (see, for examples, the letters between pp. 280 and 284). In 1792 he made a new acquaintance, which proved a very important one.

*Wm. Hayley*, his future biographer, a native of Chester, was born in 1745, and died in 1820. He first made Cowper's acquaintance through hearing that the latter was engaged on an edition of Milton's works. The circumstances are told in the following letter, which, as it forms the opening of a very important friendship, we quote at length :—

"*February* 7, 1792,
"EARTHAM, *near* CHICHESTER.

"DEAR SIR—I have often been tempted, by affectionate admiration of your poetry, to trouble you with a letter; but I have repeatedly checked myself, in recollecting that the vanity of believing ourselves distantly related in spirit to a man of genius, is but a sorry apology for intruding on his time.

"Though I resisted my desire of professing myself your friend, that I might not disturb you with intrusive familiarity, I cannot resist a desire, equally affectionate, of disclaiming an idea which I am told is imputed to me, of considering myself, on a recent occasion, as an antagonist to you. Allow me, therefore, to say, I was solicited to write a Life of Milton, for Boydell and Nicholl, before I had the least idea that you and Mr. Fuseli were concerned in a project similar to theirs. When I first heard of your intention, I was apprehensive that we might undesignedly thwart each other; but on seeing your proposals, I am agreeably persuaded that our respective labours will be far from clashing, as it is your design to illustrate Milton with a series of notes, and I only mean to execute a more candid life of him than his late biographer has given us, upon a plan that will, I flatter myself, be particularly pleasing to those who love the author as we do.

"As to the pecuniary interest of those persons who venture large sums in expensive decoration of Milton, I am persuaded his expanding glory will support them all. Every splendid edition, where the merits of the pencil are in any degree worthy of the poet, will, I think, be secure of success. I wish it cordially to all; as I have great affection for the arts, and a sincere regard for those whose talents reflect honour upon them.

"To you, my dear sir, I have a grateful attachment, for the infinite delight which your writings have afforded me; and if, in the course of your work, I have any opportunity to serve or oblige you, I shall seize it with that friendly spirit which has impelled me at present to assure you, both in prose and rhyme, that I am your very cordial admirer, W. HAYLEY.

"*P.S.*—I wrote the enclosed sonnet on being told that our names had been idly printed together, in a newspaper, *as hostile competitors.* Pray forgive its partial defects for its affectionate sincerity.

# INTRODUCTION. xxi

"From my ignorance of your address, I send this to your booksellers, by a person commissioned to place my name in the list of your subscribers; and let me add, if you ever wish to form a new collection of names for any similar purpose, I entreat you to honour me so far as to rank *mine*, of your own accord, among those of your sincerest friends. Adieu!"

## SONNET
## TO WILLIAM COWPER, ESQ.

ON HEARING THAT OUR NAMES HAD BEEN IDLY MENTIONED IN A NEWSPAPER AS COMPETITORS IN A LIFE OF MILTON.

>Cowper! delight of all who justly prize
>  The splendid magic of a strain divine,
>  That sweetly tempts th' enlighten'd soul to rise,
>As sunbeams lure an eagle to the skies.
>  Poet! to whom I feel my heart incline
>As to a friend endear'd by virtue's ties;
>  Ne'er shall my name in pride's contentious line
>  With hostile emulation cope with thine!
>No! let us meet, with kind fraternal aim,
>  Where Milton's shrine invites a votive throng.
>With thee I share a passion for his fame,
>His zeal for truth, his scorn of venal blame:
>  But thou hast rarer gifts,—to thee belong
>  His harp of highest tone, his sanctity of song.

This letter lay at the booksellers some weeks before Cowper received it, but as soon as he had done so, he wrote a very genial letter back, which Hayley has not published. His first published letter to his brother poet will be found at p. 253. Very shortly afterwards Hayley came to visit him at Weston, and during this visit Mrs. Unwin was seized with paralysis (see p. 255).

At the end of July following Cowper visited Hayley at Eartham, a "tremendous exploit," as he well called it, considering the recluse life that he had been leading for twenty years. Hayley returned more than once to Weston, and his advice and assistance proved most valuable when the heavy gloom was settling down finally on the mind of the poor poet.

*Charlotte Smith* was introduced to the poet at Eartham, who delighted in her novels. The allusion at the end of the letter on p. 298 is to her pleasant story of *The Old Manor-House*. That which is spoken of as dedicated to him is *The Emigrants*. She died in 1806.

*Mrs. King* of Pertenhall, in Cambridgeshire, had been a friend of his brother John, and in the beginning of 1788 sent to him some unpublished poems of his in his own handwriting. They were gladly welcomed, and produced some very interesting letters. The poet, as will be seen, expresses much anxiety about her health, which was well founded, for she died in 1793.

*Rev. Walter Bagot* and four of his brothers had been school-fellows of Cowper at Westminster, "and very amiable and valuable boys they were," writes the poet. Correspondence, however, had ceased between the friends until Cowper began to translate Homer, when Bagot called upon him at Olney, and brought a subscription for £20 towards the undertaking. The brother so frequently referred to by Cowper was Lewis, who became successively Bishop of Bristol, Norwich, and St. Asaph.

*Rev. John Johnson*—not to be confounded with Cowper's publisher of the same name—was grandson of his mother's brother, Roger Donne, rector of Catfield. Cowper had heard nothing of his mother's relations since his childhood, until John Johnson, a young man of twenty, a Cambridge undergraduate, called on him in 1790, and caused him as much delight as the renewed correspondence with Lady Hesketh had done. Cowper's letters to him are particularly charming, because of the sympathy they display with the young man's love of fun and frolic, as well as of the wisdom of the advice which he gives concerning the sacred profession for which Johnson is preparing. From their first introduction Cowper clung to him, and his vacations were spent at Weston.

*Mrs. Bodham*, Cowper's first cousin, and his playfellow in youth, was brought to renew the acquaintance through Johnson, who returned from his first visit to Weston with rapturous accounts of his reception there. It was this account which led her to send him with an affectionate letter his mother's picture. Of the lovely poem thereby produced we need not speak here.

*The Rev. J. Hurdis* was rector of Bishopstone in Sussex (his birthplace), and professor of poetry at Oxford. He was author of *The Village Curate*, and a tragedy on Sir Thomas More.

*The Rev. J. Buchanan*, curate of Ravenstone, near Weston. The poem alluded to on p. 231 was *The Four Ages of Man*, which Buchanan had sketched out as a suggestion to him (see *Globe*, p. lxvii).

*Rev. W. Greathead* was a Dissenting minister at Newport Pagnell.

V. In July 1795 his cousin, Mr. Johnson, finding Cowper growing daily more wretched, removed the two invalids to Norfolk, in hope that change to a more bracing climate might benefit them. How futile this hope was is shown in the whole of the Norfolk letters. No light seems to gleam through the darkness. They went first to Tuddenham, then to Mundsley, then to Dereham, where in December 1796 Mrs. Unwin died. Three years and a half later Cowper was buried by her side.

# COWPER'S LETTERS.

## LETTERS WRITTEN IN LONDON,
## 1762.

### TO CLOTWORTHY ROWLEY.

*September* 2, 1762.

DEAR ROWLEY—Your letter has taken me just in the crisis; to-morrow I set off for Brighthelmstone, and there I stay till the winter brings us all to town again. This world is a shabby fellow, and uses us ill; but a few years hence there will be no difference between us and our fathers of the tenth generation upwards. I could be as splenetick as you, and with more reason, if I thought proper to indulge that humour; but my resolution is (and I advise you to adopt it), never to be melancholy while I have a hundred pounds in the world to keep up my spirits. God knows how long that will be; but in the meantime *Io Triumphe!* If a great man struggling with misfortune is a noble object, a little man that despises them is no contemptible one; and this is all the philosophy I have in the world at present. It savours pretty much of the ancient Stoic; but till the Stoics became coxcombs they were, in my opinion, a very sensible sect.

If my resolution to be a great man was half so strong as it is to despise the shame of being a little one, I should not despair of a house in Lincoln's Inn Fields, with all its appurtenances; for there is nothing more certain, and I could prove it by a thousand instances, than that every man may be rich if he will. What is the industry of half the industrious men in the world but avarice? and, call it by which name you will, it almost always succeeds. But this provokes me, that a covetous dog, who will work by candle-light in the morning, to get what he does not want, shall be praised for his thriftiness, while a gentleman shall be abused for submitting to his wants, rather than work like an ass to relieve them. Did you ever in your life know a man who was guided in the general course of his actions by anything but his natural temper? And yet we blame each other's conduct as freely as if that temper was the most tractable beast in the world, and we had nothing to do but to twitch the rein to the right or the left, and go just as we are directed by others! All this is nonsense, and nothing better.

There are some sensible folks who, having great estates, have wisdom enough too to spend them properly; there are others who are not less wise, perhaps, as knowing how to do without them. Between these two degrees are they who spend their money dirtily, or get it so. If you ask me where they are to be placed who amass much wealth in an honest way, you must be so good as to find them first, and then I'll answer the question. Upon the whole, my dear Rowley, there is a degree of poverty that has no disgrace belonging to it; that degree of it, I mean, in which a man enjoys clean linen and good company; and if I never sink below this degree of it, I care not if I never rise above it. This is a strange epistle, nor can I imagine how the devil I came to write it; but here it is, such as it is, and much good may you do with it. I have no estate, as it happens; so if it should fall into bad hands, I shall be in no danger of a commission of lunacy. Adieu! Carr is well, and gives his love to you.—Yours ever, WM. COWPER.

TO LADY HESKETH.

THE TEMPLE, *August* 9, 1763.

MY DEAR COUSIN—Having promised to write to you, I make haste to be as good as my word. I have a pleasure in writing to you at any time, but especially at the present, when my days are spent in reading the journals, and my nights in dreaming of them—an employment not very agreeable to a head that has long been habituated to the luxury of choosing its subject, and has been as little employed upon business as if it had grown upon the shoulders of a much wealthier gentleman. But the numskull pays for it now, and will not presently forget the discipline it has undergone lately. If I succeed in this doubtful piece of promotion, I shall have at least this satisfaction to reflect upon, that the volumes I write will be treasured up with the utmost care for ages, and will last as long as the English constitution—a duration which ought to satisfy the vanity of any author who has a spark of love for his country. Oh, my good cousin! if I was to open my heart to you, I could show you strange sights; nothing, I flatter myself, that would shock you, but a great deal that would make you wonder. I am of a very singular temper, and very unlike all the men that I have ever conversed with. Certainly I am not an absolute fool; but I have more weakness than the greatest of all the fools I can recollect at present. In short, if I was as fit for the next world as I am unfit for this—and God forbid I should speak it in vanity!—I would not change conditions with any saints in Christendom.

My destination is settled at last, and I have obtained a furlough. Margate is the word, and what do you think will ensue, cousin? I know what you expect, but ever since I was born I have been good at disappointing the most natural expectations. Many years ago, cousin, there was a possibility I might prove a very different thing from what I am at present. My character is now fixed, and riveted fast upon me; and, between friends, is not a very splendid one, or likely to be guilty of much fascination.

Adieu! my dear cousin. So much as I love you, I wonder how the deuce it has happened that I was never in love with you. Thank Heaven that I never was; for at this time I have had a pleasure in writing to you, which in that case I should have forfeited. Let me hear from you, or I shall reap but half the reward that is due to my noble indifference.—Yours ever and evermore,

W. C.

# LETTERS FROM HUNTINGDON,
## 1765-1767.

### TO JOSEPH HILL.

HUNTINGDON, *June* 24, 1765.

DEAR JOE—The only recompense I can make you for your kind attention to my affairs during my illness, is to tell you that, by the mercy of God, I am restored to perfect health, both of mind and body.  This, I believe, will give you pleasure, and I would gladly do anything from which you could receive it.

I left St. Albans on the 17th, and arrived that day at Cambridge, spent some time there with my brother, and came hither on the 22d.  I have a lodging that puts me continually in mind of our summer excursions; we have had many worse, and, except the size of it (which, however, is sufficient for a single man), but few better.  I am not quite alone, having brought a servant with me from St. Albans, who is the very mirror of fidelity and affection for his master.  And whereas the Turkish Spy says, he kept no servant, because he would not have an enemy in his house, I hired mine, because I would have a friend.  Men do not usually bestow these encomiums on their lackeys, nor do they usually deserve them; but I have had experience of mine, both in sickness and in health, and never saw his fellow.

The river Ouse—I forget how they spell it—is the most agreeable circumstance in this part of the world: at this town it is, I believe, as wide as the Thames at Windsor; nor does the silver Thames better deserve that epithet, nor has it more flowers upon its banks, these being attributes which, in strict truth, belong to neither. Fluellen would say, they are as like as my fingers to my fingers, and there is salmon in both. It is a noble stream to bathe in, and I shall make that use of it three times a week, having introduced myself to it for the first time this morning.

I beg you will remember me to all my friends, which is a task will cost you no great pains to execute—particularly remember me to those of your own house, and believe me your very affectionate W. C.

TO LADY HESKETH.

HUNTINGDON, *July* 1, 1765.

MY DEAR LADY HESKETH—Since the visit you were so kind as to pay me in the Temple (the only time I ever saw you without pleasure), what have I not suffered! And since it has pleased God to restore me to the use of my reason, what have I not enjoyed! You know, by experience, how pleasant it is to feel the first approaches of health after a fever; but, oh, the fever of the brain! To feel the quenching of that fire is indeed a blessing, which I think it impossible to receive without the most consummate gratitude. Terrible as this chastisement is, I acknowledge in it the hand of an infinite justice; nor is it at all more difficult for me to perceive in it the hand of an infinite mercy likewise. When I consider the effect it has had upon me, I am exceedingly thankful for it, and, without hypocrisy, esteem it the greatest blessing, next to life itself, I ever received from the divine bounty. I pray God that I may ever retain this sense of it, and then I am sure I shall continue to be, as I am at present, really happy.

I write thus to you that you may not think me a forlorn and wretched creature, which you might be apt to do, considering my very distant removal from every friend I have in the world,—a circumstance which, before this event befell me, would undoubtedly have made me so; but my affliction has taught me a road to happiness which, without it, I should never have found; and I know, and have experience of it every day, that the mercy of God, to him who believes himself the object of it, is more than sufficient to compensate for the loss of every other blessing.

You may now inform all those whom you think really interested in my welfare, that they have no need to be apprehensive on the score of my happiness at present. And you yourself will believe that my happiness is no dream, because I have told you the foundation on which it is built. What I have written would appear like enthusiasm to many, for we are apt to give that name to every warm affection of the mind in others which we have not experienced in ourselves; but to you, who have so much to be thankful for, and a temper inclined to gratitude, it will not appear so.

I beg you will give my love to Sir Thomas, and believe that I am obliged to you both for inquiring after me at St. Albans.—Yours ever, W. C.

### TO THE SAME.

HUNTINGDON, *July* 4, 1765.

BEING just emerged from the Ouse, I sit down to thank you, my dear cousin, for your friendly and comfortable letter. What could you think of my unaccountable behaviour to you in that visit I mentioned in my last? I remember I neither spoke to you, nor looked at you. The solution of the mystery, indeed, followed soon after, but at the time it must have been inexplicable. The uproar within was even then begun, and my silence was only the sulkiness of a thunderstorm before it opens. I am glad, however, that the only instance in which I knew not how to value your company was, when I was not in my senses. It was the first of the kind, and I trust in God it will be the last.

I reckon it one instance of the providence that has attended me throughout this whole event, that, instead of being delivered into the hands of one of the London physicians—who were so much nearer that I wonder I was not—I was carried to Doctor Cotton. I was not only treated by him with the greatest tenderness while I was ill, and attended with the utmost diligence, but when my reason was restored to me, and I had so much need of a religious friend to converse with, to whom I could open my mind upon the subject without reserve, I could hardly have found a fitter person for the purpose. My eagerness and anxiety to settle my opinions upon that long-neglected point made it necessary that, while my mind was yet weak, and my spirits uncertain, I should have some assistance. The doctor was as ready to administer relief to me in this article likewise, and as well qualified to do it, as in that which was more immediately his province. How many physicians would have thought this an irregular appetite, and a symptom of remaining madness! But if it were so, my friend was as mad as myself, and it is well for me that he was so.

My dear cousin, you know not half the deliverances I have received; my brother is the only one in the family who does. My recovery is, indeed, a signal one; but a greater, if possible, went before it. My future life must express my thankfulness, for by words I cannot do it.

I pray God to bless you and my friend Sir Thomas.—
Yours ever, W. C.

TO THE SAME.

HUNTINGDON, *September* 14, 1765.

MY DEAR COUSIN—The longer I live here, the better I like the place, and the people who belong to it. I am upon very good terms with no less than five families, besides two or three odd scrambling fellows like myself. The last acquaintance I made here is with the race of the Unwins, consisting of father and mother, son and daughter, the most comfortable, social folks you ever knew. The son is about twenty-one years of age, one of the most unreserved and amiable young men I ever conversed with. He has not yet arrived at that time of life when suspicion recommends itself to us in the form of wisdom, and sets everything but our own dear selves at an immeasurable distance from our esteem and confidence. Consequently he is known almost as soon as seen, and, having nothing in his heart that makes it necessary for him to keep it barred and bolted, opens it to the perusal even of a stranger. The father is a clergyman, and the son is designed for orders. The design, however, is quite his own, proceeding merely from his being, and having always been, sincere in his belief and love of the Gospel. Another acquaintance I have lately made is with a Mr. Nicholson, a north country divine, very poor, but very good and very happy. He reads prayers here twice a day, all the year round, and travels on foot to serve two churches every Sunday through the year, his journey out and home again being sixteen miles. I supped with him last night. He gave me bread and cheese, and a black jug of ale of his own brewing, and, doubtless, brewed by his own hands. Another of my acquaintance is Mr. ——, a thin, tall, old man, and as good as he is thin. He drinks nothing but water, and eats no flesh; partly, I believe, from a religious scruple (for he is very religious), and partly in the spirit of a valetudinarian. He is to be met with every morning of his life, at about six o'clock, at a fountain of very fine water, about a mile from the town, which is reckoned extremely like the Bristol spring. Being both early risers, and the only early walkers in the place, we soon became acquainted. His great piety can be equalled by nothing but his great regularity, for he is the most perfect timepiece in the world. I have received a visit likewise from Mr. ——. He is very much a gentleman, well read, and sensible. I am persuaded, in short, that if I had had the choice of all England, where to fix my abode, I could not have chosen better for myself, and most likely I should not have chosen so well.

You say you hope it is not necessary for salvation to undergo the same afflictions that I have undergone. No! my dear cousin. God deals with His children as a merciful father; He does not, as He Himself tells us, afflict willingly the sons of men. Doubtless there are many who, having been placed by His good providence out of the reach of any great evil, and the influence of bad example, have, from their very infancy been partakers of the grace of His Holy Spirit, in such a manner as never to have allowed themselves in any grievous offence against Him. May you love Him more and more day by day, as every day, while you think upon Him, you will find Him more worthy of your love; and may you be finally accepted by Him, for His sake, whose intercession for all His faithful servants cannot but prevail!—Yours ever, W. C.

TO JOSEPH HILL.

HUNTINGDON, *July* 3, 1765.

DEAR JOE—Whatever you may think of the matter, it is no easy thing to keep house for two people. A man cannot always live upon sheep's heads and liver and lights, like the lions in the tower; and a joint of meat, in so small a family, is an endless encumbrance. My butcher's bill for last week amounted to four shillings and tenpence. I set off with a leg of lamb, and was forced to give part of it away to my washerwoman. Then I made an experience upon a sheep's heart, and that was too little. Next I put three pounds of beef into a pie, and this had like to have been too much, for it lasted three days, though my landlord was admitted to a share of it. Then as to small beer, I am puzzled to pieces about it. I have bought as much for a shilling as will serve us at least a month, and it is grown sour already. In short, I never knew how to pity poor housekeepers before; but now I cease to wonder at the politic cast which their occupation usually gives to their countenance, for it is really a matter full of perplexity.

I have received but one visit since here I came. I don't mean that I have refused any, but that only one has been offered. This was from my woollen draper—a very healthy, wealthy, sensible, sponsible man, and extremely civil. He has a cold bath, and has promised me a key of it, which I shall probably make use of in the winter. He has undertaken, too, to get me the *St. James's Chronicle* three times a week, and to show me Hinchinbrook House, and to do every service for me in his power; so that I did not exceed the truth, you see, when I spoke of his civility. Here is a card-assembly, and a dancing assembly, and a horse-race, and a club, and a bowling-green—so that I am well off, you perceive, in point of diversions; especially as I shall go to 'em just as much as I should if I lived a thousand miles off. But no matter for that; the spectator at a play is more entertained than the actor, and in real life it is much the same. You will say, perhaps, that if I never frequent these places I shall not come within the description of a spectator; and you will say right. I have made a blunder, which shall be corrected in the next edition.

You are an old dog at a bad tenant; witness all my uncle's and your mother's geese and gridirons. There is something so extremely impertinent in entering upon a man's premises, and using them without paying for 'em, that I could easily resent it if I would. But I rather choose to entertain myself with thinking how you will scour the man about, and worry him to death, if once you begin with him. Poor toad! I leave him entirely to your mercy.

My dear Joe, you desire me to write long letters—I have neither matter enough nor perseverance enough for the purpose. However, if you can contrive to be tired of reading as soon as I am of writing, we shall find that short ones answer just as well; and, in my opinion, this is a very practical measure.

My friend Colman has had good fortune; I wish him better fortune still; which is, that he may make a right use of it. The tragedies of Lloyd and Bensley are both very deep. If they are not of use to the surviving part of the society it is their own fault.

I was debtor to Bensley seven pounds, or nine, I forget which. If you can find out his brother, you will do him a great favour if you will pay him for me; but do it at your leisure.—Yours and theirs, W. C.

## TO THE SAME.

*August* 14, 1765.

DEAR JOE—Both Lady Hesketh and my brother have apprised me of your intention to give me a call; and herein I find they were both mistaken. But they both informed me, likewise, that you were already set out for Warwickshire; in consequence of which latter intelligence I have lived in continual expectation of seeing you any time this fortnight. Now how these two ingenuous personages (for such they are both) should mistake an expedition to French Flanders for a journey to Warwickshire is more than I, with all my ingenuity, can imagine. I am glad, however, that I have still a chance of seeing you, and shall treasure it up amongst my agreeable expectations. In the meantime you are welcome to the British shoe, as the song has it, and I thank you for your epitome of your travels. You don't tell me how you escaped the vigilance of the custom-house officers, though I daresay you were knuckle-deep in contrabands, and had your boots stuffed with all manner of unlawful wares and merchandises.

You know, Joe, that I am very deep in debt to my little physician at St. Alban's, and that the handsomest thing I can do will be to pay him *le plutot qu'il sera possible* (this is vile French, I believe, but you can now correct it). My brother informs me that you have such a quantity of cash in your hands, on my account, that I may venture to send him forty pounds immediately. This, therefore, I shall be obliged if you will manage for me; and when you receive the hundred pounds, which my brother likewise brags you are shortly to receive, I shall be glad if you will discharge the remainder of that debt, without waiting for any further advice from your humble servant.

I am become a professed horseman, and do hereby assume to myself the style and title of the Knight of the Bloody Spur. It has cost me much to bring this point to bear; but I think I have at last accomplished it. My love to all your family.—Yours ever, W. C.

### TO THE SAME.

*October* 25, 1765.

DEAR JOE—I am afraid the month of October has proved rather unfavourable to the *belle assemblée* at Southampton, high winds and continual rains being bitter enemies to that agreeable lounge, which you and I are equally fond of. I have very cordially betaken myself to my books and my fireside, and seldom leave them, unless for exercise. I have added another family to the number of those I was acquainted with when you were here. Their name is Unwin,—the most agreeable people imaginable; quite sociable, and as free from the ceremonious civility of country gentlefolks as any I ever met with. They treat me more like a near relation than a stranger, and their house is always open to me. The old gentleman carries me to Cambridge in his chaise. He is a man of learning and good sense, and as simple as Parson Adams. His wife has a very uncommon understanding, has read much to excellent purpose, and is more polite than a duchess. The son, who belongs to Cambridge, is a most amiable young man; and the daughter quite of a piece with the rest of the family. They see but little company, which suits me exactly; go when I will, I find a house full of peace and cordiality in all its parts, and am sure to hear no scandal, but such discourse instead of it as we are all better for.  You remember Rousseau's description of an English morning; such are the mornings I spend with these good people; and the evenings differ from them in nothing, except that they are still more snug and quieter.  Now I know them, I wonder that I liked Huntingdon so well before I knew them, and am apt to think I should find every place disagreeable that had not an Unwin belonging to it.

This incident convinces me of the truth of an observation I have often made, that when we circumscribe our estimate of all that is clever within the limits of our own acquaintance (which I at least have been always apt to do), we are guilty of a very uncharitable censure upon the rest of the world, and of a narrowness of thinking disgraceful to ourselves.  Wapping and Redriff may contain some of the most amiable persons living, and such as one would go to Wapping and Redriff to make acquaintance with.  You remember Gray's Stanza:—

>   Full many a gem of purest ray serene
>   The deep unfathom'd caves of ocean bear;
>   Full many a flower is born to blush unseen,
>   And waste its sweetness on the desert air.

Yours, dear Joe, W. C.

### TO MRS. COWPER.

HUNTINGDON, *October* 20, 1766.

MY DEAR COUSIN—I am very sorry for poor Charles's illness, and hope you will soon have cause to thank God for his complete recovery.  We have an epidemical fever in this country likewise, which leaves behind it a continual sighing, almost to suffocation; not that I have seen any instance of it, for, blessed be God ! our family have hitherto escaped it; but such was the account I heard of it this morning.

I am obliged to you for the interest you take in my welfare, and for your inquiring so particularly after the manner in which my time passes here. As to amusements—I mean what the world calls such—we have none; the place, indeed, swarms with them, and cards and dancing are the professed business of almost all the *gentle* inhabitants of Huntingdon. We refuse to take part in them, or to be accessories to this way of murdering our time, and by so doing have acquired the name of Methodists. Having told you how we *do not* spend our time, I will next say how we do. We breakfast commonly between eight and nine; till eleven we read either the Scripture, or the sermons of some faithful preacher of those holy mysteries; at eleven we attend divine service, which is performed here twice every day; and from twelve to three we separate, and amuse ourselves as we please. During that interval I either read in my own apartment, or walk, or ride, or work in the garden. We seldom sit an hour after dinner; but, if the weather permits, adjourn to the garden, where, with Mrs. Unwin and her son, I have generally the pleasure of religious conversation till tea-time. If it rains, or is too windy for walking, we either converse within doors, or sing some hymns of Martin's collection; and by the help of Mrs. Unwin's harpsichord, make up a tolerable concert, in which our hearts, I hope, are the best and most musical performers. After tea we sally forth to walk in good earnest. Mrs. Unwin is a good walker, and we have generally travelled about four miles before we see home again. When the days are short, we make this excursion in the former part of the day, between church-time and dinner. At night we read and converse, as before, till supper, and commonly finish the evening either with hymns or a sermon, and last of all the family are called to prayers. I need not tell *you* that such a life as this is consistent with the utmost cheerfulness; accordingly we are all happy, and dwell together in unity as brethren. Mrs. Unwin has almost a maternal affection for me, and I have something very like a filial one for her; and her son and I are brothers. Blessed be the God of our salvation for such companions, and for such a life; above all, for a heart to like it!

I have had many anxious thoughts about taking orders, and I believe every new convert is apt to think himself called upon for that purpose; but it has pleased God, by means which there is no need to particularise, to give me full satisfaction as to the propriety of declining it; indeed they who have the least idea of what I have suffered from the dread of public exhibitions, will readily excuse my never attempting them hereafter. In the meantime, if it please the Almighty, I may be an instrument of turning many to the truth in a private way, and I hope that my endeavours in this way have not been entirely unsuccessful. Had I the zeal of Moses, I should want an Aaron to be my spokesman.—Yours ever, my dear cousin, W. C.

TO JOSEPH HILL, ESQ.

*May 14, 1767.*

MY DEAR JOE—I only know that I was once the happy owner of a red leather trunk, and that my brother, when I first saw him at Cambridge, upon my inquiring after my papers, etc., told me that in a red leather trunk they were all safely deposited. The whole contents of it are little worth, and if I never see them more I shall be but very moderately afflicted by the loss, though I fancy the trunk upon the road will prove to be the very trunk in question.

Together with your letter came a bill from my quondam

hosier in Fleet Street, Mr. Reynolds, for the sum of two pounds ten shillings, desiring present payment, cash being scarce. I sent him an order for the money by this day's post. My future expenses in the hosiery line will be small, for Mrs. Unwin knits all my stockings, and would knit my hats too, if that were possible.

I imagine my brother will be in town about midsummer, when he will be able to confer with you upon the subject of the inexorable Mr. E——, more to the purpose than I can by letter.

Having commenced gardener, I study the arts of pruning, sowing, planting, and enterprise everything in that way, from melons down to cabbages. I have a large garden to display my abilities in; and were we twenty miles nearer London, I might turn higgler, and serve your honour with cauliflowers and broccoli at the best hand. I shall possibly now and then desire you to call at the seed shop, in your way to Westminster, though sparingly. Should I do it often, you would begin to think you had a mother-in-law at Berkhampstead.—Yours, dear Joe,                                              WM. COWPER.

### TO THE SAME.

*July 16, 1767.*

DEAR JOE—Your wishes that the newspapers may have misinformed you are vain. Mr. Unwin is dead, and died in the manner there mentioned. At nine o'clock on Sunday morning he was in perfect health, and as likely to live twenty years as either of us, and before ten was stretched speechless and senseless upon a flock bed, in a poor cottage, where (it being impossible to remove him) he died on Thursday evening. I heard his dying groans, the effect of great agony, for he was a strong man, and much convulsed in his last moments. The few short intervals of sense that were indulged him he spent in earnest prayer, and in expressions of a firm trust and confidence in the only Saviour. To that stronghold we must all resort at last, if we would have hope in our death; when every other refuge fails, we are glad to fly to the only shelter to which we can repair to any purpose; and happy is it for us when, the false ground we have chosen for ourselves being broken under us, we find ourselves obliged to have recourse to the rock which can never be shaken : when this is our lot, we receive great and undeserved mercy.

Our society will not break up, but we shall settle in some other place ; where, is at present uncertain.—Yours,

W. C.

# LETTERS FROM OLNEY.
## 1767-1786.

### TO JOSEPH HILL, ESQ.

OLNEY, *October* 10, 1767.

DEAR JOE—I am obliged to you for complying with my request, and shall be glad to have the matter expedited as fast as may be.

One more law question, and I believe the last. A man holds land in right of his wife—the rents payable half-yearly, viz. at Lady Day and Michaelmas—dies in July, are not the rising rents the property of the widow? I mean the rent of the whole last half-year. You are a better counsellor than I was, but I think you have not such a client in me as I had in Dick Harcourt. Much good may you do with me!

Neither have I any map to consult at present, but by what remembrance I have of the situation of this place in the last I saw, it lies at the northernmost point of the country. We are just five miles beyond Newport Pagnell. I am willing to suspect that you make this inquiry with a *view* to an *interview* when time shall serve. We may possibly be settled in our own house in about a month, where so good a friend of mine will be extremely welcome to Mrs. Unwin. We shall have a bed and a warm fireside at your service, if you can come before next summer, and if not, a parlour that looks the north wind full in the face, where you may be as cool as in the groves of Valombrosa.—Yours, my dear Sephus, affectionately ever,

WM. COWPER.

*P.S.*—The stock is in the 3 per cent. consols. You may send the letter of attorney by the waggon from the *George* in Smithfield. It sets out on Tuesday morning early. But upon recollection, it had better come by the post.

TO MRS. COWPER.

OLNEY, *August* 31, 1769.

MY DEAR COUSIN—A letter from your brother Frederic brought me yesterday the most afflicting intelligence that has reached me these many years. I pray to God to comfort you, and to enable you to sustain this heavy stroke with that resignation to His will which none but Himself can give, and which He gives to none but His own children. How blessed and happy is your lot, my dear friend, beyond the common lot of the greater part of mankind, that you know what it is to draw near to God in prayer, and are acquainted with a throne of grace! You have resources in the infinite love of a dear Redeemer, which are withheld from millions; and the promises of God, which are yea and amen in Jesus, are sufficient to answer all your necessities, and to sweeten the bitterest cup which your heavenly Father will ever put into your hand. May He now give you liberty to drink at these wells of salvation, till you are filled with consolation and peace in the midst of trouble! He has said, "When thou passest through the fire I will be with thee, and when through the floods, they shall not overflow thee." You have need of such a word as this, and

He knows your need of it, and the time of necessity is the time when He will be sure to appear in behalf of those who trust in Him. I bear you and yours upon my heart before Him night and day, for I never expect to hear of distress which shall call upon me with a louder voice to pray for the sufferer. I know the Lord hears me for myself, vile and sinful as I am, and believe and am sure that He will hear me for you also. He is the friend of the widow, and the father of the fatherless, even God in His holy habitation; in all our afflictions He is afflicted, and He chastens us in mercy. Surely He will sanctify this dispensation to you, do you great and everlasting good by it, make the world appear like dust and vanity in your sight, as it truly is, and open to your view the glories of a better country, where there shall be no more death, neither sorrow nor pain, but God shall wipe away all tears from your eyes for ever. O that comfortable word! "I have chosen thee in the furnaces of affliction;" so that our very sorrows are evidences of our calling, and He chastens us because we are His children.

My dear cousin, I commit you to the word of His grace, and to the comforts of His Holy Spirit. Your life is needful for your family: may God in mercy to them prolong it, and may He preserve you from the dangerous effects which a stroke like this might have upon a frame so tender as yours. I grieve with you—I pray for you: could I do more, I would; but God must comfort you. —Yours, in our dear Lord Jesus, W. C.

TO MRS. MADAN, STAFFORD ROW, WESTMINSTER.

OLNEY, *March* 24, 1770.

DEAR AUNT—You may possibly by this time have heard of the death of my dear brother. I should not have left you to learn it from any but myself had I had either spirits or opportunity to write sooner. He died on Tuesday last, the 20th. It was not judged proper that I should attend the funeral; I therefore took leave of the melancholy scene as soon as possible, and returned to Olney on Thursday. He has left me to sing of mercy and judgment. Greater sufferings than he underwent are seldom seen, greater mercy than he received, I believe, never. His views of Gospel grace were as clear, and his sense of his interest in Christ as strong, as if he had been exercised in the Christian walk and warfare many years. This is my consolation, and great consolation I find it, that he is gone to his Father and my Father, to his God and my God.

He is to be buried at his living, about seven miles from Cambridge, at his own desire, this day; the masters and fellows attend the funeral.

I shall be obliged to you, my dear aunt, if the next time you write to dear Mrs. Cowper at York, you will be so good as to inform her of this event.

I am, my dear aunt, yours affectionately in the Lord,

WM. COWPER.

### TO JOSEPH HILL, ESQ.

*September* 25, 1770.

DEAR JOE—I have not done conversing with terrestrial objects, though I should be happy were I able to hold more continual converse with a Friend above the skies. He has my heart, but He allows a corner in it for all who show me kindness, and therefore one for you. The storm of sixty-three made a wreck of the friendships I had contracted in the course of many years, yours excepted, which has survived the tempest.

I thank you for your repeated invitation. Singular

thanks are due to you for so *singular* an instance of your regard. I could not leave Olney, unless in a case of absolute necessity, without much inconvenience to myself and others. W. C.

TO THE SAME.

*November* 12, 1776.

DEAR FRIEND—The very agreeable contents of your last came safe to hand in the shape of two notes for thirty pounds. I am to thank you likewise for a barrel of very good oysters, received about a fortnight ago. One to whom fish is so welcome as it is to me, can have no great occasion to distinguish the sorts. In general, therefore, whatever fish are likely to think a jaunt into the country agreeable, will be sure to find me ready to receive them: butts, plaice, flounder, or any other. If herrings are yet to be had, as they cannot be had at Olney till they are good for nothing, they will be welcome too. We have seen none this year, except a parcel Mrs. Unwin sent for, and the fishmonger sent stale ones, a trick they are apt to play upon their customers at a distance.

Having suffered so much from nervous fevers myself, I know how to congratulate Ashley upon his recovery. Other distempers only batter the walls; but *they* creep slowly into the citadel, and put the garrison to the sword.

You see I have not made a squeamish use of your obliging offer. The remembrance of past years, and of the sentiments formerly exchanged in our evening walks, convinces me still that an unreserved acceptance of what is graciously offered is the handsomest way of dealing with one of your character.—Believe me yours,

WM. COWPER.

The Wellingborough diligence passes our door every Tuesday, Thursday, and Saturday; and inns at the *Cross Keys*, St. John's Street, Smithfield.

As to the frequency, which you leave to my choice too, you have no need to exceed the number of your former remittances.

If it were to rain pupils, perhaps I might catch a tubful; but till it does, the fruitlessness of my inquiries makes me think I must keep my Greek and Latin to myself.—Yours affectionately, WM. COWPER.

TO THE REV. W. UNWIN.

*July* 18, 1778.

MY DEAR FRIEND—I hurry you into the midst of things at once, which, if it be not much in the epistolary style, is acknowledged, however, to be very sublime. Mr. Morley, *videlicet*, the grocer, is guilty of such neglect and carelessness, and has lately so much disappointed your mother that she is at last obliged to leave him, and begs you will send her Mr. Rawlinson's address, that she may transfer her custom to him. She adds, moreover, that she was well aware of the unseasonableness of salmon, and did not mean that you should order any to Olney till the spring.

We are indebted to you for your political intelligence, but have it not in our power to pay you in kind. Proceed, however, to give us such information as cannot be learned from the newspaper, and when anything arises at Olney which is not in the threadbare style of daily occurrences, you shall hear of it in return. Nothing of this sort has happened lately, except that a lion was imported here at a fair, seventy years of age, and as tame as a goose. Your mother and I saw him embrace his keeper with his paws, and lick his face. Others saw him receive his head in his mouth, and restore it to him again unhurt—a sight we chose not to be favoured with, but rather advised the honest man to discontinue the practice—a practice hardly reconcileable to prudence, unless he had a head to spare. The beast, however, was a very magnificent one, and much more royal in his appearance than those I have seen in the Tower.

The paper tells us that the Chancellor is frequently at the Register Office, having conceived a design to shorten the proceedings in his court. If he has indeed such a purpose in view, he is so industrious and so resolute that he will never let it drop unaccomplished. Perhaps the practitioners will have no reason to regret it, as they may gain in such an event more by the multiplicity of suits than they do at present by the length of them.

Your mother joins me in affectionate respects—I should have said love—to yourself, Mrs. Unwin, Miss Shuttleworth, and little John. If you will accept this for a letter, perhaps I may be able to furnish more such upon occasion.—Yours, with thanks for your last,

WM. COWPER.

### TO THE SAME.

*May* 26, 1779.

MY DEAR FRIEND—I must beg your assistance in a design I have formed to cheat the glazier. Government has laid a tax upon glass, and he has trebled it. I want as much as will serve for a large frame, but am unwilling to pay an exorbitant price for it. I shall be obliged to you, therefore, if you will inquire at a glass-manufacturer's how he sells his Newcastle glass, such as is used for frames and hothouses. If you will be so good as to send me this information, and at the same time the manufacturer's address, I will execute the rest of the business myself, without giving you any further trouble.

I am obliged to you for the Poets; and though I little thought that I was translating so much money out of your pocket into the bookseller's when I turned Prior's poem into Latin, yet I must needs say, that if you think it worth while to purchase the English classics at all, you cannot possess yourself of them upon better terms. I have looked into some of the volumes, but, not having yet finished the Register, have merely looked into them. A few things I have met with, which, if they had been burned the moment they were written, it would have been better for the author, and at least as well for his readers. There is not much of this, but a little is too much. I think it a pity the editor admitted any; the English muse would have lost no credit by the omission of such trash. Some of them, again, seem to me to have but a very disputable right to a place among the classics; and I am quite at a loss, when I see them in such company, to conjecture what is Dr. Johnson's idea or definition of classical merit. But if he inserts the poems of some who can hardly he said to deserve such an honour, the purchaser may comfort himself with the hope that he will exclude none that do.

Your mother sends her love and affectionate remembrance to all at Stock, from the tallest to the shortest there, in which she is accompanied by yours,

W. C.

### TO THE SAME.

*July*, 1779.

My dear Friend—If you please, you may give my service to Mr. James Martin, glazier, and tell him that I have furnished myself with glass from Bedford for half the money.

When I was at Margate it was an excursion of pleasure to go to see Ramsgate. The pier, I remember, was accounted a most excellent piece of stonework, and such I found it. By this time, I suppose, it is finished; and surely it is no small advantage that you have an opportunity of observing how nicely those great stones are put together, as often as you please, without trouble or expense. But you think Margate more lively. So is a Cheshire cheese, full of mites, more lively than a sound one; but that very liveliness only proves its rottenness. I remember, too, that Margate, though full of company, was generally filled with such company as people who were nice in the choice of their company were rather fearful of keeping company with. The hoy went to London every week, loaded with mackerel and herrings, and returned loaded with company. The cheapness of the conveyance made it equally commodious for dead fish and lively company. So, perhaps, your solitude at Ramsgate may turn out another advantage, at least I should think it one.

There was not, at that time, much to be seen in the Isle of Thanet besides the beauty of the country, and the fine prospects of the sea, which are nowhere surpassed except in the Isle of Wight, or upon some parts of the coast of Hampshire. One sight, however, I remember, engaged my curiosity, and I went to see it—a fine piece of ruins, built by the late Lord Holland at a great expense, which, the day after I saw it, tumbled down for nothing. Perhaps, therefore, it is still a ruin; and if it is, I would advise you by all means to visit it, as it must have been much improved by this fortunate incident. It is hardly possible to put stones together with that air of wild and magnificent disorder which they are sure to acquire by falling of their own accord.

We heartily wish that Mrs. Unwin may receive the

utmost benefit of bathing. At the same time we caution *you* against the use of it, however the heat of the weather may seem to recommend it. It is not safe for thin habits hectically inclined.

I remember (the fourth and last thing I mean to remember on this occasion) that Sam Cox, the counsel, walking by the seaside as if absorbed in deep contemplation, was questioned about what he was musing on. He replied: "I was wondering that such an almost infinite and unwieldy element should produce a *sprat.*"

Our love attends your whole party.—Yours affectionately, W. C.

*P.S.*—You are desired to purchase three pounds of sixpenny white worsted at a shop well recommended for that commodity. The Isle of Thanet is famous for it, beyond any other place in the kingdom.

TO THE SAME.

*July* 17, 1779.

MY DEAR FRIEND—We envy you your sea breezes. In the garden we feel nothing but the reflection of the heat from the walls, and in the parlour from the opposite houses. I fancy Virgil was so situated when he wrote those two beautiful lines :—

> " Oh quis me gelidis in vallibus Hæmi
> Sistat, et ingenti ramorum protegat umbra !"

The worst of it is, that though the sunbeams strike as forcibly upon my harp-strings as they did upon his, they elicit no such sounds, but rather produce such groans as they are said to have drawn from those of the statue of Memnon.

As you have ventured to make the experiment, your own experience will be your best guide in the article of bathing. An inference will hardly follow, though one should pull at it with all one's might, from Smollett's case to yours. He was corpulent, muscular, and strong—whereas if you were either stolen or strayed such a description of you in an advertisement would hardly direct an enquirer with sufficient accuracy and exactness. But if bathing does not make your head ache, or prevent your sleeping at night, I should imagine it could not hurt you.

I remember taking a walk upon the strand at Margate where the cliff is high and perpendicular. At long intervals there are cartways cut through the rock down to the beach, and there is no other way of access to it or from it. I walked near a mile upon the water edge without observing that the tide was rising fast upon it. When I *did* observe it, it was almost too late. I ran every step of the way back again, and had much ado to save my distance. I mention this as a caution, lest you should happen at any time to be surprised as I was. It would be very unpleasant to be forced to cling like a cat to the side of a precipice, and perhaps hardly possible to do it for four hours without any respite.

It seems a trifle, but it is a real disadvantage, to have no better name to pass by than the gentleman you mention. Whether we suppose him settled and promoted in the army, the church, or the law, how uncouth the sound — Captain Twopenny! Bishop Twopenny! Judge Twopenny! The abilities of Lord Mansfield would hardly impart a dignity to such a name. Should he perform deeds worthy of poetical panegyric, how difficult would it be to ennoble the sound of Twopenny!

> Muse! place him high upon the lists of Fame,
> The wondrous man, and Twopenny his name!

But to be serious, if the French should land in the Isle of Thanet, and Mr. Twopenny should fall into their hands, he will have a fair opportunity to Frenchify his name, and may call himself Monsieur Deux Sous, which, when he comes to be exchanged by Cartel, will easily resume an English form, and slide naturally into Two Shoes, in my mind a considerable improvement.—Yours affectionately, W. C.

TO THE SAME.

*September* 21, 1779.

AMICO MIO — Be pleased to buy me a glazier's diamond pencil. I have glazed the two frames designed to receive my pine plants. But I cannot mend the kitchen windows till by the help of that implement I can reduce the glass to its proper dimensions. If I were a plumber I should be a complete glazier; and possibly the happy time may come when I shall be seen trudging away to the neighbouring towns with a shelf of glass hanging at my back. If Government should impose another tax upon that commodity, I hardly know a business in which a gentleman might more successfully employ himself. A Chinese of ten times my fortune would avail himself of such an opportunity without scruple; and why should not I, who want money as much as any mandarin in China? Rousseau would have been charmed to have seen me so occupied, and would have exclaimed with rapture, "that he had found the Emilius who, he supposed, had subsisted only in his own idea." I would recommend it to you to follow my example. You will presently qualify yourself for the task, and may not only amuse yourself at home, but may even exercise your skill in mending the church windows; which, as it would save money to the parish, would conduce, together with your other ministerial accomplishments, to make you extremely popular in the place.

I have eight pair of tame pigeons. When I first enter the garden in the morning, I find them perched upon the wall, waiting for their breakfast; for I feed them always upon the gravel walk. If your wish should be accomplished, and you should find yourself furnished with the wings of a dove, I shall undoubtedly find you amongst them. Only be so good, if that should be the case, as to announce yourself by some means or other. For I imagine your crop will require something better than tares to fill it.

Your mother and I last week made a trip in a post-chaise to Gayhurst, the seat of Mr. Wright, about four miles off. He understood that I did not much affect strange faces, and sent over his servant on purpose to inform me that he was going into Leicestershire, and that, if I chose to see the gardens, I might gratify myself without danger of seeing the proprietor. I accepted the invitation, and was delighted with all I found there. The situation is happy, the gardens elegantly disposed, the hothouse in the most flourishing state, and the orange-trees the most captivating creatures of the kind I ever saw. A man, in short, had need have the talents of Cox or Langford, the auctioneers, to do the whole scene justice. Our love attends you all.—Yours,    W. C.

TO JOSEPH HILL, ESQ.

*October 2, 1779.*

MY DEAR FRIEND—You begin to count the remaining days of the vacation, not with impatience, but through unwillingness to see the end of it. For the mind of man, at least of most men, is equally busy in anticipating the evil and the good. That word *anticipation* puts me in remembrance of the pamphlet of that name, which, if you purchased, I should be glad to borrow. I have seen only an extract from it in the Review, which made me laugh heartily, and wish to peruse the whole.

The newspaper informs me of the arrival of the Jamaica fleet. I hope it imports some pine-apple plants for me. I have a good frame and a good bed prepared to receive them. I send you annexed a fable, in which the pine-apple makes a figure, and shall be glad if you like the taste of it. Two pairs of soles, and shrimps, which arrived last night, demand my acknowledgments. You have heard that when Orion performed upon the harp the fish followed him. I really have no design to fiddle you out of more fish, but if you should esteem my verses worthy of such a price,—though I shall never be so renowned as he was—I shall think myself equally indebted to the muse that helps me.

My affectionate respects attend Mrs. Hill. She has put Mr. Wright to the expense of building a new hot-house, the plants produced by the seed she gave me having grown so large as to require an apartment by themselves.—Yours,           WM. COWPER.

### TO THE REV. WILLIAM UNWIN.

*October* 31, 1779.

MY DEAR FRIEND—I wrote my last letter merely to inform you that I had nothing to say, in answer to which you have said nothing. I admire the propriety of your conduct, though I am a loser by it. I will endeavour to say something now, and shall hope for something in return.

I have been well entertained with Johnson's biography, for which I thank you: with one exception, and that a swinging one, I think he has acquitted himself with his usual good sense and sufficiency. His treatment of Milton is unmerciful to the last degree. A pensioner is not likely to spare a republican, and the Doctor, in order, I suppose, to convince his royal patron of the sincerity of his monarchical principles, has belaboured that great poet's character with the most industrious cruelty. As a man, he has hardly left him the shadow of one good quality. Churlishness in his private life, and a rancorous hatred of everything royal in his public, are the two colours with which he has smeared all the canvas. If he had any virtues, they are not to be found in the Doctor's picture of him, and it is well for Milton that some sourness in his temper is the only vice with which his memory has been charged; it is evident enough that if his biographer could have discovered more, he would not have spared him. As a poet, he has treated him with severity enough, and has plucked one or two of the most beautiful feathers out of his Muse's wing, and trampled them under his great foot. He has passed sentence of condemnation upon Lycidas, and has taken occasion, from that charming poem, to expose to ridicule (what is indeed ridiculous enough) the childish prattlement of pastoral compositions, as if Lycidas was the prototype and pattern of them all. The liveliness of the description, the sweetness of the numbers, the classical spirit of antiquity that prevails in it, go for nothing. I am convinced, by the way, that he has no ear for poetical numbers, or that it was stopped by prejudice against the harmony of Milton's. Was there ever anything so delightful as the music of the *Paradise Lost?* It is like that of a fine organ; has the fullest and the deepest tones of majesty, with all the softness and elegance of the Dorian flute: variety without end, and never equalled, unless perhaps by Virgil. Yet the Doctor has little or nothing to say upon this copious theme, but talks something about the unfitness of the English language for blank verse, and how apt it is, in the mouth of some readers, to degenerate into declamation. Oh! I could thrash his old jacket till I made his pension jingle in his pockets.

I could talk a good while longer, but I have no room. Our love attends yourself, Mrs. Unwin, and Miss Shuttleworth, not forgetting the two miniature pictures at your elbow.—Yours affectionately, W. C.

### TO THE SAME.

*February* 27, 1780.

MY DEAR FRIEND—As you are pleased to desire my letters, I am the more pleased with writing them, though, at the same time, I must needs testify my surprise that you should think them worth receiving, as I seldom send one that I think favourably of myself. This is not to be understood as an imputation upon your taste or judgment, but as an encomium upon my own modesty and humility, which I desire you to remark well. It is a just observation of Sir Joshua Reynolds, that though men of ordinary talents may be highly satisfied with their own productions, men of true genius never are. Whatever be their subject, they always seem to themselves to fall short of it, even when they seem to others most to excel. And for this reason,—because they have a certain sublime sense of perfection, which other men are strangers to, and which they themselves in their performances are not able to exemplify. Your servant, Sir Joshua ! I little thought of seeing you when I began, but as you have popped in, you are welcome.

When I wrote last, I was a little inclined to send you a copy of verses entitled the Modern Patriot, but was not quite pleased with a line or two which I found it difficult to mend, therefore did not. At night I read Mr. Burke's speech in the newspaper, and was so well pleased with his proposals for a reformation, and with the temper in which he made them, that I began to think better of his cause, and burnt my verses. Such is the lot of the man who writes upon the subject of the day; the aspect of affairs changes in an hour or two, and his opinion with it; what was just and well-deserved satire in the morning, in the evening becomes a libel; the author commences his own judge, and while he condemns with unrelenting severity what he so lately approved, is sorry to find that he has laid his leaf-gold upon touchwood, which crumbled away under his fingers. Alas! what can I do with my wit? I have not enough to do great things with, and these little things are so fugitive, that while a man catches at the subject, he is only filling his hand with smoke. I must do with it as I do with my linnet: I keep him for the most part in a cage, but now and then set open the door that he may whisk about the room a little, and then shut him up again. My whisking wit has produced the following, the subject of which is more important than the manner in which I have treated it seems to imply, but a fable may speak truth, and all truth is sterling; I only premise, that in the philosophical tract in the Register, I found it asserted that the glow-worm is the nightingale's proper food.

Have you heard?—Who has not? for a recommendatory advertisement of it is already published—that a certain relation of your humble servant has written a tract, now in the press, to prove polygamy a divine institution. A plurality of wives is intended, but not of husbands. The end proposed by the author is to remedy the prevailing practice of adultery by making the female delinquent *pro facto* the lawful wife of the male.

The officer of a regiment, part of which is quartered here, gave one of the soldiers leave to be drunk six weeks, in hopes of curing him by satiety. He *was* drunk six weeks, and is so still, as often as he can find an opportunity. One vice may swallow up another, but no coroner in the state of ethics ever brought in his verdict, when a vice died, that it was—*felo de se.*

They who value the man are sorry for his book, the rest say—

> Solvuntur risu tabulae, tu missus abibis.

Thanks for all you have done, and all you intend; the biography will be particularly welcome. My truly affectionate respects attend you all.—Yours,

WM. COWPER.

When you feel postage a burden, send me some franks.

### TO THE REV. JOHN NEWTON.

*May* 3, 1780.

DEAR SIR—You indulge me in such a variety of subjects, and allow me such a latitude of excursion in this scribbling employment, that I have no excuse for silence. I am much obliged to you for swallowing such boluses as I send you, for the sake of my gilding, and verily believe I am the only man alive from whom they would be welcome to a palate like yours. I wish I could make them more splendid than they are, more alluring to the eye at least, if not more pleasing to the taste; but my leaf-gold is tarnished, and has received such a tinge from the vapours that are ever brooding over my mind, that I think it no small proof of your partiality to me that you will read my letters. I am not fond of long-winded metaphors; I have always observed that they halt at the latter end of their progress, and so does mine. I deal much in ink, indeed, but not such ink as is employed by poets and writers of essays. Mine is a harmless fluid, and guilty of no deceptions but such as may prevail without the least injury to the person imposed on. I draw mountains, valleys, woods, and streams, and ducks, and dab-chicks. I admire them myself, and Mrs. Unwin admires them; and her praise and my praise put together are fame enough for me. Oh! I could spend whole days and moonlight nights in feeding upon a lovely prospect! My eyes drink the rivers as they flow. If every human being upon earth could think, for one quarter of an hour, as I have done for many years, there might perhaps be many miserable men among them, but not an unawakened one would be found, from the Arctic to the Antarctic circle. At present, the difference between them and me is greatly to their advantage. I delight in baubles, and know them to be so; for rested in, and viewed without a reference to their Author, what is the earth, what are the planets, what is the sun itself but a bauble? Better for a man never to have seen them, or to see them with the eyes of a brute, stupid and unconscious of what he beholds, than not to be able to say, "The Maker of all these wonders is my friend!" Their eyes have never been opened to see that they are trifles; mine have been, and will be till they are closed for ever. They think a fine estate, a large conservatory, a hothouse rich as a West Indian garden, things of consequence; visit them with pleasure, and muse upon them with ten times more. I am pleased with a frame of four lights, doubtful whether the few pines it contains will ever be worth a farthing; amuse myself with a greenhouse which Lord Bute's gardener could take upon his back and walk away with; and when I have paid it the accustomed visit, and watered it, and given it air, I say to myself—"This is not mine, 'tis a plaything lent me for the present; I must leave it soon."

W. C.

TO THE REV. WILLIAM UNWIN.

*July* 27, 1780.

MY DEAR FRIEND—As two men sit silent, after having exhausted all their topics of conversation, one says, "It is very fine weather;" and the other says, "Yes;" one blows his nose, and the other rubs his eyebrows—by the way, this is very much in Homer's manner :—such seems to be the case between you and me. After a silence of some days, I wrote you a long something that, I suppose, was nothing to the purpose, because it has not afforded you materials for an answer. Nevertheless, as it often happens in the case above stated, one of the distressed parties, being deeply sensible of the awkwardness of a dumb duet, breaks silence again, and resolves to speak, though he has nothing to say. So it fares with me : I am with you again in the form of an epistle, though, considering my present emptiness, I have reason to fear that your only joy upon the occasion will be, that it is conveyed to you in a frank.

When I began I expected no interruption. But if I had expected interruptions without end, I should have been less disappointed. First came the barber, who, after having embellished the outside of my head, has left the inside just as unfurnished as he found it. Then came Olney Bridge, not into the house, but into the conversation. The cause relating to it was tried on Tuesday at Buckingham. The judge directed the jury to find a verdict favourable to Olney. The jury consisted of one knave and eleven fools. The last-mentioned followed the afore-mentioned, as sheep follow a bell-wether, and decided in direct opposition to the said judge. Then a flaw was discovered in the indictment. The indictment was quashed, and an order made for a new trial. The new trial will be in the King's Bench, where said knave and said fools will have nothing to do with it. So the men of Olney fling up their caps, and assure themselves of a complete victory. A victory will save me and your mother many shillings, perhaps some pounds, which, except that it has afforded me a subject to write upon, was the only reason why I have said so much about it. I know you take an interest in all that concerns us, and will consequently rejoice with us in the prospect of an event in which we are concerned so nearly.

I will say of that book what I never said, and what no man ought to say of any other, that I could answer it without reading it, deriving all my arguments from principles of mere humanity, fidelity, and domestic expediency. My respects with your mother's love attend yourself and the ladies; the children are never forgot.—Yours affectionately,

W. C.

My franks are out.

### TO THE REV. JOHN NEWTON.

*August* 21, 1780.

The following occurrence ought not to be passed over in silence, in a place where so few notable ones are to be met with. Last Wednesday night, while we were at supper, between the hours of eight and nine, I heard an unusual noise in the back parlour, as if one of the hares was entangled, and endeavouring to disengage herself. I was just going to rise from table when it ceased. In about five minutes a voice on the outside of the parlour door inquired if one of my hares had got away. I immediately rushed into the next room, and found that my poor favourite Puss had made her escape. She had gnawed in sunder the strings of the lattice-work, with which I thought I had sufficiently secured the window, and which I preferred to any other sort of blind, because it admitted plenty of air. From thence I hastened to the kitchen, where I saw the redoubtable Thomas Freeman, who told me, that having seen her, just after she dropped into the street, he attempted to cover her with his hat, but she screamed out, and leaped directly over his head. I then desired him to pursue as fast as possible, and added Richard Coleman to the chase, as being nimbler, and carrying less weight than Thomas; not expecting to see her again, but desirous to learn, if possible, what became of her. In something less than an hour Richard returned, almost breathless, with the following account: That soon after he began to run, he left Tom behind him, and came in sight of a most numerous hunt of men, women, children, and dogs; that he did his best to keep back the dogs, and presently outstripped the crowd, so that the race was at last disputed between himself and Puss—she ran right through the town, and down the lane that leads to Dropshort—a little before she came to the house, he got the start and turned her; she pushed for the town again, and soon after she entered it sought shelter in Mr. Wagstaff's tanyard, adjoining to old Mr. Drake's—Sturge's harvest men were at supper, and saw her from the opposite side of the way. There she encountered the tan-pits full of water; and while she was struggling out of one pit and plunging into another, and almost drowned, one of the men drew her out by the ears and secured her. She was then well washed in a bucket, to get the lime out of her coat, and brought home in a sack at ten o'clock.

This frolic cost us four shillings, but you may believe we did not grudge a farthing of it. The poor creature received only a little hurt in one of her claws, and in one of her ears, and is now almost as well as ever.

I do not call this an answer to your letter, but such as

it is I send it, presuming upon that interest which I know you take in my minutest concerns, which I cannot express better than in the words of Terence a little varied—*Nihil mei a te alienum putas.*—Yours, my dear friend,

W. C.

### TO THE SAME.

*January* 21, 1781.

MY DEAR SIR—I am glad that the *Progress of Error* did not err in its progress, as I feared it had; and that it has reached you safe; and still more pleased that it has met with your approbation; for if it had not I should have wished it had miscarried, and had been sorry that the bearer's memory had served him so well upon the occasion. I knew him to be that sort of genius which, being busied in making excursions of the imaginary kind, is not always present to its own immediate concerns, much less to those of others; and having reposed the trust in him, began to regret that I had done so, when it was too late. But I did it to save a frank, and as the affair has turned out, that end was very well answered. This is committed to the hands of a less volatile person, and therefore more to be depended on.

As to the poem called *Truth*, which is already longer than its elder brother, and is yet to be lengthened by the addition of perhaps twenty lines, perhaps more, I shrink from the thought of transcribing it at present. But as there is no need to be in any hurry about it, I hope that in some rainy season, which the next month will probably bring with it, when perhaps I may be glad of employment, the undertaking will appear less formidable.

I suppose you know that Mr. Scott will be in town on Tuesday. He is likely to take possession of the vicarage at last, with the best grace possible; at least, if he and

Mr. Browne can agree upon the terms. The old gentleman, I find, would be glad to let the house and abridge the stipend; in other words, to make a good bargain for himself, and starve his curate.—Yours, my dear friend,

WM. COWPER.

TO THE REV. WILLIAM UNWIN.

*February* 6, 1781.

MY DEAR FRIEND—It is high time you should consult your own peace of mind, and not suffer the insatiable demands and unreasonable expectations of other men to be a source of unhappiness to yourself. You have lived long enough in the world to know that it swarms with people who are always ready to take advantage of the generosity of such men as you; who say in their hearts, when they meet with such disinterested treatment as every one receives from your hands: "Now is the time;—the man has a gentlemanly regard for his character, he loves peace more than money, and will make any concessions, so that he may but approve himself to his own conscience. Let us squeeze him; he will yield well; the more he complies the more we will insist, and make him pay dear for the character he wishes to deserve." I cannot doubt but your predecessor's curate is of this stamp; his demand wants nothing but a cocked pistol to make it felony, without benefit of clergy.

As to your proposal to the executors, if it does not give contentment, it must be for the reasons above mentioned; in which case I would recommend it to you by all means, to pay them exactly what they can lawfully demand for glebe and tithe, and not a farthing more, and in return to insist upon every penny you lay out in necessary repairs, and not a farthing less. It is wrong not to deal liberally with persons who themselves act upon liberal and honest principles; but it is weakness to be the willing dupe of artifice, and to sacrifice one's own interest for the sake of satisfying the insatiable or unjust.

We are obliged to you for the rugs, a commodity that can never come to such a place as this at an unseasonable time. We have given one to an industrious poor widow with four children whose sister overheard her shivering in the night, and with some difficulty brought her to confess the next morning that she was half perished for want of sufficient covering. Her said sister borrowed a rug for her at a neighbour's immediately, which she had used but one night when yours arrived. And I doubt not but we shall meet with others equally indigent, and deserving of your bounty.

I hear this morning, *via tonsoris*, that Lord George [Gordon] is acquitted. I take it for granted you was at the trial, for three reasons: First, because you was in town so lately; Secondly, because you have a laudable curiosity, that acts as a spur upon your spirits on all such occasions; and Thirdly, because you are slender and slim, and take up so little room that you are sure of a place when men of ampler dimensions are necessarily excluded. Tell us all that passed; and if he is indeed acquitted, let us know upon what point his acquittal turned, for at present I am rather at a loss to conceive how he could escape if the law was allowed to take its course, uninterrupted by fear and uncontrolled by a spirit of party.

Much good may your humanity do you, as it does so much good to others. You can nowhere find objects more entitled to your pity than where your pity seeks them. A man whose vices and irregularities have brought his liberty and life into danger will always be viewed with an eye of compassion by those who understand what human nature is made of. And while we acknowledge the severity of the law to be founded upon principles of necessity and justice, and are glad that there is such a barrier provided for the peace of society, if we consider that the difference between ourselves and the culprit is not of our own making, we shall be, as you are, tenderly affected with the view of his misery, and not the less so because he has brought it upon himself. I look upon the worst man in Chelmsford gaol with a more favourable eye than upon a certain curate, who claims a servant's wages from one who never was his master.

What goes before was written in the morning. This evening I have read the trial as related in the *General Evening*, and can only add to what I said before, in the words of Horace—

—— " Miror quo facto judicium illud fugerit."

I give you joy of your own hair. No doubt you are a considerable gainer in your appearance by being disperiwigged. The best wig is that which most resembles the natural hair; why then should he that has hair enough of his own have recourse to imitation? I have little doubt but that if an arm or a leg could have been taken off with as little pain as attends the amputation of a curl or a lock of hair, the natural limb would have been thought less becoming, or less convenient, by some men, than a wooden one, and have been disposed of accordingly.

Thanks for the salmon; it was perfectly good, as were the two lobsters; and the two guineas came safe. Having some verses to transcribe, and being rather weary, I add no more, except our love to the whole family, jointly and severally. Having begun my letter with a miserable pen, I was not willing to change it for a better, lest my writing should not be all of a piece, but it has worn me and my patience quite out.—Yours ever,

WM. COWPER.

TO JOSEPH HILL, ESQ.

OLNEY, *February* 3, 1781.

MY DEAR FRIEND—It is possible that Mrs. Hill may not be herself a sufferer by the late terrible catastrophe[1] in the Islands, but I should suppose by her correspondence with those parts she may be connected with some that are. In either case, I condole with her; for it is reasonable to imagine that, since the first tour that Columbus made into the Western world, it never before experienced such a convulsion, perhaps never since the foundation of the globe. You say that the state grows old, and discovers many symptoms of decline. A writer possessed of a genius for hypothesis, like that of Burnet, might construct a plausible argument to prove that the world itself is in a state of superannuation, if there be such a word. If not, there must be such a one as superannuity. When that just equilibrium which has hitherto supported all things seems to fail, when the elements burst the chain that had bound them, the wind sweeping away the works of man, and man himself together with his works, and the ocean seeming to overleap the command, "Hitherto shalt thou come and no further, and here shall thy proud waves be stayed,"—these irregular and prodigious vagaries seemed to bespeak a decay, and forebode, perhaps, not a very distant dissolution. This thought has so run away with my attention that I have left myself no room for the little politics that have only Great Britain for their object. Who knows but that while a thousand and ten thousand tongues are employed in adjusting the scale of our national concerns, in complaining of new taxes, and funds loaded with the debt of accumulating millions, the consummation

---

[1] The most destructive hurricane ever remembered in the West Indies.

of all things may discharge it in a moment, and the scene of all this bustle disappear, as if it had never been. Charles Fox would say, perhaps, he thought it very unlikely. I question if he could prove even that. I am sure, however, he could not prove it to be impossible.—
Yours, W. C.

TO THE REV. JOHN NEWTON.

OLNEY, *February* 18, 1781.

MY DEAR FRIEND—I send you *Table Talk*. It is a medley of many things, some that may be useful, and some that, for ought I know, may be very diverting. I am merry that I may decoy people into my company, and grave that they may be the better for it. Now and then I put on the garb of a philosopher, and take the opportunity that disguise procures me to drop a word in favour of religion. In short, there is some froth, and here and there a bit of sweetmeat, which seems to entitle it justly to the name of a certain dish the ladies call a trifle. I did not choose to be more facetious, lest I should consult the taste of my readers at the expense of my own approbation; nor more serious than I have been, lest I should forfeit theirs. A poet in my circumstances has a difficult part to act: one minute obliged to bridle his humour, if he has any; and the next to clap a spur to the sides of it; now ready to weep from a sense of the importance of his subject, and on a sudden constrained to laugh, lest his gravity should be mistaken for dulness. If this be not violent exercise for the mind, I know not what is; and if any man doubt it, let him try. Whether all this management and contrivance be necessary I do not know, but am inclined to suspect that if my nurse was to go forth clad in Quaker colour, without one bit of riband to enliven her appearance, she might walk from one end of London to the other as little noticed as if she were one of the sisterhood indeed.

You had been married thirty-one years last Monday. When you married I was eighteen years of age, and had just left Westminster school. At that time I valued a man according to his proficiency and taste in classical literature, and had the meanest opinion of all other accomplishments unaccompanied by that. I lived to see the vanity of what I had made my pride, and in a few years found that there were other attainments which would carry a man more handsomely through life than a mere knowledge of what Homer and Virgil had left behind them. In measure as my attachment to these gentry wore off, I found a more welcome reception among those whose acquaintance it was more my interest to cultivate. But all this time was spent in painting a piece of wood that had no life in it. At last, I began to think *indeed;* I found myself in possession of many baubles, but not one grain of solidity in all my treasures. Then I learned the truth, and then I lost it, and there ends my history. I would no more than you wish to live such a life over again, but for one reason. He that is carried to execution, though through the roughest road, when he arrives at the destined spot would be glad, notwithstanding the many jolts he met with, to repeat his journey.—Yours, my dear Sir, with our joint love,

W. C.

TO THE REV. WILLIAM UNWIN.

*February* 27, 1781.

MY DEAR FRIEND—In the first place my paper is insufferably bad, so that though this is the second sheet on which I have begun to write, and taken from another quire, I can hardly flatter myself that I shall be able to persevere to the end of it.

I thank you for your relation of Mr. Fytche's dispute with the Bishop; it affords matter for some reflections not altogether favourable to the episcopal order, as it is easy to see that if his Lordship had the power, he does not want the inclination to use the thunder of the Vatican, and anathematise a poor gentleman that dares to oppose him, without mercy. I know not in what part of Scripture he will find it revealed that a patron, by taking a bond of resignation from the person he presents, forfeits all hope of mercy in this world and that which is to come. Yet he asserts it as gravely as if he knew it to be true; but the laity at this time of day are wiser than when they gave their bishops credit for omnipotence; that cheat will pass no longer.

Alas, poor Vestris! what a pitiable object, how truly French in his humiliation, when he bowed his head down to the stage and held it there, as if he never meant to raise it more! As humble in his abasement as exalted in his capers, equally French in both. Which is most entitled to compassion, the dancer who is obliged, at the expense of all that is called dignity in man, to stoop to the arbitrary requisitions of an enraged assembly, or that assembly themselves who think it worth their while to spend hours in bellowing for satisfaction from the concessions of a dancer? Considering that life does not last for ages, and they know it, it is not unreasonable to say that both he and they might set a higher value upon their time, and devote it to a better purpose. It is possible, too, you may think, that the maker of this wise reflection might himself have been better employed than in writing what follows upon the subject. I subscribe to the truth of the animadversion, and can only say, in my excuse, that the composition is short, did not cost me much time, and may perhaps provoke a longer, which is not always useless.  If you please, you may send it to the Poet's Corner :—

[A Card, *Poems*, p. 336.]

I have not forgot, though when I wrote last I did not think of answering, your kind invitation.  I can only say at present that Stock shall be my first visit, but that visiting at this time would be attended with insupportable awkwardness to me, and with such as the visited themselves would assuredly feel the weight of.  My witticisms are only current upon paper now, and that sort of paper currency must serve, like the Congress dollars, for want of the more valuable coin—myself.

We thank you for the intended salmon, and beg you would get yourself made Bishop of Chichester as soon as possible, that we may have to thank you for every kind of eatable fish the British coast produces.—Yours ever,

WM. COWPER.

I have hurried to the end as fast as possible, being weary of a letter that is one continued blot.

TO THE SAME.

*May* 1, 1781.

Your mother says I *must* write, and *must* admits of no apology; I might otherwise plead that I have nothing to say, that I am weary, that I am dull, that it would be more convenient therefore for you, as well as for myself, that I should let it alone; but all these pleas, and whatever pleas besides either disinclination, indolence, or necessity might suggest, are overruled, as they ought to be, the moment a lady adduces her irrefragable argument, *you must.*  You have still, however, one comfort left, that what I must write you may, or may not, read, just as it shall please you; unless Lady Anne at your elbow should say you must read it, and then, like a true knight, you will obey without looking out for a remedy.

I do not love to harp upon strings that, to say the least, are not so musical as one would wish, but you I know have many a time sacrificed your own feelings to those of others, and where an act of charity leads you, are not easily put out of your way. This consideration encourages me just to insinuate that your silence on the subject of a certain nomination is distressful to more than you would wish; in particular to the little boy whose clothes are outgrown and worn out; and to his mother, who is unwilling to furnish him with a new suit, having reason to suppose that the long blue petticoat would soon supersede it if she should.

In the press, and speedily will be published, in one volume octavo, price three shillings, Poems, by William Cowper, of the Inner Temple, Esq. You may suppose, by the size of the publication, that the greatest part of them have been long kept secret, because you yourself have never seen them; but the truth is, that they are most of them, except what you have in your possession, the produce of the last winter. Two-thirds of the compilation will be occupied by four pieces, the first of which sprung up in the month of December, and the last of them in the month of March. They contain, I suppose, in all about two thousand and five hundred lines; are known, or are to be known in due time, by the names of *Table-Talk*, *The Progress of Error*, *Truth*, *Expostulation*. Mr. Newton writes a Preface, and Johnson is the publisher. The principal, I may say the only, reason why I never mentioned to you, till now, an affair which I am just going to make known to all the world (if *that* Mr. All-the-world should think it worth his knowing), has been this,—that, till within these few days, I had not the honour to know it myself. This may seem strange, but it is true; for, not knowing where to find underwriters who would choose to insure them, and not finding it convenient to a purse like mine to run any hazard, even upon the credit of my own ingenuity, I was very much in doubt for some weeks whether any bookseller would be willing to subject himself to an ambiguity that might prove very expensive in case of a bad market. But Johnson has heroically set all peradventures at defiance, and takes the whole charge upon himself. So out I come. I shall be glad of my Translations from Vincent Bourne in your next frank. My muse will lay herself at your feet immediately on her first public appearance.— Yours, my dear friend, with your mother's love,

W. C.

TO JOSEPH HILL, ESQ.

*May* 9, 1781.

MY DEAR SIR—I am in the press, and it is vain to deny it. But how mysterious is the conveyance of intelligence from one end to the other of your great city! Not many days since, except one man, and he but little taller than yourself, all London was ignorant of it; for I do not suppose that the public prints have yet announced the most agreeable tidings; the title-page, which is the basis of the advertisement, having so lately reached the publisher; and now it is known to you, who live at least two miles distant from my confidant upon the occasion.

My labours are principally the production of the last winter; all, indeed, except a few of the minor pieces. When I can find no other occupation I think, and when I think I am very apt to do it in rhyme. Hence it comes to pass, that the season of the year which generally pinches off the flowers of poetry unfolds mine, such as they are, and crowns me with a winter garland. In this respect, therefore, I and my contemporary bards are by no means upon a par. They write when the delightful influences of fine weather, fine prospects, and a brisk motion of the animal spirits, make poetry almost the language of Nature; and I, when icicles depend from all the leaves of the Parnassian laurel, and when a reasonable man would as little expect to succeed in verse as to hear a blackbird whistle. This must be my apology to you for whatever want of fire and animation you may observe in what you will shortly have the perusal of. As to the public, if they like me not, there is no remedy. A friend will weigh and consider all disadvantages, and make as large allowances as an author can wish, and larger, perhaps, than he has any right to expect; but not so the world at large; whatever they do not like they will not by any apology be persuaded to forgive, and it would be in vain to tell *them* that I wrote my verses in January, for they would immediately reply, "Why did you not write them in May?" A question that might puzzle a wiser head than we poets are generally blessed with.  W. C.

TO THE REV. WILLIAM UNWIN.

*May* 10, 1781.

MY DEAR FRIEND—It is Friday; I have just drunk tea, and just perused your letter; and, though this answer to it cannot set off till Sunday, I obey the warm impulse I feel, which will not permit me to postpone the business till the regular time of writing.

I expected you would be grieved; if you had not been so, those sensibilities which attend you upon every other occasion must have left you upon this. I am sorry that I have given you pain, but not sorry that you have felt it. A concern of that sort would be absurd, because it would be to regret your friendship for me, and to be dissatisfied with the effect of it. Allow yourself, however, three minutes only for reflection, and your penetration must necessarily dive into the motives of my conduct. In the first place, and by way of preface, remember that I do not (whatever your partiality may incline you to do) account it of much consequence to any friend of mine, whether he is, or is not, employed by me upon such an occasion. But all affected renunciations of poetical merit apart (and all unaffected expressions of the sense I have of my own littleness in the poetical character too), the obvious and only reason why I resorted to Mr. Newton, and not to my friend Unwin, was this—that the former lived in London, and the latter at Stock; the former was upon the spot to correct the press, to give instructions respecting any sudden alterations, and to settle with the publisher everything that might possibly occur in the course of such a business; the latter could not be applied to for these purposes without what I thought would be a manifest encroachment on his kindness; because it might happen that the troublesome office might cost him now and then a journey, which it was absolutely impossible for me to endure the thought of.

When I wrote to you for the copies you have sent me, I told you I was making a collection, but not with a design to publish. There is nothing truer than that at that time I had not the smallest expectation of sending a volume of poems to the press. I had several small pieces that might amuse, but I would not, when I publish, make the amusement of the reader my only object. When the winter deprived me of other employments, I began to compose, and seeing six or seven months before me, which would naturally afford me much leisure for such a purpose, I undertook a piece of some length;

that finished, another; and so on, till I had amassed the number of lines I mentioned in my last.

Believe of me what you please, but not that I am indifferent to you, or your friendship for me, on any occasion. We have no franks.—Yours, W. C.

TO THE SAME.

*May* 23, 1781.

MY DEAR FRIEND—If a writer's friends have need of patience, how much more the writer! Your desire to see my muse in public, and mine to gratify you, must both suffer the mortification of delay. I expected that my trumpeter would have informed the world by this time of all that is needful for them to know upon such an occasion; and that an advertising blast, blown through every newspaper, would have said — "The poet is coming!"— But man, especially man that writes verse, is born to disappointments, as surely as printers and booksellers are born to be the most dilatory and tedious of all creatures. The plain English of this magnificent preamble is, that the season of publication is just elapsed, that the town is going into the country every day, and that my book cannot appear till they return,—that is to say, not till next winter. This misfortune, however, comes not without its attendant advantage: I shall now have, what I should not otherwise have had, an opportunity to correct the press myself; no small advantage upon any occasion, but especially important where poetry is concerned! A single erratum may knock out the brains of a whole passage, and that perhaps which, of all others, the unfortunate poet is the most proud of. Add to this, that now and then there is to be found in a printing house a presumptuous intermeddler, who will fancy himself a poet too, and what is still worse, a better than he that employs him. The consequence is, that with cobbling, and tinkering, and patching on here and there a shred of his own, he makes such a difference between the original and the copy, that an author cannot know his own work again. Now, as I choose to be responsible for nobody's dulness but my own, I am a little comforted when I reflect that it will be in my power to prevent all such impertinence; and yet not without your assistance. It will be quite necessary that the correspondence between me and Johnson should be carried on without the expense of postage, because proof-sheets would make double or treble letters, which expense, as in every instance it must occur twice, first when the packet is sent, and again when it is returned, would be rather inconvenient to me, who, you perceive, am forced to live by my wits, and to him, who hopes to get a little matter no doubt by the same means. Half a dozen franks therefore to me, and *totidem* to him, will be singularly acceptable, if you can, without feeling it in any respect a trouble, procure them for me—Johnson, Bookseller, S. Paul's Churchyard.

My neckcloths being all worn out, I intend to wear stocks, but not unless they are more fashionable than the former. In that case, I shall be obliged to you if you will buy me a handsome stock-buckle for a very little money; for twenty or twenty-five shillings perhaps a second-hand affair may be purchased that will make a figure at Olney.

I am much obliged to you for your offer to support me in a translation of Bourne. It is but seldom, however, and never, except for my amusement, that I translate, because I find it disagreeable to work by another man's pattern; I should at least be sure to find it so in a business of any length. Again, *that* is epigrammatic and witty in Latin which would be perfectly insipid in

English; and a translator of Bourne would frequently find himself obliged to supply what is called the turn, which is in fact the most difficult and the most expensive part of the whole composition, and could not perhaps, in many instances, be done with any tolerable success. If a Latin poem is neat, elegant, and musical, it is enough; but English readers are not so easily satisfied. To quote myself, you will find, on comparing the Jackdaw with the original, that I was obliged to sharpen a point which, though smart enough in the Latin, would, in English, have appeared as plain and blunt as the tag of a lace. I love the memory of Vinny Bourne. I think him a better Latin poet than Tibullus, Propertius, Ausonius, or any of the writers in *his* way, except Ovid, and not at all inferior to *him*. I love him, too, with a love of partiality, because he was usher of the fifth form at Westminster when I passed through it. He was so good-natured, and so indolent, that I lost more than I got by him; for he made me as idle as himself. He was such a sloven, as if he had trusted to his genius as a cloak for everything that could disgust you in his person; and indeed in his writings he has almost made amends for all. His humour is entirely original; he can speak of a magpie or a cat in terms so exquisitely appropriated to the character he draws, that one would suppose him animated by the spirit of the creature he describes. And with all this drollery there is a mixture of rational, and even religious, reflection at times, and always an air of pleasantry, good-nature, and humanity, that makes him, in my mind, one of the most amiable writers in the world. It is not common to meet with a writer who can make you smile, and yet at nobody's expense; who is always entertaining, and yet always harmless; and who, though always elegant, and classical to a degree not always found even in the classics themselves, charms more by the simplicity and playfulness of his ideas, than by the neatness and purity of his verse; yet such was poor Vinny. I remember seeing the Duke of Richmond set fire to his greasy locks, and box his ears to put it out again.

I am delighted with your project, but not with the view I have of its success. If the world would form its opinion of the clerical character at large, from yours in particular, I have no doubt but the event would be as prosperous as you could wish. But I suppose there is not a member of either house who does not see within the circle of his own acquaintance a minister, perhaps many ministers, whose integrity would contribute but little to the effects of such a bill. Here are seven or eight in the neighbourhood of Olney who have shaken hands with sobriety, and who would rather suppress the Church, were it not for the emoluments annexed, than discourage the sale of strong beer in a single instance. Were I myself in Parliament, I am not sure that I could favour your scheme; are there not to be found within five miles of almost every neighbourhood, parsons who would purchase well accustomed public-houses, because they could secure them a license, and patronise them when they had done? I think no penalty would prevent the abuse, on account of the difficulty of proof, and that no ingenuity could guard against all the possible abuses. To sum up all in a few words, the generality of the clergy, especially within these last twenty or thirty years, have worn their circingles so loose, that I verily believe no measure that proposed an accession of privilege to an order which the laity retain but little respect for would meet with the countenance of the Legislature. You will do me the justice to suppose that I do not say these things to gratify a splenetic humour or a censorious turn of mind; far from it,—it may add, perhaps, to the severity of the foregoing observations to assert, but if it does, I cannot help asserting, that I verily believe them to be founded upon fact, and that I am sure, partly from my own knowledge, and partly from the report of those whose veracity I can depend upon, that in this part of the world at least, many of the most profligate characters are the very men to whom the morals, and even the souls, of others are entrusted; and I cannot suppose that the diocese of Lincoln, or this part of it in particular, is more unfortunate in that respect than the rest of the kingdom.

Since I began to write long poems I seem to turn up my nose at the idea of a short one. I have lately entered upon one, which, if ever finished, cannot easily be comprised in much less than a thousand lines! But this must make part of a second publication, and be accompanied in due time by others not yet thought of; for it seems (which I did not know until the bookseller had occasion to tell me so) that single pieces stand no chance, and that nothing less than a volume will go down. You yourself afford me a proof of the certainty of this intelligence by sending me franks which nothing less than a volume can fill. I have accordingly sent you one, but am obliged to add, that had the wind been in any other point of the compass, or, blowing as it does from the east, had it been less boisterous, you must have been contented with a much shorter letter, but the abridgment of every other occupation is very favourable to that of writing.

Our love attends all the family at Stock. I am glad I did not expect to hear from you by this post, for the boy has lost the bag in which your letter must have been enclosed;— another reason for my prolixity!—Yours affectionately, WM. COWPER.

TO THE REV. JOHN NEWTON.

*July* 12, 1781.

MY VERY DEAR FRIEND—I am going to send, what

when you have read, you may scratch your head, and say, I suppose, there's nobody knows, whether what I have got, be verse or not—by the tune and the time, it ought to be rhyme; but if it be, did you ever see, of late or of yore, such a ditty before?

I have writ *Charity*, not for popularity, but as well as I could, in hopes to do good; and if the reviewer should say, "To be sure, the gentleman's muse, wears Methodist shoes; you may know by her pace, and talk about grace, that she and her bard have little regard, for the taste and fashions, and ruling passions, and hoydening play, of the modern day; and though she assume a borrowed plume, and now and then wear a tittering air, 'tis only her plan to catch, if she can, the giddy and gay, as they go that way, by a production, on a new construction; she has baited her trap, in hopes to snap all that may come, with a sugar plum."—His opinion in this will not be amiss; 'tis what I intend, my principal end; and if I succeed, and folks should read, till a few are brought to a serious thought, I shall think I am paid, for all I have said, and all I have done, though I have run, many a time, after a rhyme, as far as from hence to the end of my sense, and by hook or crook, write another book, if I live and am here, another year.

I have heard before, of a room with a floor, laid upon springs, and such like things, with so much art, in every part, that when you went in, you was forced to begin a minuet pace, with an air and a grace, swimming about, now in and now out, with a deal of state, in a figure of eight, without pipe or string, or any such thing; and now I have writ, in a rhyming fit, what will make you dance, and as you advance, will keep you still, though against your will, dancing away, alert and gay, till you come to an end of what I have penned; which that you may do, ere Madam and you are quite worn out with jigging

about, I take my leave, and here you receive a bow profound, down to the ground, from your humble me,
W. C.

TO THE SAME.
*August* 16, 1781.

MY DEAR FRIEND—I might date my letter from the greenhouse, which we have converted into a summer parlour. The walls hung with garden mats, and the floor covered with a carpet, it affords us by far the pleasantest retreat in Olney. We eat, drink, and sleep where we always did; but here we spend all the rest of our time, and find that the sound of the wind in the trees and the singing of birds are much more agreeable to our ears than the incessant barking of dogs and screaming of children. Not to mention the exchange of a sweet-smelling garden for the putrid exhalations of Silver End. It is an observation that naturally occurs upon the occasion, and which many other occasions furnish an opportunity to make, that people long for what they have not, and overlook the good in their possession. This is so true in the present instance, that for years past I should have thought myself happy to enjoy a retirement even less flattering to my natural taste than this in which I am now writing; and have often looked wistfully at a snug cottage, which, on account of its situation at a distance from noise and disagreeable objects, seemed to promise me all I could wish or expect, so far as happiness may be said to be local, never once adverting to this comfortable nook, which affords me all that could be found in the most sequestered hermitage, with the advantage of having all those accommodations at hand which no hermitage could possibly afford me. People imagine they should be happy in circumstances which they would feel insupportably burthensome in less than a week. A man that has been clothed in fine linen, and fared sumptuously every day, envies the peasant under a thatched hovel; who, in return, envies him as much his palace and his pleasure-ground. Could they change situations, the fine gentleman would find his ceilings too low, and that his casements admitted too much wind; that he had no cellar for his wine, and no wine to put in his cellar. These, with a thousand other mortifying deficiencies, would shatter his romantic project into innumerable fragments in a moment. The clown, at the same time, would find the accession of so much unwieldy treasure an encumbrance quite incompatible with an hour's ease. His choice would be puzzled by variety. He would drink to excess, because he would foresee no end to his abundance; and he would eat himself sick for the same reason. He would have no idea of any other happiness than sensual gratification; would make himself a beast, and die of his good fortune. The rich gentleman had perhaps, or might have had, if he pleased, at the shortest notice, just such a recess as this; but if he had it, he overlooked it, or, if he had it not, forgot that he might command it whenever he would. The rustic, too, was actually in possession of some blessings, which he was a fool to relinquish, but which he could neither see nor feel, because he had the daily and constant use of them; such as good health, bodily strength, a head and a heart that never ached, and temperance, to the practice of which he was bound by necessity, that, humanely speaking, was a pledge and a security for the continuance of them all.

Thus I have sent you a schoolboy's theme. When I write to you I do not write without thinking, but always without premeditation; the consequence is, that such thoughts as pass through my head when I am not writing make the subject of my letters to you.

Johnson sent me lately a sort of apology for his printer's negligence, with his promise of greater diligence for the future. There was need enough of both. I have received but one sheet since you left us. Still, indeed, I see that there is time enough before us; but I see likewise that no length of time can be sufficient for the accomplishment of a work that does not go forward. I know not yet whether he will add "Conversation" to those poems already in his hand, nor do I care much. No man ever wrote such quantities of verse, as I have written this last year, with so much indifference about the event, or rather, with so little ambition of public praise. My pieces are such as may possibly be made useful. The more they are approved, the more likely they are to spread, and consequently the more likely to attain the end of usefulness, which, as I said once before, except my present amusement, is the only end I propose. And even in the pursuit of this purpose, commendable as it is in itself, I have not the spur I should once have had;—my labour must go unrewarded, and, as Mr. Raban once said, I am raising a scaffold before a house that others are to live in, and not I.

I have left myself no room for politics, which I thought, when I began, would have been my principal theme.

Mr. Symonds's letters certainly are not here. Our servants never touch a paper without leave, and are so observant of our injunction in this particular, that, unless I burn the covers of the news, they accumulate till they make a litter.—Yours, my dear Sir,

WM. COWPER.

### TO THE SAME.

*August* 21, 1781.

MY DEAR FRIEND—You wish you could employ your time to better purpose, yet are never idle. In all that you say or do; whether you are alone, or pay visits, or receive them; whether you think or write, or walk or sit still—the state of your mind is such as discovers even to yourself, in spite of all its wanderings, that there is a principle at bottom whose determined tendency is towards the best things. I do not at all doubt the truth of what you say, when you complain of that crowd of trifling thoughts that pesters you without ceasing; but then you always have a serious thought standing at the door of your imagination, like a justice of the peace, with the Riot Act in his hand, ready to read it, and disperse the mob. Here lies the difference between you and me. My thoughts are clad in a sober livery, for the most part as grave as that of a bishop's servants. They turn, too, upon spiritual subjects, but the tallest fellow, and the loudest among them all, is he who is continually crying with a loud voice, *Actum est de te; periisti!* You wish for more attention, I for less. Dissipation itself would be welcome to me so it were not a vicious one; but however earnestly invited, is coy, and keeps at a distance. Yet with all this distressing gloom upon my mind I experience, as you do, the slipperiness of the present hour, and the rapidity with which time escapes me. Everything around us, and everything that befalls us, constitutes a variety, which, whether agreeable or otherwise, has still a thievish propensity, and steals from us days, months, and years, with such unparalleled address that even while we say they are here, they are gone. From infancy to manhood is rather a tedious period, chiefly, I suppose, because at that time we act under the control of others, and are not suffered to have a will of our own. But thence downward into the vale of years is such a declivity that we have just an opportunity to reflect upon the steepness of it, and then find ourselves at the bottom.

Here is a new scene opening, which, whether it perform what it promises or not, will add fresh plumes to the wings of time,—at least while it continues to be a subject of contemplation. If the project takes effect, a thousand varieties will attend the change it will make in our situation at Olney. If not, it will serve, however, to speculate and converse on, and steal away many hours, by engaging our attention, before it be entirely dropped. Lady Austen, very desirous of retirement, especially of a retirement near her sister, an admirer of Mr. Scott as a preacher, and of your two humble servants now in the greenhouse as the most agreeable creatures in the world, is at present determined to settle here. That part of our great building which is at present occupied by Dick Coleman, his wife, child, and a thousand rats, is the corner of the world she chooses above all others as the place of her future residence. Next spring twelvemonth she begins to repair and beautify, and the following winter (by which time the lease of her house in town will determine) she intends to take possession. I am highly pleased with the plan, upon Mrs. Unwin's account, who, since Mrs. Newton's departure, is destitute of all female connexion, and has not, in any emergency, a woman to speak to. Mrs. Scott is indeed in the neighbourhood, and an excellent person, but always engaged by a close attention to her family, and no more than ourselves a lover of visiting. But these things are all at present in the clouds. Two years must intervene, and in two years not only this project, but all the projects in Europe, may be disconcerted.

[Cocoa-nut naught, *Poems*, p. 336.]

Yours, my dear Sir, W. C.

TO THE SAME.

*September* 9, 1781.

MY DEAR FRIEND—I am not willing to let the post set off without me, though I have nothing material to put into his bag. I am writing in the greenhouse, where my myrtles, ranged before the windows, make the most agreeable blind imaginable, where I am undisturbed by noise, and where I see none but pleasing objects. The situation is as favourable to my purpose as I could wish, but the state of my mind is not so, and the deficiencies I feel there are not to be remedied by the stillness of my retirement, or the beauty of the scene before me. I believe it is in part owing to the excessive heat of the weather that I find myself so much at a loss when I attempt either verse or prose; my animal spirits are depressed, and dulness is the consequence. That dulness, however, is all at your service; and the portion of it that is necessary to fill up the present epistle I send you without the least reluctance.

I am sorry to find that the censure I passed upon Occiduus is even better founded than I supposed. Lady Austin has been at his sabbatical concerts, which, it seems, are composed of song-tunes and psalm-tunes indiscriminately; music without words—and I suppose one may say, consequently, without devotion. On a certain occasion, when her niece was sitting at her side, she asked his opinion concerning the lawfulness of such amusements as are to be found at Vauxhall or Ranelagh, meaning only to draw from him a sentence of disapprobation, that Miss Green might be the better reconciled to the restraint under which she was held when she found it warranted by the judgment of so famous a divine. But she was disappointed; he accounted them innocent, and recommended them as useful. Curiosity, he said, was natural to young persons; and it was wrong to deny them a gratification which they might be indulged in with the greatest safety; because the denial being unreasonable, the desire of it would still subsist. It was but a walk, and a walk was as harmless in one place as another; with other arguments of a similar import, which might have proceeded with more grace, at least with less offence, from the lips of a sensual layman. He seems, together with others of our acquaintance, to have suffered considerably in his spiritual character by his attachment to music. The lawfulness of it, when used with moderation, and in its proper place, is unquestionable; but I believe that wine itself, though a man be guilty of habitual intoxication, does not more debauch and befool the natural understanding than music,—always music, music in season and out of season,—weakens and destroys the spiritual discernment. If it is not used with an unfeigned reference to the worship of God, and with a design to assist the soul in the performance of it, which cannot be the case when it is the only occupation, it degenerates into a sensual delight and becomes a most powerful advocate for the admission of other pleasures, grosser perhaps in degree, but in their kind the same.

Mr. Monk, though a simple, honest, good man,—such, at least, he appears to us,—is not likely to give general satisfaction. He preaches the truth, it seems, but not the whole truth; and a certain member of that church, who signed the letter of invitation, which was conceived in terms sufficiently encouraging, is likely to prove one of his most strenuous opposers. The little man, however, has an independent fortune, and has nothing to do but to trundle himself away to some other place where he may find hearers neither so nice nor so wise as we are at Olney.—Yours, my dear sir, with our united love,

W. C.

### TO THE SAME.

*The Greenhouse, September* 18, 1781.

MY DEAR FRIEND—I return your preface, with many thanks for so affectionate an introduction to the public. I have observed nothing that in my judgment required alteration except a single sentence in the first paragraph, which I have not obliterated, that you may restore it if you please, by obliterating my interlineation. My reason for proposing an amendment of it was, that your meaning did not strike me, which therefore I have endeavoured to make more obvious. The rest is what I would wish it to be. You say, indeed, more in my commendation than I can modestly say of myself, but something will be allowed to the partiality of friendship on so interesting an occasion.

I have no objection in the world to your conveying a copy to Dr. Johnson; though I well know that one of his pointed sarcasms, if he should happen to be displeased, would soon find its way into all companies, and spoil the sale. He writes, indeed, like a man that thinks a great deal, and that sometimes thinks religiously; but report informs me that he has been severe enough in his animadversions on Dr. Watts, who was nevertheless, if I am in any degree a judge of verse, a man of true poetical ability: careless, indeed, for the most part, and inattentive too often to those niceties which constitute elegance of expression, but frequently sublime in his conceptions, and masterly in his execution. Pope, I have heard, had placed him once in the *Dunciad*, but on being advised to read before he judged him, was convinced that he deserved other treatment, and thrust somebody's blockhead into the gap, whose name, consisting of a monosyllable, happened to fit it. Whatever faults, however,

I may be chargeable with as a poet, I cannot accuse myself of negligence. I never suffer a line to pass till I have made it as good as I can; and though my doctrines may offend this king of critics, he will not, I flatter myself, be disgusted by slovenly inaccuracy, either in the numbers, rhymes, or language. Let the rest take its chance. It is possible he may be pleased; and if he should, I shall have engaged on my side one of the best trumpeters in the kingdom. Let him only speak as favourably of me as he has spoken of Sir Richard Blackmore (who, though he shines in his poem called "Creation," has written more absurdities in verse than any writer of our country), and my success will be secured.

I have often promised myself a laugh with you about your pipe, but have always forgotten it when I have been writing, and at present I am not much in a laughing humour. You will observe, however, for your comfort and the honour of that same pipe, that it hardly falls within the line of my censure. You never fumigate the ladies, or force them out of company; nor do you use it as an incentive to hard drinking. Your friends, indeed, have reason to complain that it frequently deprives them of the pleasure of your own conversation, while it leads you either into your study or your garden; but in all other respects it is as innocent a pipe as can be. Smoke away, therefore, and remember that if one poet has condemned the practice, a better than he (the witty and elegant Hawkins Browne) has been warm in the praise of it.

"Retirement" grows, but more slowly than any of its predecessors. Time was when I could with ease produce fifty, sixty, or seventy lines in a morning; now I generally fall short of thirty, and am sometimes forced to be content with a dozen. It consists at present, I suppose, of between six and seven hundred; so that there are hopes of an end, and I daresay Johnson will give me time enough to finish it.

> I add nothing to this, but *still I am*
> Your most affectionate and humble WILLIAM.

### TO THE SAME.

*November* 7, 1781.

MY DEAR FRIEND—So far as Johnson is to be depended on, and I begin to hope that he is now in earnest, I think myself warranted to furnish you with an answer to the question which you say so often meets you. Mr. Unwin made the same inquiry at his shop on his way to Stock from Brighthelmstone, when he assured him that the book would be printed off in a month, and ready for publication after the holidays. For some time past the business has proceeded glibly, and if he perseveres at the same rate, it is probable his answer will prove a true one. In my last despatches I sent him a new edition of the title-page, having discarded the Latin paradox which stood at the head of the former, and added a French motto to that from Virgil. It is taken from a volume of the excellent Caraccioli, called *Jouissance de soi-même*.

Mr. Bull is an honest man. We have seen him twice since he received your orders to march hither, and faithfully told us it was in consequence of those orders that he came. He dined with us yesterday; we were all in pretty good spirits, and the day passed very agreeably. It is not long since he called on Mr. Scott. Mr. Raban came in. Mr. Bull began, addressing himself to the former: "My friend, you are in trouble, you are unhappy; I read it in your countenance." Mr. Scott replied he had been so, but he was better. "Come, then," says Mr. Bull, "I will expound to you the cause of all your anxiety. You are too common; you make yourself cheap. Visit your people less, and converse more with your own heart. How often do you speak to them in the week?" "Thrice." "Ay, there it is! Your sermons are an old ballad; your prayers are an old ballad; and you are an old ballad too." "I would wish to tread in the steps of Mr. Newton." "You do well to follow his steps in all other instances, but in this instance you are wrong, and so was he. Mr. Newton trod a path which no man but himself could have used so long as he did, and he wore it out long before he went from Olney. Too much familiarity and condescension cost him the estimation of his people. He thought he should ensure their love, to which he had the best possible title, and by those very means he lost it. Be wise, my friend; take warning; make yourself scarce if you wish that persons of little understanding should know how to prize you."

When he related to us this harangue, so nicely adjusted to the case of the third person present, it did us both good, and as Jacques says,

"It made my lungs to crow like chanticleer."

Mrs. Unwin wishes me to inform you that the character of Thomas ——— is no longer a doubtful one in Olney. He is much addicted to public-houses, and everybody knows it. Geary Ball led him home drunk from one of them not long since, where he had been playing at quoits, and regaling himself with drink till he was unable to stand unsupported. She thought it the part of a friend to communicate to you this piece of intelligence, that you may not lend him money and lose it. He used frequently to borrow of us, but we intend henceforth to discontinue our aids of that sort.

I have only seen Mr. Jones since I received your last, and have had no opportunity to mention to him your inquiry. He was alive yesterday, however, and not long spoke of an intended journey to London.

We wish your letter to your parishioners may have the best effects, and shall be glad to read it. Many thanks for three couple of mackerel, perfectly fresh. Our love of you both, though often sent to London, is still with us. If it is not an inexhaustible well (there is but one love that can, with propriety, be called so), it is, however, a very deep one, and not likely to fail while we are living.—Yours, my dear Sir, W. C.

TO JOSEPH HILL, ESQ.

*November* 30, 1781.

MY DEAR FRIEND—Though I have a deal of wit, and Mrs. Unwin has much more, it would require more than our joint stock amounts to, to answer all the demands of these gloomy days and long evenings. Books are the only remedy I can think of, but books are a commodity we deal but little in at Olney. If, therefore, it may consist with your other multifarious concerns, I shall be obliged to you if you will be so good as to subscribe for me to some well-furnished circulating library, and leave my address upon the counter written in a legible hand, and order them to send me down a catalogue. Their address you will be so good as to transmit to me, and then you shall have no further trouble.

This being merely a letter of business, I add no more but that I am yours, WM. COWPER.

TO THE REV. WILLIAM UNWIN.

*January* 5, 1782.

MY DEAR FRIEND—Did I allow myself to plead the common excuse of idle correspondents, and esteem it a sufficient reason for not writing that I have nothing to write about, I certainly should not write now. But I have so often found, on similar occasions, when a great penury of matter has seemed to threaten me with an utter impossibility of hatching a letter, that nothing is necessary but to put pen to paper, and go on, in order to conquer all difficulties; that, availing myself of past experience, I now begin with a most assured persuasion that sooner or later, one idea naturally suggesting another, I shall come to a most prosperous conclusion.

In the last "Review,"—I mean in the last but one,—I saw Johnson's critique upon Prior and Pope. I am bound to acquiesce in his opinion of the latter, because it has always been my own. I could never agree with those who preferred him to Dryden; nor with others (I have known such, and persons of taste and discernment too) who could not allow him to be a poet at all. He was certainly a mechanical maker of verses, and in every line he ever wrote we see indubitable marks of most indefatigable industry and labour. Writers who find it necessary to make such strenuous and painful exertions are generally as phlegmatic as they are correct; but Pope was, in this respect, exempted from the common lot of authors of that class. With the unwearied application of a plodding Flemish painter, who draws a shrimp with the most minute exactness, he had all the genius of one of the first masters. Never, I believe, were such talents and such drudgery united. But I admire Dryden most, who has succeeded by mere dint of genius, and in spite of a laziness and carelessness almost peculiar to himself. His faults are numberless, and so are his beauties. His faults are those of a great man, and his beauties are such (at least sometimes) as Pope, with all his touching and retouching, could never equal. So far, therefore, I have no quarrel with Johnson. But I cannot subscribe to what he says of Prior. In the first place, though my memory may fail me, I do not recollect that he takes any notice of his Solomon—in my mind the best poem, whether we consider the subject of it, or the execution, that he ever wrote. In the next place, he condemns him for introducing Venus and Cupid into his love verses, and concludes it impossible his passion could be sincere, because when he would express it he has recourse to fables. But when Prior wrote those deities were not so obsolete as they are at present. His contemporary writers, and some that succeeded him, did not think them beneath their notice. Tibullus, in reality, disbelieved their existence as much as we do; yet Tibullus is allowed to be the prince of all poetical inamoratos, though he mentions them in almost every page. There is a fashion in these things, which the Doctor seems to have forgotten. But what shall we say of his fusty-rusty remarks upon Henry and Emma? I agree with him, that, morally considered, both the knight and his lady are bad characters, and that each exhibits an example which ought not to be followed. The man dissembles in a way that would have justified the woman had she renounced him; and the woman resolves to follow him, at the expense of delicacy, propriety, and even modesty itself. But when the critic calls it a dull dialogue, who but a critic will believe him? There are few readers of poetry of either sex in this country who cannot remember how that enchanting piece has bewitched them—who do not know, that instead of finding it tedious, they have been so delighted with the romantic turn of it, as to have overlooked all its defects, and to have given it a consecrated place in their memories, without ever feeling it a burden. I wonder almost, that as the Bacchanals served Orpheus, the boys and girls do not tear this husky, dry commentator limb from limb, in resentment of such an injury done to their darling poet.

I admire Johnson as a man of great erudition and sense; but when he sets himself up for a judge of writers upon the subject of love, a passion which I suppose he never felt in his life, he might as well think himself qualified to pronounce upon a treatise on horsemanship, or the art of fortification.

The next packet I receive will bring me, I imagine, the last proof-sheet of my volume, which will consist of about three hundred and fifty pages honestly printed.—My public *entrée*, therefore, is not far distant.—Yours,

W. C.

TO THE SAME.

*April* 1, 1782.

MY DEAR FRIEND—I could not have found a better trumpeter. Your zeal to serve the interest of my volume, together with your extensive acquaintance, qualify you perfectly for that most useful office. Methinks I see you with the long tube at your mouth, proclaiming to your numerous connexions my poetical merits, and at proper intervals levelling it at Olney, and pouring into my ear the welcome sound of their approbation. I need not encourage you to proceed—your breath will never fail in such a cause; and thus encouraged, I myself perhaps may proceed also, and when the versifying fit returns, produce another volume. Alas! we shall never receive such commendations from him on the woolsack, as your good friend has lavished upon us. Whence I learn, that however important I may be in my own eyes, I am very insignificant in his. To make me amends, however, for this mortification, Mr. Newton tells me that my book is likely to run, spread, and prosper; that the grave cannot help smiling, and the gay are struck with the truth of it; and that it is likely to find its way into his Majesty's hands, being put into a proper course for that purpose. Now if the King should fall in love with my muse, and with you for her sake, such an event would make us ample amends for the Chancellor's indifference, and you might be the first divine that ever reached a mitre from the shoulders of a poet. But, I believe, we must be content,—I with my gains, if I gain anything, and you with the pleasure of knowing that I am a gainer.

We laughed heartily at your answer to little John's question; and yet I think you might have given him a direct answer—"There are various sorts of cleverness, my dear—I do not know that mine lies in the poetical way, but I can do ten times more towards the entertainment of company in the way of conversation than our friend at Olney. He can rhyme, and I can rattle. If he had my talent, or I had his, we should be too charming, and the world would almost adore us."—Yours,

W. C.

### TO THE SAME.

*August* 3, 1782.

MY DEAR FRIEND—Entertaining some hope that Mr. Newton's next letter would furnish me with the means of satisfying your inquiry on the subject of Dr. Johnson's opinion, I have till now delayed my answer to your last; but the information is not yet come, Mr. Newton having intermitted a week more than usual since his last writing. When I receive it, favourable or not, it shall be communicated to you; but I am not over sanguine in my expectations from that quarter. Very learned and very critical heads are hard to please. He may, perhaps, treat me with lenity for the sake of the subject and design, but the composition, I think, will hardly escape his censure. Though all doctors may not be of the same mind, there is one doctor at least, whom I have lately discovered, my professed admirer. He, too, like Johnson, was with difficulty persuaded to read, having an aversion to all poetry, except the "Night Thoughts," which on a certain occasion, when being confined on board a ship, he had no other employment, he got by heart. He was, however, prevailed upon, and read me several times over; so that if my volume had sailed with him, instead of Dr. Young's, I perhaps might have occupied that shelf in his memory which he then allotted to the Doctor.

It is a sort of paradox, but it is true,—we are never more in danger than when we think ourselves most secure, nor in reality more secure than when we seem to be most in danger. Both sides of this apparent contradiction were lately verified in my experience: Passing from the greenhouse to the barn, I saw three kittens (for we have so many in our retinue) looking with fixed attention on something which lay on the threshold of a door nailed up. I took but little notice of them at first, but a loud hiss engaged me to attend more closely, when behold—a viper! the largest that I remember to have seen, rearing itself, darting its forked tongue, and ejaculating the aforesaid hiss at the nose of a kitten, almost in contact with his lips. I ran into the hall for a hoe with a long handle, with which I intended to assail him, and returning in a few seconds missed him: he was gone, and I feared had escaped me. Still, however, the kittten sat watching immovably upon the same spot. I concluded therefore that, sliding between the door and the threshold, he had found his way out of the garden into the yard—I went round immediately, and there found him in close conversation with the old cat, whose curiosity, being excited by so novel an appearance, inclined her to pat his head repeatedly with her fore foot, with her claws, however, sheathed, and not in anger, but in the way of philosophic inquiry and examination. To prevent her falling a victim to so laudable an exercise of her talents, I interposed in a moment with the hoe, and performed upon him an act of decapitation, which though not immediately mortal proved so in the end. Had he slid into the passages, where it is dark, or had he, when in the yard, met with no interruption from the cat, and secreted himself in any of the outhouses, it is hardly possible but that some of the family must have been bitten; he might have been trodden upon without being perceived, and have slipped away before the sufferer could have distinguished what foe had wounded him. Three years ago we discovered one in the same place, which the barber slew with a trowel.

Our proposed removal to Mr. Small's was, as you suppose, a jest, or rather a joco-serious matter. We never looked upon it as entirely feasible, yet we saw in it something so like practicability, that we did not esteem it altogether unworthy of our attention. It was one of those projects which people of lively imaginations play with, and admire for a few days, and then break in pieces. Lady Austen returned on Thursday from London, where she spent the last fortnight, and whither she was called by an unexpected opportunity to dispose of the remainder of her lease. She has therefore no longer any connexion with the great city, and no house but at Olney. Her abode is to be at the vicarage, where she has hired as much room as she wants, which she will embellish with her own furniture, and which she will occupy as soon as the minister's wife has produced another child, which is expected to make its entry in October.

Mr. Bull, a dissenting minister of Newport, a learned, ingenious, good-natured, pious friend of ours, who sometimes visits us, and whom we visited last week, has put into my hands three volumes of French poetry, composed by Madame Guyon—a quietist, say you, and a fanatic; I will have nothing to do with her.—'Tis very well, you are welcome to have nothing to do with her; but in the meantime her verse is the only French verse I ever read that I found agreeable; there is a neatness in it equal to that which we applaud with so much reason in the compositions of Prior. I have translated several of them, and shall proceed in my translations till I have filled a Liliputian paper book I happen to have by me, which, when filled, I shall present to Mr. Bull. He is her passionate admirer; rode twenty miles to see her picture in the house of a stranger, which stranger politely insisted on his acceptance of it, and it now hangs over his chimney. It is a striking portrait, too characteristic not to be a strong resemblance, and, were it encompassed with a glory, instead of being dressed in a nun's hood, might pass for the face of an angel.—Yours, W. C.

TO MRS. NEWTON.

*November* 23, 1782.

MY DEAR MADAM—The soles with which you favoured us were remarkably fine. Accept our thanks for them; thanks likewise for the trouble you take in vending my poems, and still more for the interest you take in their success. My authorship is undoubtedly pleased when I hear that they are approved either by the great or the small; but to be approved by the great, as Horace observed many years ago, is fame indeed. Having met with encouragement, I consequently wish to write again; but wishes are a very small part of the qualifications necessary for such a purpose. Many a man who has succeeded tolerably well in his first attempt has spoiled all by the second. But it just occurs to me that I told you so once before, and if my memory had served me with the intelligence a minute sooner, I would not have repeated the observation now.

The winter sets in with great severity. The rigour of the season, and the advanced price of grain, are very threatening to the poor. It is well with those that can feed upon a promise, and wrap themselves up warm in the robe of salvation. A good fireside, and a well-spread table, are but very indifferent substitutes for these better accommodations; so very indifferent, that I would gladly exchange them both for the rags and the unsatisfied hunger of the poorest creature that looks forward with hope to a better world, and weeps tears of joy in the midst of penury and distress. What a world is this! How mysteriously governed, and, in appearance, left to itself! One man, having squandered thousands at a gaming-table, finds it convenient to travel; gives his estate to somebody to manage for him; amuses himself a few years in France and Italy; returns, perhaps, wiser than he went, having acquired knowledge which, but for his follies, he would never have acquired; again makes a splendid figure at home, shines in the senate, governs his country as its minister, is admired for his abilities, and, if successful, adored, at least by a party. When he dies, he is praised as a demi-god, and his monument records everything but his vices. The exact contrast of such a picture is to be found in many cottages at Olney. I have no need to describe them; you know the characters I mean. They love God, they trust him, they pray to him in secret, and though he means to reward them openly, the day of recompense is delayed. In the meantime they suffer everything that infirmity and poverty can inflict upon them. Who would suspect, that has not a spiritual eye to discern it, that the fine gentleman was one whom his Maker had in abhorrence, and the wretch last mentioned dear to him as the apple of his eye? It is no wonder that the world who are not in the secret, find themselves obliged, some of them, to doubt a Providence, and others absolutely to deny it, when almost all the real virtue there is in it is to be found living and dying in a state of neglected obscurity, and all the vices of others cannot exclude them from the privilege of worship and honour! But behind the curtain the matter is explained, very little, however, to the satisfaction of the great.

If you ask me why I have written thus, and to you especially, to whom there was no need to write thus, I can only reply, that having a letter to write, and no news to communicate, I picked up the first subject I found, and pursued it as far as was convenient for my purpose.

Mr. Newton and I are of one mind on the subject of patriotism. Our dispute was no sooner begun than it ended. It would be well, perhaps, if, when two disputants begin to engage, their friends would hurry each into a separate chaise, and order them to opposite points of the compass. Let one travel twenty miles east; the other as many west; then let them write their opinions by the post. Much altercation and chafing of the spirit would be prevented; they would sooner come to a right understanding, and, running away from each other, would carry on the combat more judiciously, in exact proportion to the distance.

My love to that gentleman, if you please; and tell him that, like him, though I love my country, I hate its follies and its sins, and had rather see it scourged in mercy than judicially hardened by prosperity.

Mrs. Unwin is not very well, but better than she has been. She adds her love to both. — Yours, my dear madam, as ever, WM. COWPER.

TO JOSEPH HILL, ESQ.

*December* 7, 1782.

MY DEAR FRIEND—At 7 o'clock this evening, being the 7th of December, I imagine I see you in your box at the coffee-house. No doubt the waiter, as ingenious and adroit as his predecessors were before him, raises the tea-pot to the ceiling with his right hand, while in his left the tea-cup, descending almost to the floor, receives a limpid stream; limpid in its descent, but no sooner has it reached its destination, than, frothing and foaming to the view, it becomes a roaring syllabub. This is the nineteenth winter since I saw you in this situation ; and if nineteen more pass over me before I die, I shall still remember a circumstance we have often laughed at.

How different is the complexion of your evenings and mine !—yours, spent amid the ceaseless hum that proceeds from the inside of fifty noisy and busy periwigs; mine, by a domestic fireside, in a retreat as silent as retirement can make it ; where no noise is made but what we make for our own amusement. For instance, here are two rustics and your humble servant in company. One of the ladies has been playing on the harpsichord, while I, with the other, have been playing at battledore and shuttlecock. A little dog, in the meantime, howling under the chair of the former, performed, in the vocal way, to admiration. This entertainment over, I began my letter, and having nothing more important to communicate, have given you an account of it. I know you love dearly to be idle, when you can find an opportunity to be so ; but as such opportunities are rare with you, I thought it possible that a short description of the idleness I enjoy might give you pleasure. The happiness we cannot call our own, we yet seem to possess while we sympathise with our friends who can.

The papers tell me that peace is at hand, and that it is at a great distance; that the siege of Gibraltar is abandoned, and that it is still to be continued. It is happy for me that, though I love my country, I have but little curiosity. There was a time when these contradictions would have distressed me, but I have learnt by experience that it is best for little people like myself to be patient, and to wait till time affords the intelligence which no speculations of theirs can ever furnish.

I thank you for a fine cod with oysters, and hope that, ere long, I shall have to thank you for procuring me Elliot's medicines. Every time I feel the least uneasiness in either eye I tremble lest, my Æsculapius being departed, my infallible remedy should be lost for ever. Adieu. My respects to Mrs. Hill.—Yours faithfully,

WM. COWPER.

TO THE REV. JOHN NEWTON.

*January 26, 1783.*

MY DEAR FRIEND—It is reported among persons of the best intelligence at Olney—the barber, the schoolmaster, and the drummer of a corps quartered at this place—that the belligerent powers are at last reconciled, the articles of the treaty adjusted, and that peace is at the door. I saw this morning, at nine o'clock, a group of about twelve figures very closely engaged in a conference, as I suppose, upon the same subject. The scene of consultation was a blacksmith's shed, very comfortably screened from the wind, and directly opposed to the morning sun. Some held their hands behind them, some had them folded across their bosom, and others had thrust them into their breeches pockets. Every man's posture bespoke a pacific turn of mind; but the distance being too great for their words to reach me, nothing transpired. I am willing, however, to hope that the secret will not be a secret long, and that you and I, equally interested in the event, though not, perhaps, equally well informed, shall soon have an opportunity to rejoice in the completion of it. The powers of Europe have clashed with each other to a fine purpose; that the Americans, at length declared independent, may keep themselves so if they can; and that what the parties, who have thought proper to dispute upon that point, have wrested from each other in the course of the conflict may be, in the issue of it, restored to the proper owner. Nations may be guilty of a conduct that would render an individual infamous for ever, and yet carry their heads high, talk of their glory, and despise their neighbours. Your opinions and mine, I mean our political ones, are not exactly of a piece, yet I cannot think otherwise upon this subject than I have always done. England, more perhaps through the fault of her generals than her councils, has in some instances acted with a spirit of cruel animosity she was never chargeable with till now. But this is the worst that can be said. On the other hand, the Americans, who, if they had contented themselves with a struggle for lawful liberty, would have deserved applause, seem to me to have incurred the guilt of parricide by renouncing their parent, by making her ruin their favourite object, and by associating themselves with her worst enemy for the accomplishment of their purpose. France and, of course, Spain have acted a treacherous, a thievish part. They have stolen America from England, and whether they are able to possess themselves of that jewel or not hereafter, it was doubtless what they intended. Holland appears to me in a meaner light than any of them. They quarrelled with a friend for an enemy's sake. The French led them by the nose, and the English have thrashed them for suffering it. My view of the contest being, and having been always such, I have consequently brighter hopes for England than her situation some time since seemed to justify. She is the only injured party. America may perhaps call her the aggressor, but if she were so, America has not only repelled the injury, but done a greater. As to the rest, if perfidy, treachery, avarice, and ambition can prove their cause to have been a rotten one, those proofs are found upon them. I think, therefore, that whatever scourge may be prepared for England on some future day, her ruin is not yet to be expected.

Acknowledge, now, that I am worthy of a place under the shed I described, and that I should make no small figure among the *quidnuncs* of Olney.

I wish the society you have formed may prosper. Your subjects will be of greater importance, and discussed with more sufficiency. The earth is a grain of sand, but the spiritual interests of man are commensurate with the heavens.

Pray remind Mr. Bull, who has too much genius to have a good memory, that he has an account to settle for Mrs. Unwin with her grocer, and give our love to him. Accept for yourself and Mrs. Newton your just share of the same commodity, with our united thanks for a very fine barrel of oysters. This, indeed, is rather commending the barrel than its contents. I should say, therefore, for a barrel of very fine oysters.—Yours, my dear friend, as ever, W. C.

TO THE REV. WILLIAM UNWIN.

*May* 12, 1783.

MY DEAR FRIEND—A letter written from such a place as this is a creation; and creation is a work for which mere mortal man is very indifferently qualified. *Ex nihilo nihil fit* is a maxim that applies itself in every case where Deity is not concerned. With this view of the matter, I should charge myself with extreme folly for pretending to work without materials did I not know that although nothing could be the result, even that nothing will be welcome. If I can tell you no news, I can tell you at least that I esteem you highly; that my friendship with you and yours is the only balm of my life, a comfort sufficient to reconcile me to an existence destitute of every other. This is not the language of to-day, only the effect of a transient cloud suddenly brought over me, and suddenly to be removed, but punctually expressive of my habitual frame of mind, such as it has been these ten years.

In the "Review" of last month I met with an account of a sermon preached by Mr. Paley at the consecration of his friend, Bishop Law. The critic admires and extols the preacher, and devoutly prays the Lord of the Harvest to send forth more such labourers into his vineyard. I rather differ from him in opinion, not being able to conjecture in what respect the vineyard will be benefited by such a measure. He is certainly ingenious, and has stretched his ingenuity to the uttermost in order to exhibit the Church established, consisting of bishops, priests, and deacons, in the most favourable point of view. I lay it down for a rule, that when much ingenuity is necessary to gain an argument credit, that argument is unsound at bottom. So is his, and so are all the petty devices by which he seeks to enforce it. He says first, "that the appointment of various orders in the Church is attended with this good consequence,—that each class of people is supplied with a clergy of their own level and description, with whom they may live and associate on terms of equality." But in order to effect this good purpose there ought to be at least three parsons in every parish,—one for the gentry, one for traders and mechanics, and one for the lowest of the vulgar. Neither is it easy to find many parishes where the laity at large have any society with their minister at all. This, therefore, is fanciful, and a mere invention. In the next place, he says it gives a dignity to the ministry itself, and the clergy share in the respect paid to their superiors. Much good may such participation do them ! They themselves know how little it amounts to. The dignity a parson derives from the lawn sleeves and square cap of his diocesan will never endanger his humility.

Pope says truly—

> Worth makes the man, and want of it the fellow;
> The rest is all but leather or prunello.

Again—"Rich and splendid situations in the Church have been justly regarded as prizes, held out to invite persons of good hopes and ingenious attainments." Agreed. But the prize held out in the Scripture is of a very different kind; and our ecclesiastical baits are too often snapped by the worthless, and persons of no attainments at all. They are, indeed, incentives to avarice and ambition, but not to those acquirements by which only the ministerial function can be adorned,—zeal for the salvation of men, humility, and self-denial. Mr. Paley and I, therefore, cannot agree.—Yours, my dear friend,

W. C.

TO THE REV. WM. BULL.

*June* 3, 1783.

MY DEAR FRIEND—My greenhouse, fronted with myrtles, and where I hear nothing but the pattering of a fine shower, and the sound of distant thunder, wants only the fumes of your pipe to make it perfectly delightful. Tobacco was not known in the Golden Age. So much the worse for the Golden Age. This age of iron, or lead, would be insupportable without it; and therefore we may reasonably suppose that the happiness of those better days would have been much improved by the use of it. We hope that you and your son are perfectly recovered. The season has been most unfavourable to animal life; and I, who am merely animal, have suffered much by it.

Though I should be glad to write, I write little or nothing. The time for such fruit is not yet come; but I expect it, and I wish for it. I want amusement, and, deprived of that, have none to supply the place of it. I send you, however, according to my promise to send you everything, two stanzas composed at the request of Lady Austen. She wanted words to a tune she much admired, and I gave her these on Peace.—Yours,   W.C.

### TO THE REV. WILLIAM UNWIN.

*June* 8, 1783.

MY DEAR WILLIAM—Our severest winter, commonly called the spring, is now over, and I find myself seated in my favourite recess, the greenhouse. In such a situation, so silent, so shady, where no human foot is heard, and where only my myrtles presume to peep in at the window, you may suppose I have no interruption to complain of, and that my thoughts are perfectly at my command. But the beauties of the spot are themselves an interruption, my attention being called upon by those very myrtles, by a double row of grass pinks just beginning to blossom, and by a bed of beans already in bloom; and you are to consider it, if you please, as no small proof of my regard, that though you have so many powerful rivals, I disengage myself from them all, and devote this hour entirely to you.

You are not acquainted with the Rev. Mr. Bull of Newport; perhaps it is as well for you that you are not. You would regret still more than you do that there are so many miles interposed between us. He spends part of the day with us to-morrow. A Dissenter, but a liberal one; a man of letters and of genius; master of a fine imagination, or rather not master of it—an imagination which, when he finds himself in the company he loves, and can confide in, runs away with him into such fields of speculation as amuse and enliven every other imagination that has the happiness to be of the party! At other times he has a tender and delicate sort of melancholy in his disposition, not less agreeable in its way. No men are better qualified for companions in such a world as this than men of such a temperament. Every scene of life has two sides, a dark and a bright one, and the mind that has an equal mixture of melancholy and vivacity is best of all qualified for the contemplation of either. He can be lively without levity, and pensive without dejection. Such a man is Mr. Bull. But—he smokes tobacco— nothing is perfect—

*Nihil est ab omni*
*Parte beatum.*

I find that your friend Mr. Fytche has lost his cause; and, more mortifying still, has lost it by a single voice. Had I been a peer, he should have been secure of mine; for I am persuaded that if conditional presentations were in fashion, and if every minister held his benefice, as the judges their office, upon the terms of *quamdiu bene se gesserit*, it would be better for the cause of religion, and more for the honour of the Establishment. There ought to be discipline somewhere; and if the Bishops will not exercise it, I do not see why lay patrons should have their hands tied.  If I remember the state of your case (and I never heard it stated but by you), my reflections upon it are pertinent.  It is, however, long since we talked about it, and I may possibly misconceive it at present; if so, they go for nothing.  I understand that he presented upon condition that if the parson proved immoral or negligent, he should have liberty to call upon him either for his resignation, or the penalty.  If I am wrong, correct me.—Yours, W. C.

TO THE SAME.

*August* 4, 1783.

MY DEAR WILLIAM — I feel myself sensibly obliged by the interest you take in the success of my productions. Your feelings upon the subject are such as I should have myself, had I an opportunity of calling Johnson aside to make the inquiry you propose.  But I am pretty well prepared for the worst, and so long as I have the opinion of a few capable judges in my favour, and am thereby convinced that I have neither disgraced myself nor my subject, shall not feel myself disposed to any extreme anxiety about the sale.  To aim with success at the spiritual good of mankind, and to become popular by writing on scriptural subjects, were an unreasonable ambition even for a poet to entertain in days like these. Verse may have many charms, but has none powerful enough to conquer the aversion of a dissipated age to such instruction.  Ask the question therefore boldly, and be not mortified even though he should shake his head and drop his chin; for it is no more than we have reason to expect.  We will lay the fault upon the vice of the times, and we will acquit the poet.

I am glad you were pleased with my Latin ode, and

indeed with my English dirge, as much as I was myself. The tune laid me under a disadvantage, obliging me to write in Alexandrines; which I suppose would suit no ear but a French one; neither did I intend anything more than that the subject and the words should be sufficiently accommodated to the music. The ballad is a species of poetry I believe peculiar to this country, equally adapted to the drollest and the most tragical subjects. Simplicity and ease are its proper characteristics. Our forefathers excelled in it; but we moderns have lost the art. It is observed that we have few good English odes. But to make amends, we have many excellent ballads, not inferior perhaps in true poetical merit to some of the very best odes that the Greek or Latin languages have to boast of. It is a sort of composition I was ever fond of, and if graver matters had not called me another way, should have addicted myself to it more than to any other. I inherit a taste for it from my father, who succeeded well in it himself, and who lived at a time when the best pieces in that way were produced. What can be prettier than Gay's ballad, or rather Swift's, Arbuthnot's, Pope's, and Gay's, in the What-do-ye-call-it—"''Twas when the seas were roaring?" I have been well informed that they all contributed, and that the most celebrated association of clever fellows this country ever saw did not think it beneath them to unite their strength and abilities in the composition of a song. The success, however, answered their wishes. The ballads that Bourne has translated, beautiful in themselves, are still more beautiful in his version of them, infinitely surpassing in my judgment all that Ovid or Tibullus have left behind them. They are quite as elegant, and far more touching and pathetic, than the tenderest strokes of either.

So much for ballads and ballad-writers. "A worthy subject," you will say, "for a man whose head might be filled with better things:"—and it is filled with better things, but to so ill a purpose, that I thrust into it all manner of topics that may prove more amusing; as for instance, I have two goldfinches, which in the summer occupy the greenhouse. A few days since, being employed in cleaning out their cages, I placed that which I had in hand upon the table, while the other hung against the wall; the windows and the doors stood wide open. I went to fill the fountain at the pump, and on my return was not a little surprised to find a goldfinch sitting on the top of the cage I had been cleaning, and singing to and kissing the goldfinch within. I approached him, and he discovered no fear; still nearer, and he discovered none. I advanced my hand towards him, and he took no notice of it. I seized him, and supposed I had caught a new bird, but casting my eye upon the other cage perceived my mistake. Its inhabitant, during my absence, had contrived to find an opening, where the wire had been a little bent, and made no other use of the escape it afforded him than to salute his friend, and to converse with him more intimately than he had done before. I returned him to his proper mansion, but in vain. In less than a minute he had thrust his little person through the aperture again, and again perched upon his neighbour's cage, kissing him, as at the first, and singing, as if transported with the fortunate adventure. I could not but respect such friendship as, for the sake of its gratification, had twice declined an opportunity to be free, and, consenting to their union, resolved that for the future one cage should hold them both. I am glad of such incidents. For at a pinch, and when I need entertainment, the versification of them serves to divert me.         W. C.

TO THE SAME.

MY DEAR FRIEND—It is hard upon us striplings who have uncles still living (N.B. I myself have an uncle still alive), that those venerable gentlemen should stand in our way, even when the ladies are in question; that I, for instance, should find in one page of your letter a hope that Miss Shuttleworth would be of your party, and be told in the next that she is engaged to your uncle. Well, we may perhaps never be uncles, but we may reasonably hope that the time is coming when others, as young as we are now, shall envy us the privileges of old age, and see us engross that share in the attention of the ladies to which their youth must aspire in vain. Make our compliments, if you please, to your sister Eliza, and tell her that we are both mortified at having missed the pleasure of seeing her.

Balloons are so much the mode, that even in this country we have attempted a balloon. You may possibly remember that at a place called Weston, a little more than a mile from Olney, there lives a family whose name is Throckmorton. The present possessor of the estate is a young man whom I remember a boy. He has a wife, who is young, genteel, and handsome. They are Papists, but much more amiable than many Protestants. We never had any intercourse with the family, though ever since we lived here we have enjoyed the range of their pleasure-grounds, having been favoured with a key, which admits us into all. When this man succeeded to the estate on the death of his elder brother, and came to settle at Weston, I sent him a complimentary card, requesting the continuance of that privilege, having till then enjoyed it by favour of his mother, who on that occasion went to finish her days at Bath. You may conclude that he

granted it, and for about two years nothing more passed
between us. A fortnight ago I received an invitation in
the civilest terms, in which he told me that the next day
he should attempt to fill a balloon, and if it would be any
pleasure to me to be present, should be happy to see me.
Your mother and I went. The whole country were there,
but the balloon could not be filled. The endeavour was,
I believe, very philosophically made, but such a process
depends for its success upon such niceties as make it very
precarious. Our reception, was, however, flattering to
a great degree, insomuch that more notice seemed to be
taken of us than we could possibly have expected, indeed
rather more than of any of his other guests. They even
seemed anxious to recommend themselves to our regards.
We drank chocolate, and were asked to dine, but were
engaged. A day or two afterwards Mrs. Unwin and I
walked that way, and were overtaken in a shower. I
found a tree that I thought would shelter us both, a large
elm, in a grove that fronts the mansion. Mrs. T. observed
us, and, running towards us in the rain, insisted on our
walking in. He was gone out. We sat chatting with
her till the weather cleared up, and then at her instance
took a walk with her in the garden. The garden is almost
their only walk, and is certainly their only retreat in which
they are not liable to interruption. She offered us a key
of it in a manner that made it impossible not to accept it,
and said she would send us one. A few days afterwards,
in the cool of the evening, we walked that way again.
We saw them going toward the house, and exchanged
bows and curtsies at a little distance, but did not join them.
In a few minutes, when we had passed the house, and had
almost reached the gate that opens out of the park into
the adjoining field, I heard the iron gate belonging to the
courtyard ring, and saw Mr. T. advancing hastily towards
us; we made equal haste to meet him; he presented to us

the key, which I told him I esteemed a singular favour, and after a few such speeches as are made on such occasions we parted. This happened about a week ago. I concluded nothing less than that all this civility and attention was designed on their part as a prelude to a nearer acquaintance; but here at present the matter rests. I should like exceedingly to be on an easy footing there, to give a morning call, and now and then to receive one, but nothing more. For though he is one of the most agreeable men I ever saw, I could not wish to visit him in any other way; neither our house, furniture, servants, nor income, being such as qualify us to make entertainments; neither would I on any account be introduced to the neighbouring gentry, which must be the consequence of our dining there, there not being a man in the country except himself with whom I could endure to associate. They are squires—merely such—purse-proud, and sportsmen. Mr. T. is altogether a man of fashion, and respectable on every account.

I have told you a long story. Farewell. We number the days as they pass, and are glad that we shall see you and your sister soon.—Yours, etc., W. C.

TO THE REV. JOHN NEWTON.

*November* 30, 1783.

MY DEAR FRIEND—I have neither long visits to pay nor to receive, nor ladies to spend hours in telling me that which might be told in five minutes, yet often find myself obliged to be an economist of time, and to make the most of a short opportunity. Let our station be as retired as it may, there is no want of playthings and avocations, nor much need to seek them, in this world of ours. Business, or what presents itself to us under that imposing character, will find us out, even in the stillest retreat, and plead its importance, however trivial in reality, as a just demand upon our attention. It is wonderful how, by means of such real or seeming necessities, my time is stolen away. I have just time to observe that time is short, and by the time I have made the observation time is gone. I have wondered in former days at the patience of the antediluvian world; that they could endure a life almost millenary with so little variety as seems to have fallen to their share. It is probable that they had much fewer employments than we. Their affairs lay in a narrower compass; their libraries were indifferently furnished; philosophical researches were carried on with much less industry and acuteness of penetration; and fiddles, perhaps, were not even invented. How then could seven or eight hundred years of life be supportable? I have asked this question formerly, and been at a loss to resolve it; but I think I can answer it now. I will suppose myself born a thousand years before Noah was born or thought of. I rise with the sun; I worship; I prepare my breakfast; I swallow a bucket of goat's milk, and a dozen good sizeable cakes. I fasten a new string to my bow, and my youngest boy, a lad of about thirty years of age, having played with my arrows till he has stript off all the feathers, I find myself obliged to repair them. The morning is thus spent in preparing for the chase, and it is become necessary that I should dine. I dig up my roots; I wash them; I boil them; I find them not done enough; I boil them again; my wife is angry; we dispute; we settle the point; but in the meantime the fire goes out and must be kindled again. All this is very amusing. I hunt; I bring home the prey; with the skin of it I mend an old coat, or I make a new one. By this time the day is far spent; I feel myself fatigued, and retire to rest. Thus what with tilling the ground and eating the fruit of it, hunting, and walking, and running, and mending old clothes, and sleeping and rising again, I can suppose an inhabitant of the primæval world so much occupied as to sigh over the shortness of life, and to find at the end of many centuries that they had all slipped through his fingers, and were passed away like a shadow. What wonder then that I, who live in a day of so much greater refinement, when there is so much more to be wanted, and wished, and to be enjoyed, should feel myself now and then pinched in point of opportunity, and at some loss for leisure to fill four sides of a sheet like this. Thus, however, it is; and if the ancient gentlemen to whom I have referred, and their complaints of the disproportion of time to the occasions they had for it, will not serve me as an excuse, I must even plead guilty, and confess that I am often in haste when I have no good reason for being so.

This by way of introduction; now for my letter. Mr. Scott is desired by Mr. De Coetlegon to contribute to the *Theological Review*, of which, I suppose, that gentleman is a manager. He says he has insured your assistance, and at the same time desires mine, either in prose or verse. He did well to apply to you, because you can afford him substantial help; but as for me, had he known me better, he would never have suspected me for a theologian, either in rhyme or otherwise.

Lord Dartmouth's Mr. Wright spent near two hours with me this morning: a respectable old man, whom I always see with pleasure, both for his master's sake and for his own. I was glad to learn from him that his lordship has better health than he has enjoyed for some years. —Believe me, my dear friend, your affectionate,

WM. COWPER.

TO THE REV. WILLIAM UNWIN.

*March* 21, 1784.

MY DEAR WILLIAM—I thank you for the entertainment you have afforded me. I often wish for a library; often regret my folly in selling a good collection; but I have one in Essex. It is rather remote; indeed, too distant for occasional reference; but it serves the purpose of amusement, and a waggon being a very suitable vehicle for an author, I find myself commodiously supplied. Last night I made an end of reading Johnson's Prefaces; but, the number of poets whom he has vouchsafed to chronicle being fifty-six, there must be many with whose history I am not yet acquainted. These, or some of these, if it suits you to give them a part of your chaise, when you come, will be heartily welcome. I am very much the biographer's humble admirer. His uncommon share of good sense, and his forcible expression, secure to him that tribute from all his readers. He has a penetrating insight into character, and a happy talent of correcting the popular opinion upon all occasions where it is erroneous; and this he does with the boldness of a man who will think for himself, but, at the same time, with a justness of sentiment that convinces us he does not differ from others through affectation, but because he has a sounder judgment. This remark, however, has his narrative for its object, rather than his critical performance. In the latter I do not think him always just when he departs from the general opinion. He finds no beauties in Milton's *Lycidas*. He pours contempt upon Prior to such a degree, that, were he really as undeserving of notice as he represents him, he ought no longer to be numbered among the poets. These, indeed, are the two capital instances in which he has offended me. There are others less important, which I have not room to enumerate, and in which I am less confident that he is wrong. What suggested to him the thought that the *Alma* was written in imitation of *Hudibras*, I cannot conceive. In former years they were both favourites of mine, and I often read them; but never saw in them the least resemblance to each other; nor do I now, except that they are composed in verse of the same measure. After all, it is a melancholy observation, which it is impossible not to make after having run through this series of poetical lives, that, where there were such shining talents, there should be so little virtue. These luminaries of our country seem to have been kindled into a brighter blaze than others, only that their spots might be more noticed! So much can nature do for our intellectual part, and so little for our moral. What vanity, what petulance in Pope! How painfully sensible of censure, and yet how restless in provocation! To what mean artifices could Addison stoop in hopes of injuring the reputation of his friend! Savage, how sordidly vicious, and the more condemned for the pains that are taken to palliate his vices. Offensive as they appear through a veil, how would they disgust without one. What a sycophant to the public taste was Dryden; sinning against his feelings, lewd in his writings, though chaste in his conversation. I know not but one might search these eight volumes with a candle, as the prophet says, to find a man, and not find one, unless, perhaps, Arbuthnot were he.

I shall begin Beattie this evening, and propose to myself much satisfaction in reading him. In him, at least, I shall find a man whose faculties have now and then a glimpse from Heaven upon them,—a man, not indeed in possession of much evangelical light, but faithful to what he has, and never neglecting an opportunity to use it.

How much more respectable such a character than that of thousands who would call him blind, and yet have not the grace to practise half his virtues! He, too, is a poet, and wrote the *Minstrel*. The specimen which I have seen of it pleased me much. If you have the whole, I should be glad to read it. I may, perhaps, since you allow me the liberty, indulge myself here and there with a marginal annotation, but shall not use that allowance wantonly so as to deface the volumes.

Your mother wishes you to buy for her ten yards and a half of yard-wide Irish, from two shillings to two shillings and sixpence per yard; and my head will be equally obliged to you for a hat, of which I enclose a string that gives you the circumference. The depth of the crown must be four inches and one-eighth. Let it not be a round slouch, which I abhor, but a smart, well-cocked, fashionable affair. A fashionable hat likewise for your mother; a black one if they are worn; otherwise, chip.—Yours, my dear William,                                          W. C.

TO THE REV. JOHN NEWTON.

*March* 29, 1784.

MY DEAR FRIEND—It being his Majesty's pleasure that I should yet have another opportunity to write before he dissolves the Parliament, I avail myself of it with all possible alacrity. I thank you for your last, which was not the less welcome for coming, like an extraordinary gazette, at a time when it was not expected.

As, when the sea is uncommonly agitated, the water finds its way into creeks and holes of rocks, which in its calmer state it never reaches, in like manner, the effect of these turbulent times is felt even at Orchardside, where in general we live as undisturbed by the political element, as shrimps or cockles that have been accidentally deposited in some hollow beyond the water-mark by the usual dashing of the waves. We were sitting yesterday after dinner—the two ladies and myself—very composedly, and without the least apprehension of any such intrusion, in our snug parlour, one lady knitting, the other netting, and the gentleman winding worsted, when, to our unspeakable surprise, a mob appeared before the window, a smart rap was heard at the door, the boys hallooed, and the maid announced Mr. Grenville. Puss[1] was unfortunately let out of her box, so that the candidate, with all his good friends at his heels, was refused admittance at the grand entry, and referred to the back door, as the only possible way of approach.

Candidates are creatures not very susceptible of affronts, and would rather, I suppose, climb in at a window than be absolutely excluded. In a minute the yard, the kitchen, and the parlour were filled. Mr. Grenville, advancing towards me, shook me by the hand with a degree of cordiality that was extremely seducing. As soon as he and as many more as could find chairs were seated, he began to open the intent of his visit. I told him I had no vote, for which he readily gave me credit. I assured him I had no influence, which he was not equally inclined to believe, and the less, no doubt, because Mr. Ashburner, the drapier, addressing himself to me at that moment, informed me that I had a great deal. Supposing that I could not be possessed of such a treasure without knowing it, I ventured to confirm my first assertion by saying that if I had any I was utterly at a loss to imagine where it could be, or wherein it consisted. Thus ended the conference. Mr. Grenville squeezed me by the hand again, kissed the ladies, and withdrew. He kissed likewise the maid in the kitchen,

[1] His tame hare.

and seemed upon the whole a most loving, kissing, kind-hearted gentleman. He is very young, genteel, and handsome. He has a pair of very good eyes in his head, which not being sufficient, as it should seem, for the many nice and difficult purposes of a senator, he has a third also, which he wore suspended by a riband from his button-hole. The boys hallooed, the dogs barked, Puss scampered; the hero, with his long train of obsequious followers, withdrew. We made ourselves very merry with the adventure, and in a short time settled into our former tranquillity, never probably to be thus interrupted more. I thought myself, however, happy in being able to affirm truly that I had not that influence for which he sued; and for which, had I been possessed of it, with my present views of the dispute between the Crown and the Commons, I must have refused him, for he is on the side of the former. It is comfortable to be of no consequence in a world where one cannot exercise any without disobliging somebody. The town, however, seems to be much at his service, and, if he be equally successful throughout the county, he will undoubtedly gain his election. Mr. Ashburner, perhaps, was a little mortified, because it was evident that I owed the honour of this visit to his misrepresentation of my importance. But had he thought proper to assure Mr. Grenville that I had three heads, I should not, I suppose, have been bound to produce them.

Mr. Scott, who you say was so much admired in your pulpit, would be equally admired in his own, at least by all capable judges, were he not so apt to be angry with his congregation. This hurts him, and, had he the understanding and eloquence of Paul himself, would still hurt him. He seldom, hardly ever indeed, preaches a gentle, well-tempered sermon, but I hear it highly commended; but warmth of temper, indulged to a degree that may be called scolding, defeats the end of preaching.

It is a misapplication of his powers, which it also cripples, and teases away his hearers. But he is a good man, and may perhaps outgrow it.

Many thanks for the worsted, which is excellent. We are as well as a spring hardly less severe than the severest winter will give us leave to be. With our united love, we conclude ourselves yours and Mrs. Newton's affectionate and faithful
W. C.
M. V.

TO THE SAME.

*April* 26, 1784.

MY DEAR FRIEND—We are truly sorry that you have been indisposed. It is well, however, to have passed through such a season, and to have fared no worse. A cold and a sore throat are troublesome things, but in general an ague is more troublesome; and in this part of the world few have escaped one. I have lately been an invalid myself, and have just recovered from a rheumatic pain in my back, the most excruciating of the sort I ever felt. There was talk of bleeding and blistering, but I escaped with only an embrocation and a box of pills. Mr. Grindon attended me, who, though he fidgets about the world as usual, is, I think, a dying man, having had some time since a stroke of apoplexy and lately a paralytic one. His loss will be felt in this country. Though I do not think him absolutely an Æsculapius, I believe him to be as skilful as most of his fraternity in the neighbourhood; besides which he has the merit of being extremely cautious, a very necessary quality in a practitioner upon the constitutions of others.

We are glad that your book runs. It will not, indeed, satisfy those whom nóthing could satisfy but your accession to their party; but the liberal will say you do well, and it is in the opinion of such men only that you can feel yourself interested.

I have lately been employed in reading Beattie, and Blair's Lectures. The latter I have not yet finished. I find the former the most agreeable of the two, indeed the most entertaining writer upon dry subjects that I ever met with. His imagination is highly poetical, his language easy and elegant, and his manner so familiar, that we seem to be conversing with an old friend, upon terms of the most sociable intercourse, while we read him. Blair is, on the contrary, rather stiff; not that his style is pedantic, but his air is formal. He is a sensible man, and understands his subjects, but too conscious that he is addressing the public, and too solicitous about his success, to indulge himself for a moment in that play of fancy which makes the other so agreeable. In Blair we find a scholar, in Beattie both a scholar and an amiable man; indeed so amiable that I have wished for his acquaintance ever since I read his book. Having never in my life perused a page of Aristotle, I am glad to have had an opportunity of learning more than, I suppose, he would have taught me, from the writings of two modern critics. I felt myself, too, a little disposed to compliment my own acumen upon the occasion. For, though the art of writing and composing was never much my study, I did not find that they had any great news to tell me. They have assisted me in putting my own observations into some method, but have not suggested many, of which I was not by some means or other previously apprised. In fact, critics did not originally beget authors; but authors made critics. Common-sense dictated to writers the necessity of method, connexion, and thoughts congruous to the nature of their subject; genius prompted them with embellishments; and then came the critics. Observing the good effects of an attention to these items, they enacted laws for the observance of them in time to come; and, having drawn their rules for good writing from what was actually well written, boasted themselves the inventors of an art which yet the authors of the day had already exemplified. They are, however, useful in their way, giving us at one view a map of the boundaries which propriety sets to fancy; and serving as judges to whom the public may at once appeal when pestered with the vagaries of those who have had the hardiness to transgress them.

The candidates for this county have set an example of economy which other candidates would do well to follow, having come to an agreement on both sides to defray the expenses of their voters, but to open no houses for the entertainment of the rabble; a reform, however, which the rabble did not at all approve of, and testified their dislike of it by a riot. A stage was built, from which the orators had designed to harangue the electors. This became the first victim of their fury. Having very little curiosity to hear what gentlemen could say, who would give them nothing better than words, they broke it in pieces, and threw the fragments upon the hustings. The sheriff, the members, the lawyers, the voters, were instantly put to flight. They rallied, but were again routed by a second assault, like the former. They then proceeded to break the windows of the inn to which they had fled; and, a fear prevailing that at night they would fire the town, a proposal was made by the freeholders to face about and endeavour to secure them. At that instant a rioter, dressed in a Merry Andrew's jacket, stepped forward, and challenged the best man among them. Olney sent the hero to the field, who made him repent of his presumption. Mr. Ashburner was he. Seizing him by the throat, he shook him, he threw him to the earth, he made the hollowness of his skull resound by the application of his fists, and dragged him into custody without the least damage to his person. Animated by this example, the other freeholders followed it; and in five minutes twenty-eight out of thirty ragamuffins were safely lodged in jail.

Adieu, my dear friend; writing makes my back ache, and my paper is full.—We love you, and are yours,

W. & M.

### TO THE REV. WM. UNWIN.

*July* 3, 1784.

MY DEAR WILLIAM—I was sorry that I could only take a flying leave of you. When the coach stopped at the door, I thought you had been in your chamber; my dishabille would not otherwise have prevented my running down for the sake of a more suitable parting. We rejoice that you had a safe journey, and though we should have rejoiced still more had you had no occasion for a physician, we are glad that having had need of one, you had the good fortune to find him. Let us hear soon that his advice has proved effectual, and that you are delivered from all ill symptoms.

Thanks for the care you have taken to furnish me with a dictionary. It is rather strange that at my time of life, and after a youth spent in classical pursuits, I should want one; and, stranger still, that, being possessed at present of only one Latin author in the world, I should think it worth while to purchase one. I say that it is strange, and indeed I think it so myself. But I have thought that when my present labours of the pen are ended, I may go to school again, and refresh my spirits by a little intercourse with the Mantuan and the Sabine bard, and perhaps by a reperusal of some others, whose works we generally lay by at that period of life when we are best qualified to read them, when, the judgment and the taste being formed, their beauties are least likely to be overlooked.

This change of wind and weather comforts me, and I

should have enjoyed the first fine morning I have seen this month with a peculiar relish, if our new tax-maker had not put me out of temper. I am angry with him, not only for the matter, but for the manner of his proposal. When he lays his impost upon horses, he is even jocular, and laughs, though, considering that wheels, and miles, and grooms, were taxed before, a graver countenance upon the occasion would have been more decent. But he provokes me still more by reasoning as he does on the justification of the tax upon candles. Some families, he says, will suffer little by it. Why? Because they are so poor that they cannot afford themselves more than ten pounds in the year. Excellent! they can use but few, therefore they will pay but little, and consequently will be but little burdened—an argument which for its cruelty and effrontery seems worthy of a hero; but he does not avail himself of the whole force of it, nor, with all his wisdom, had sagacity enough to see that it contains, when pushed to its utmost extent, a free discharge and acquittal of the poor from the payment of any tax at all: a commodity, being once made too expensive for their pockets, will cost them nothing, for they will not buy it. Rejoice, therefore, O ye penniless! the minister will indeed send you to bed in the dark, but your remaining halfpenny will be safe; instead of being spent in the useless luxury of candlelight, it will buy you a roll for breakfast, which you will eat no doubt with gratitude to the man who so kindly lessens the number of your disbursements, and, while he seems to threaten your money, saves it. I wish he would remember that the halfpenny which Government imposes the shopkeeper will swell to twopence. I wish he would visit the miserable huts of our lace-makers at Olney, and see them working in the winter months, by the light of a farthing candle, from four in the afternoon till midnight. I wish he had laid his tax upon the ten thousand lamps that illuminate the Pantheon, upon the flambeaux that wait upon ten thousand chariots and sedans in an evening, and upon the wax candles that give light to ten thousand card tables. I wish, in short, that he would consider the pockets of the poor as sacred, and that to tax a people already so necessitous, is but to discourage the little industry that is left among us, by driving the laborious to despair.

A neighbour of mine, in Silverend, keeps an ass; the ass lives on the other side of the garden wall, and I am writing in the greenhouse; it happens that he is this morning most musically disposed, either cheered by the fine weather, or by some new tune which he has just acquired, or by finding his voice more harmonious than usual. It would be cruel to mortify so fine a singer; therefore I do not tell him that he interrupts and hinders me, but I venture to tell you so, and to plead his performance in excuse of my abrupt conclusion.

I send you the goldfinches, with which you will do as you see good. We have an affectionate remembrance of your late visit, and of all our friends at Stock.—Believe me ever yours, W. C.

TO THE REV. JOHN NEWTON.

*September* 18, 1784.

MY DEAR FRIEND—Following your good example, I lay before me a sheet of my largest paper. It was this moment fair and unblemished, but I have begun to blot it, and, having begun, am not likely to cease till I have spoiled it. I have sent you many a sheet, that, in my judgment of it, has been very unworthy of your acceptance; but my conscience was in some measure satisfied by reflecting, that if it were good for nothing, at the same time it cost you nothing, except the trouble of reading it. But the case is altered now. You must pay a solid price for frothy matter, and though I do not absolutely pick your pocket, yet you lose your money, and, as the saying is, are never the wiser; a saying literally fulfilled to the reader of my epistles.

My greenhouse is never so pleasant as when we are just upon the point of being turned out of it. The gentleness of the autumnal suns, and the calmness of this latter season, make it a much more agreeable retreat than we ever find it in summer; when, the winds being generally brisk, we cannot cool it by admitting a sufficient quantity of air without being at the same time incommoded by it. But now I sit with all the windows and the door wide open, and am regaled with the scent of every flower in a garden as full of flowers as I have known how to make it. We keep no bees, but if I lived in a hive I should hardly hear more of their music. All the bees in the neighbourhood resort to a bed of mignonette opposite to the window, and pay me for the honey they get out of it by a hum, which, though rather monotonous, is as agreeable to my ear as the whistling of my linnets. All the sounds that Nature utters are delightful, at least in this country. I should not, perhaps, find the roaring of lions in Africa, or of bears in Russia, very pleasing; but I know no beast in England whose voice I do not account musical, save and except always the braying of an ass. The notes of all our birds and fowls please me, without one exception. I should not, indeed, think of keeping a goose in a cage, that I might hang him up in the parlour for the sake of his melody; but a goose upon a common, or in a farmyard, is no bad performer. And as to insects, if the black beetle, and beetles, indeed, of all hues, will keep out of my way, I have no objection to any of the rest; on the contrary, in whatever key they sing, from the gnat's fine treble to the bass of the humble bee, I admire them all. Seriously, however, it strikes me as a very observable instance of providential kindness to man that such an exact accord has been contrived between his ear and the sounds with which, at least in a rural situation, it is almost every moment visited. All the world is sensible of the uncomfortable effect that certain sounds have upon the nerves, and consequently upon the spirits; and if a sinful world had been filled with such as would have curdled the blood, and have made the sense of hearing a perpetual inconvenience, I do not know that we should have had a right to complain. But now the fields, the woods, the gardens, have each their concert, and the ear of man is for ever regaled by creatures who seem only to please themselves. Even the ears that are deaf to the Gospel are continually entertained, though without knowing it, by sounds for which they are solely indebted to its Author. There is somewhere in infinite space a world that does not roll within the precincts of mercy, and as it is reasonable, and even scriptural, to suppose that there is music in heaven, in those dismal regions perhaps the reverse of it is found; tones so dismal as to make woe itself more insupportable, and to acuminate even despair. But my paper admonishes me in good time to draw the reins, and to check the descent of my fancy into deeps with which she is but too familiar. Our best love attends you both, with yours—*Sum ut semper, tui studiosissimus,*

W. C.

TO THE REV. WILLIAM UNWIN.

*October* 20, 1784.

MY DEAR WILLIAM—Your letter has relieved me from some anxiety, and given me a good deal of positive pleasure. I have faith in your judgment, and an implicit confidence in the sincerity of your approbation. The writing of so long a poem is a serious business; and the author must know little of his own heart who does not in some degree suspect himself of partiality to his own production; and who is he that would not be mortified by the discovery that he had written five thousand lines in vain? The poem, however, which you have in hand will not of itself make a volume so large as the last, or as a bookseller would wish. I say this, because when I had sent Johnson five thousand verses, he applied for a thousand more. Two years since I began a piece which grew to the length of two hundred, and there stopped. I have lately resumed it, and, I believe, shall finish it. But the subject is fruitful, and will not be comprised in a smaller compass than seven or eight hundred verses. It turns on the question whether an education at school or at home be preferable, and I shall give the preference to the latter. I mean that it shall pursue the track of the former,—that is to say, it shall visit Stock in its way to publication. My design also is to inscribe it to you. But you must see it first; and if, after having seen it, you should have any objection, though it should be no bigger than the tittle of an *i*, I will deny myself that pleasure, and find no fault with your refusal. I have not been without thoughts of adding "John Gilpin" at the tail of all. He has made a good deal of noise in the world, and perhaps it may not be amiss to show, that, though I write generally with a serious intention, I know how to be occasionally merry. The Critical Reviewers charged me with an attempt at humour. John having been more celebrated upon the score of humour than most pieces that have appeared in modern days, may serve to exonerate me from the imputation; but in this article I am entirely under your judgment, and mean to be set down by it. All these together will make an octavo like the last. I should have told you that the piece which now employs me is in rhyme. I do not intend to write any more blank. It is more difficult than rhyme, and not so amusing in the composition. If, when you make the offer of my book to Johnson, he should stroke his chin, and look up to the ceiling and cry " Humph ! "—anticipate him, I beseech you, at once, by saying—" that you know I should be sorry that he should undertake for me to his own disadvantage, or that my volume should be in any degree pressed upon him. I make him the offer merely because I think he would have reason to complain of me if I did not." But that punctilio once satisfied, it is a matter of indifference to me what publisher sends me forth. If Longman should have difficulties, which is the more probable, as I understand from you that he does not in these cases see with his own eyes, but will consult a brother poet, take no pains to conquer them. The idea of being hawked about, and especially of your being the hawker, is insupportable. Nichols, I have heard, is the most learned printer of the present day. He may be a man of taste as well as of learning ; and I suppose that you would not want a gentleman usher to introduce you. He prints the *Gentleman's Magazine*, and may serve us if the others should decline ; if not, give yourself no further trouble about the matter. I may possibly envy authors who can afford to publish at their own expense, and in that case should write no more. But the mortification would not break my heart.

I can easily see that you may have very reasonable objections to my dedicatory proposal. You are a clergyman, and I have banged your order. You are a child of *alma mater*, and I have banged her too. Lay yourself, therefore, under no constraints that I do not lay you under, but consider yourself as perfectly free.

With our best love to you all, I bid you heartily farewell. I am tired of this endless scribblement. Adieu !
—Yours, W. C.

## TO THE SAME.

*November* 1, 1784.

MY DEAR FRIEND—Were I to delay my answer, I must yet write without a frank at last, and may as well therefore write without one now, especially feeling, as I do, a desire to thank you for your friendly offices so well performed. I am glad for your sake, as well as for my own, that you succeeded in the first instance, and that the first trouble proved the last. I am willing, too, to consider Johnson's readiness to accept a second volume of mine as an argument that at least he was no loser by the former. I collect from it some reasonable hope that the volume in question may not wrong him neither. My imagination tells me (for I know you interest yourself in the success of my productions) that your heart fluttered when you approached his door, and that it felt itself discharged of a burden when you came out again. You did well to mention it at the Thornton's; they will now know that you do not pretend to a share in my confidence, whatever be the value of it, greater than you actually possess. I wrote to Mr. Newton by the last post, to tell him that I was gone to the press again. He will be surprised, and perhaps not pleased. But I think he cannot complain, for he keeps his own authorly secrets without participating them with me. I do not think myself in the least injured by his reserve; neither should I, if he were to publish a whole library without favouring me with any previous notice of his intentions. In these cases it is no violation of the laws of friendship not to communicate, though there must be a friendship where the communication is made. But many reasons may concur in disposing a writer to keep his work secret, and none of them injurious to his friends. The influence of one I have felt myself, for which none of them would blame me,—I mean the desire of surprising agreeably. And if I have denied myself this pleasure in your instance, it was only to give myself a greater, by eradicating from your mind any little weeds of suspicion that might still remain in it, that any man living is nearer to me than yourself. Had not this consideration forced up the lid of my strong box like a lever, it would have kept its contents with an inviolable closeness to the last; and the first news that either you or any of my friends would have had of the *Task*, they would have received from the public papers. But you know now, that neither as poet, nor as man, do I give to any man a precedence in my estimation at your expense.

I am proceeding with my new work (which at present I feel myself much inclined to call by the name of "Tirocinium") as fast as the muse permits. It has reached the length of seven hundred lines, and will probably receive an addition of two or three hundred more. When you see Mr. Smith, perhaps you will not find it difficult to procure from him half a dozen franks, addressed to yourself, and dated the fifteenth of December, in which case they will all go to the post filled with my lucubrations on the evening of that day. I do not name an earlier, because I hate to be hurried; and Johnson cannot want it sooner than, thus managed, it will reach him.

I am not sorry that "John Gilpin," though hitherto he has been nobody's child, is likely to be owned at last. Here and there I can give him a touch that I think will mend him, the language in some places not being quite so quaint and old-fashioned as it should be; and in one of the stanzas there is a false rhyme. When I have thus given the finishing stroke to his figure, I mean to grace him with two mottoes, a Greek and a Latin one, which, when the world shall see that I have only a little one of three words to the volume itself, and none to the books of which it consists, they will perhaps understand as a stricture upon that pompous display of literature with which some authors take occasion to crowd their titles. Knox, in particular, who is a sensible man too, has not, I think, fewer than half a dozen to his Essays.—Adieu.

W. C.

TO THE REV. JOHN NEWTON.

*November* 27, 1784.

MY DEAR FRIEND—All the interest that you take in my new publication, and all the pleas that you urge in behalf of your right to my confidence, the moment I had read your letter, struck me as so many proofs of your regard—of a friendship in which distance and time make no abatement. But it is difficult to adjust opposite claims to the satisfaction of all parties. I have done my best, and must leave it to your candour to put a just interpretation upon all that has passed, and to give me credit for it, as a certain truth, that whatever seeming defects, in point of attention and attachment to you, my conduct on this occasion may have appeared to have been chargeable with, I am in reality as clear of all real ones, as you would wish to find me.

I send you enclosed, in the first place, a copy of the advertisement to the reader, which accounts for my title, not otherwise easily accounted for; secondly, what is called an argument, or a summary of the contents of each book, more circumstantial and diffuse by far than that which I have sent to the press. It will give you a pretty accurate acquaintance with my matter, though the tenons and mortises by which the several passages are connected, and let into each other, cannot be explained in a syllabus; and lastly, an extract as you desired. The subject of it, I am sure, will please you, and, as I have admitted into my description no images but what are scriptural, and have aimed as exactly as I could at the plain and simple sublimity of the Scripture language, I have hopes the manner of it may please you too. As far as the numbers and diction are concerned, it may serve pretty well for a sample of the whole. But the subjects being so various, no single passage can in all respects be a specimen of the book at large.

My principal purpose is to allure the reader by character, by scenery, by imagery, and such poetical embellishments, to the reading of what may profit him. Subordinately to this, to combat that predilection in favour of a metropolis that beggars and exhausts the country, by evacuating it of all its principal inhabitants; and collaterally, and as far as is consistent with this double intention, to have a stroke at vice, vanity, and folly, wherever I find them. I have not spared the Universities. A letter which appeared in the *General Evening Post* of Saturday, said to have been received by a general officer, and by him sent to the press as worthy of public notice, and which has all the appearance of authenticity, would alone justify the severest censure of those bodies, if any such justification were wanted. By way of supplement to what I have written on this subject, I have added a poem, called "Tirocinium," which is in rhyme. It treats of the scandalous relaxation of discipline that obtains in almost all schools universally, but especially in the largest, which are so negligent in the article of morals, that boys are debauched, in general, the moment they are capable of being so. It recommends the office of tutor to the father, where there is no real impediment; the expedient of a domestic tutor, where there is; and the disposal of boys into the hands of a respectable country clergyman, who limits his attention to two, in all cases where they cannot be conveniently educated at home. Mr. Unwin happily affording me an instance in point, the poem is inscribed to him. You will now, I hope, command your hunger to be patient, and be satisfied with the luncheon that I send till dinner comes. That piecemeal perusal of the work, sheet by sheet, would be so disadvantageous to the work itself, and therefore so uncomfortable to me, that, I dare say, you will waive your desire of it. A poem thus disjointed cannot possibly be fit for anybody's inspection but the author's.

Tully's rule,
"Nulla dies sine linea,"
will make a volume in less time than one would suppose. I adhered to it so rigidly, that though more than once I found three lines as many as I had time to compass, still I wrote; and finding occasionally, and, as it might happen, a more fluent vein, the abundance of one day made me amends for the barrenness of another. But I do not mean to write blank verse again. Not having the music of rhyme, it requires so close an attention to the pause and the cadence, and such a peculiar mode of expression, as render it, to me at least, the most difficult species of poetry that I have ever meddled with.

I am obliged to you, and to Mr. Bacon, for your kind remembrance of me when you meet. No artist can excel as he does without the finest feelings; and every man that has the finest feelings is, and must be amiable.— Adieu, my dear friend. Affectionately yours,

W. C.

### TO THE SAME.

*December* 13, 1784.

MY DEAR FRIEND—Having imitated no man, I may reasonably hope that I shall not incur the disadvantage of a comparison with my betters. Milton's manner was peculiar. So is Thomson's. He that should write like either of them would in my judgment deserve the name of a copyist, but not of a poet. A judicious and sensible reader therefore, like yourself, will not say that my manner is not good, because it does not resemble theirs, but will rather consider what it is in itself. Blank verse is susceptible of a much greater diversification of manner than verse in rhyme; and why the modern writers of it have all thought proper to cast their numbers alike, I know not. Certainly it was not necessity that compelled them to it. I flatter myself, however, that I have avoided that sameness with others, which would entitle me to nothing but a share in one common oblivion with them all. It is possible that, as a reviewer of my former volume found cause to say that he knew not to what class of writers to refer me, the reviewer of this, whosoever he shall be, may see occasion to remark the same singularity. At any rate, though as little apt to be sanguine as most men, and more prone to fear and despond than to overrate my own productions, I am persuaded that I shall not forfeit anything by this volume that I gained by the last. As to the title, I take it to be the best that is to be had. It is not possible that a book, including such a variety of subjects, and in which no particular one is predominant, should find a title adapted to them all. In such a case it seemed almost necessary to accommodate the name to the incident that gave birth to the poem; nor does it appear to me that because I performed more than my task, therefore the *Task* is not a suitable title. A house would still be a house though the builder of it should make it ten times as big as he at first intended. I might, indeed, following the example of the Sunday newsmonger, call it the "Olio." But I should do myself wrong; for though it have much variety, it has, I trust, no confusion.

For the same reason none of the interior titles apply themselves to the contents at large of that book to which they belong. They are, every one of them, taken either from the leading (I should say the introductory) passage of that particular book, or from that which makes the most conspicuous figure in it. Had I set off with a design to write upon a gridiron, and had I actually written near two hundred lines upon that utensil, as I have upon the "Sofa," the gridiron should have been my title. But the "Sofa" being, as I may say, the starting-post from which I addressed myself to the long race that I soon conceived a design to run, it acquired a just pre-eminence in my account, and was very worthily advanced to the titular honour it enjoys, its right being at least so far a good one, that no word in the language could pretend a better.

The "Timepiece" appears to me (though by some accident the import of that title has escaped you) to have a degree of propriety beyond the most of them. The book to which it belongs is intended to strike the hour that gives notice of approaching judgment, and, dealing pretty largely in the *signs* of the *times*, seems to be denominated, as it is, with a sufficient degree of accommodation to the subject.

As to the word *worm*, it is the very appellation which Milton himself, in a certain passage of the *Paradise Lost*, gives to the serpent. Not having the book at hand, I cannot now refer to it, but I am sure of the fact. I am mistaken, too, if Shakespeare's Cleopatra do not call the asp, by which she thought fit to destroy herself, by the same name. But not having read the play these five-and-twenty years, I will not affirm it. They are, however, without all doubt, convertible terms; a worm is a small serpent, and a serpent is a large worm; and when an epithet significant of the most terrible species of those creatures is adjoined, the idea is surely sufficiently ascertained. No animal of the vermicular or serpentine kind is crested, but the most formidable of all.

We do not often see, or rather feel, so severe a frost before Christmas. Unexpected, at least by me, it had like to have been too much for my greenhouse, my myrtles having found themselves yesterday morning in an atmosphere so cold that the mercury was fallen eight degrees below the freezing point.

We are truly sorry for Mrs. Newton's indisposition, and shall be glad to hear of her recovery. We are most liable to cold at this season, and at this season a cold is most difficult of cure.

Be pleased to remember us to the young ladies, and to all under your roof and elsewhere who are mindful of us. —And believe me, your affectionate,

WILLIAM COWPER.

Your letters are gone to their address. The oysters were very good.

TO MR. JOHNSON [1] [PRINTER].

I DID not write the line that has been tampered with hastily, or without due attention to the construction of it; and what appeared to me its only merit is, in its present state, entirely annihilated.

I know that the ears of modern verse writers are delicate to an excess, and their readers are troubled with the same squeamishness as themselves. So that if a line do not run as smooth as quicksilver, they are offended. A critic of the present day serves a poem as a cook does a dead turkey, when she fastens the legs of it to a post and draws out all the sinews. For this we may thank Pope; but unless we could imitate him in the closeness and compact-

---

[1] It happened that some accidental reviser of the manuscript had taken the liberty to alter a line in a poem of Cowper's. This liberty drew from the offended poet the following very just and animated remonstrance, which I am anxious to preserve, because it elucidates, with great felicity of expression, his deliberate ideas on English versification.—NOTE BY HAYLEY.

ness of his expression, as well as in the smoothness of his numbers, we had better drop the imitation, which serves no other purpose than to emasculate and weaken all we write. Give me a manly rough line, with a deal of meaning in it, rather than a whole poem full of musical periods, that have nothing but their oily smoothness to recommend them!

I have said thus much, as I hinted in the beginning, because I have just finished a much longer poem than the last, which our common friend will receive by the same messenger that has the charge of this letter. In that poem there are many lines which an ear so nice as the gentleman's who made the above-mentioned alteration would undoubtedly condemn; and yet (if I may be permitted to say it) they cannot be made smoother without being the worse for it. There is a roughness on a plum which nobody that understands fruit would rub off, though the plum would be much more polished without it. But, lest I tire you, I will only add that I wish you to guard me from all such meddling; assuring you that I always write as smoothly as I can; but that I never did, never will, sacrifice the spirit or sense of a passage to the sound of it.

TO THE REV. WILLIAM UNWIN.

*December* 18, 1784.

MY DEAR FRIEND—I condole with you that you had the trouble to ascend St. Paul's in vain, but at the same time congratulate you that you escaped an ague. I should be very well pleased to have a fair prospect of a balloon under sail, with a philosopher or two on board, but at the same time should be very sorry to expose myself for any length of time to the rigour of the upper regions, at this season, for the sake of it. The travellers themselves, I suppose, are secured from all injuries of the weather by that fervency of spirit and agitation of mind which must needs accompany them in their flight; advantages which the more composed and phlegmatic spectator is not equally possessed of.

The inscription of the poem is more your own affair than any other person's. You have therefore an undoubted right to fashion it to your mind, nor have I the least objection to the slight alteration that you have made in it. I inserted what you have erased for a reason that was perhaps rather chimerical than solid. I feared, however, that the reviewers, or some of my sagacious readers, not more merciful than they, might suspect that there was a secret design in the wind; and that author and friend had consulted in what manner author might introduce friend to public notice as a clergyman every way qualified to entertain a pupil or two, if peradventure any gentleman of fortune were in want of a tutor for his children. I therefore added the words "and of his two sons only" by way of insinuating that you are perfectly satisfied with your present charge, and that you do not wish for more; thus meaning to obviate an illiberal construction which we are both of us incapable of deserving. But the same caution not having appeared to you to be necessary, I am very willing and ready to suppose that it is not so.

I intended in my last to have given you my reasons for the compliment I have paid Bishop Bagot, lest, knowing that I have no personal connexion with him, you should suspect me of having done it rather too much at a venture. In the first place, then, I wished the world to know that I have no objection to a bishop, *quid* bishop. In the second place, the brothers were all five my schoolfellows, and very amiable and valuable boys they were. Thirdly, Lewis, the bishop, had been rudely and coarsely treated in the *Monthly Review*, on account of a sermon, which appeared to me, when I read their extract from it, to deserve the highest commendations, as exhibiting explicit proof both of his good sense and his unfeigned piety. For these causes me thereunto moving, I felt myself happy in an opportunity to do public honour to a worthy man who had been publicly traduced; and, indeed, the reviewers themselves have since repented of their aspersions, and have travelled not a little out of their way in order to retract them, having taken occasion, by the sermon preached at the bishop's visitation at Norwich, to say everything handsome of his lordship, who, whatever might be the merit of the discourse, in that instance at least, could himself lay claim to no other than that of being a hearer.

Since I wrote I have had a letter from Mr. Newton that did not please me, and returned an answer to it that possibly may not have pleased him. His was fretful and peevish, and mine, if not chargeable with exactly the same qualities, was, however, dry and unsavoury enough. We shall come together again soon, I suppose, upon as amicable terms as usual. But at present he is in a state of mortification. He would have been pleased had the book passed out of his hands into yours, or even out of yours into his, so that he had previously had opportunity to advise a measure which I pursued without his recommendation, and had seen the poems in manuscript. But my design was to pay you a whole compliment, and I have done it. If he says more on the subject I shall speak freely, and perhaps please him less than I have done already.

We wished to have thanked you sooner for three fine cod, with shrimps and oysters, all excellent in their way, but knew not where a letter might find you.—Yours, with our love to all, W. C.

TO THE SAME.

*April* 30, 1785.

MY DEAR FRIEND—I return you thanks for a letter so

warm with the intelligence of the celebrity of "John Gilpin." I little thought when I mounted him upon my Pegasus that he would become so famous. I have learned also from Mr. Newton that he is equally renowned in Scotland, and that a lady there had undertaken to write a second part, on the subject of Mrs. Gilpin's return to London, but, not succeeding in it as she wished, she dropped it. He tells me likewise that the head master of St. Paul's school (who he is I know not) has conceived, in consequence of the entertainment that John has afforded him, a vehement desire to write to me. Let us hope he will alter his mind; for should we even exchange civilities on the occasion, *Tirocinium* will spoil all. The great estimation, however, in which this knight of the stone bottles is held may turn out a circumstance propitious to the volume of which his history will make a part. Those events that prove the prelude to our greatest success are often apparently trivial in themselves, and such as seemed to promise nothing. The disappointment that Horace mentions is reversed: we design a mug, and it proves a hogshead. It is a little hard that I alone should be unfurnished with a printed copy of this facetious story. When you visit London next you must buy the most elegant impression of it, and bring it with you. I thank you also for writing to Johnson. I likewise wrote to him myself. Your letter and mine together have operated to admiration. There needs nothing more but that the effect be lasting, and the whole will soon be printed. We now draw towards the middle of the fifth book of the *Task*. The man Johnson is like unto some vicious horses that I have known; they would not budge till they were spurred, and when they were spurred they would kick. So did he; his temper was somewhat disconcerted, but his pace was quickened, and I was contented.

I was very much pleased with the following sentence in

Mr. Newton's last :—" I am perfectly satisfied with the propriety of your proceeding as to the publication." Now, therefore, we are friends again. Now he once more inquires after the work, which, till he had disburdened himself of this acknowledgment, neither he nor I, in any of our letters to each other, ever mentioned. Some side-wind has wafted to him a report of those reasons by which I justified my conduct. I never made a secret of them ; but both your mother and I have studiously deposited them with those who we thought were most likely to transmit them to him. They wanted only a hearing, which once obtained, their solidity and cogency were such that they were sure to prevail.

You mention Bensley. I formerly knew the man you mention, but his elder brother much better. We were schoolfellows, and he was one of a club of seven Westminster men, to which I belonged, who dined together every Thursday. Should it please God to give me ability to perform the poet's part to some purpose, many whom I once called friends, but who have since treated me with a most magnificent indifference, will be ready to take me by the hand again, and some, whom I never held in that estimation, will, like Bensley (who was but a boy when I left London), boast of a connexion with me which they never had. Had I the virtues, and graces, and accomplishments of St. Paul himself, I might have them at Olney and nobody would care a button about me, yourself and one or two more excepted. Fame begets favour, and one talent, if it be rubbed a little bright by use and practice, will procure a man more friends than a thousand virtues. Dr. Johnson, I believe, in the life of one of our poets—I believe of Savage—says that he retired from the world flattering himself that he should be regretted. But the world never missed him. I think his observation upon it is that the vacancy made by the retreat of any individual is soon filled up; that a man may always be obscure if he chooses to be so; and that he who neglects the world will be by the world neglected.

Your mother and I walked yesterday in the Wilderness. As we entered the gate a glimpse of something white, contained in a little hole in the gate-post, caught my eye. I looked again, and discovered a bird's nest, with two tiny eggs in it. By and by they will be fledged, and tailed, and get wing feathers, and fly. My case is somewhat similar to that of the parent bird; my nest is in a little nook; here I brood and hatch, and in due time my progeny takes wing and whistles.

We wait for the time of your coming with pleasant expectation.—Yours truly, W. C.

TO THE REV. JOHN NEWTON.

*September* 24, 1785.

MY DEAR FRIEND—I am sorry that an excursion which you would otherwise have found so agreeable was attended with so great a drawback upon its pleasures as Miss Cunningham's illness must needs have been. Had she been able to bathe in the sea it might have been of service to her; but I knew her weakness and delicacy of habit to be such as did not encourage any very sanguine hopes that the regimen would suit her. I remember Southampton well, having spent much time there; but, though I was young, and had no objections on the score of conscience either to dancing or cards, I never was in the assembly room in my life. I never was fond of company, and especially disliked it in the country. A walk to Netley Abbey, or to Freemantle, or to Redbridge, or a book by the fireside, had always more charms for me than any other amusement that the place afforded. I was also a sailor, and, being of Sir Thomas Hesketh's party, who was himself born one, was often pressed into the service. But though I gave myself an air, and wore trousers, I had no genuine right to that honour, disliking much to be occupied in great waters, unless in the finest weather. How they contrive to elude the wearisomeness that attends a sea life who take long voyages you know better than I; but for my own part, I seldom have sailed so far as from Hampton river to Portsmouth without feeling the confinement irksome, and sometimes to a degree that was almost insupportable. There is a certain perverseness, of which I believe all men have a share, but of which no man has a larger share than I,—I mean that temper, or humour, or whatever it is to be called, that indisposes us to a situation, though not unpleasant in itself, merely because we cannot get out of it. I could not endure the room in which I now write were I conscious that the door were locked. In less than five minutes I should feel myself a prisoner, though I can spend hours in it under an assurance that I may leave it when I please, without experiencing any tedium at all. It was for this reason, I suppose, that the yacht was always disagreeable to me. Could I have stepped out of it into a cornfield or garden, I should have liked it well enough; but, being surrounded by water, I was as much confined in it as if I had been surrounded by fire; and did not find that it made me any adequate compensation for such an abridgment of my liberty. I make little doubt but Noah was glad when he was enlarged from the ark; and we are sure that Jonah was when he came out of the fish; and so was I to escape from the good sloop the " Harriet."

In my last I wrote you word that Mr. Perry was given over by his friends, and pronounced a dead man by his physician. Just when I had reached the end of the foregoing paragraph, he came in. His errand hither was to bring two letters, which I enclose; one is to yourself, in which he will give you, I doubt not, such an account both of his body and mind as will make all that I might say upon those subjects superfluous. The only consequences of his illness seem to be that he looks a little pale, and that, though always a most excellent man, he is still more angelic than he was. Illness sanctified is better than health. But I know a man who has been a sufferer by a worse illness than his almost these fourteen years, and who at present is only the worse for it.'

Mr. Scott called upon us yesterday. He is much inclined to set up a Sunday school, if he can raise a fund for the purpose. Mr. Jones has had one some time at Clifton, and Mr. Unwin writes me word that he has been thinking of nothing else day and night for a fortnight. It is a wholesome measure that seems to bid fair to be pretty generally adopted, and, for the good effects that it promises, deserves well to be so. I know not, indeed, while the spread of the Gospel continues so limited as it is, how a reformation of manners in the lower class of mankind can be brought to pass; or by what other means the utter abolition of all principle among them, moral as well as religious, can possibly be prevented. Heathenish parents can only bring up heathenish children; an assertion nowhere oftener or more clearly illustrated than at Olney, where children, seven years of age, infest the streets every evening with curses and with songs, to which it would be unseemly to give their proper epithet. Such urchins as these could not be so diabolically accomplished unless by the connivance of their parents. It is well, indeed, if in some instances their parents be not themselves their instructors. Judging by their proficiency, one can hardly suppose any other. It is therefore doubtless an act of the greatest charity to snatch them out of such hands before the inveteracy of the evil shall have made it desperate. Mr.

Teedon, I should imagine, will be employed as a teacher should this expedient be carried into effect. I know not, at least, that we have any other person among us so well qualified for the service. He is indisputably a Christian man, and miserably poor, whose revenues need improvement as much as any children in the world can possibly need instruction.

I understand that Mr. Jones is in London; it is possible that you may have seen him, and, if you have, are better acquainted with his present intentions respecting Lord Peterborough than myself. We saw him not long since, when he talked of resigning his office immediately; but I hear that he was afterwards otherwise advised, and repented of his purpose. I think it great pity that he did. A thing that a man had better never have touched cannot too soon be relinquished. While his principal kept himself at a distance his connexion with him was less offensive; but now, to all who interest themselves in his conduct as a minister of the gospel, it is an offence indeed. He seems aware of it, and we hope, therefore, will soon abandon it.

Mrs. Unwin hopes that a hare, which she sent before Mrs. Newton went her journey, arrived safe. By this week's coach she also sent three fowls and a ham, with cabbage, of whose safe arrival she will likewise be glad to hear. She has long been troubled with a pain in her side, which we take to be of the spasmodic kind, but is otherwise well. She joins with me in love to yourself and Mrs. Newton, and to the young ladies; neither do we forget Sally Johnson.—Believe me, my dear friend, with true affection, yours. W. C.

Hannah desires me to give her duty to Miss Cunningham and Miss Catlett.

TO LADY HESKETH.

*October* 12, 1785.

MY DEAR COUSIN—It is no new thing with you to give pleasure. But I will venture to say that you do not often give more than you gave me this morning. When I came down to breakfast, and found upon the table a letter franked by my uncle, and when opening that frank I found that it contained a letter from you, I said within myself—"This is just as it should be. We are all grown young again, and the days that I thought I should see no more are actually returned." You perceive, therefore, that you judged well when you conjectured that a line from you would not be disagreeable to me. It could not be otherwise than, as in fact it proved, a most agreeable surprise, for I can truly boast of an affection for you that neither years nor interrupted intercourse have at all abated. I need only recollect how much I valued you once, and with how much cause, immediately to feel a revival of the same value; if that can be said to revive which at the most has only been dormant for want of employment. But I slander it when I say that it has slept. A thousand times have I recollected a thousand scenes, in which our two selves have formed the whole of the drama, with the greatest pleasure; at times, too, when I had no reason to suppose that I should ever hear from you again. I have laughed with you at the Arabian Nights' Entertainment, which afforded us, as you well know, a fund of merriment that deserves never to be forgot. I have walked with you to Netley Abbey, and have scrambled with you over hedges in every direction; and many other feats we have performed together upon the field of my remembrance, and all within these few years. Should I say within this twelvemonth I should not transgress the truth. The hours that I have spent with you were among the pleasantest of my former days, and are therefore chronicled in my mind so deeply as to fear no erasure. Neither do I forget my poor friend Sir Thomas. I should remember him indeed, at any rate, on account of his personal kindness to myself; but the last testimony that he gave of his regard for you endears him to me still more. With his uncommon understanding (for with many peculiarities he had more sense than any of his acquaintance), and with his generous sensibilities, it was hardly possible that he should not distinguish you as he has done. As it was the last, so it was the best proof that he could give of a judgment that never deceived him when he would allow himself leisure to consult it.

You say that you have often heard of me; that puzzles me. I cannot imagine from what quarter; but it is no matter. I must tell you, however, my cousin, that your information has been a little defective. That I am happy in my situation is true; I live, and have lived these twenty years, with Mrs. Unwin, to whose affectionate care of me during the far greater part of that time it is, under Providence, owing that I live at all. But I do not account myself happy in having been for thirteen of those years in a state of mind that has made all that care and attention necessary; an attention and a care that have injured her health, and which, had she not been uncommonly supported, must have brought her to the grave. But I will pass to another subject; it would be cruel to particularise only to give pain, neither would I by any means give a sable hue to the first letter of a correspondence so unexpectedly renewed.

I am delighted with what you tell me of my uncle's good health. To enjoy any measure of cheerfulness at so late a day is much. But to have that late day enlivened with the vivacity of youth is much more, and in these post-diluvian times a rarity indeed. Happy for the most part are parents who have daughters. Daughters are not apt to outlive their natural affections, which a son has generally survived even before his boyish years are expired. I rejoice particularly in my uncle's felicity, who has three female descendants from his little person, who leave him nothing to wish for upon that head.

My dear cousin, dejection of spirits, which I suppose may have prevented many a man from becoming an author, made me one. I find constant employment necessary, and therefore take care to be constantly employed. Manual occupations do not engage the mind sufficiently, as I know by experience, having tried many. But composition, especially of verse, absorbs it wholly. I write, therefore, generally three hours in a morning, and in an evening I transcribe. I read also, but less than I write, for I must have bodily exercise, and therefore never pass a day without it.

You ask me where I have been this summer. I answer, at Olney. Should you ask me where I spent the last seventeen summers, I should still answer at Olney. Ay, and the winters also; I have seldom left it, and except when I attended my brother in his last illness, never, I believe, a fortnight together.

Adieu, my beloved cousin, I shall not always be thus nimble in reply, but shall always have great pleasure in answering you when I can.—Yours, my dear friend and cousin,   W. C.

TO THE SAME.

OLNEY, *November* 9, 1785.

MY DEAREST COUSIN, whose last most affectionate letter has run in my head ever since I received it, and which I now sit down to answer two days sooner than the post will serve me—I thank you for it, and with a warmth for which I am sure you will give me credit, though I do not spend many words in describing it. I do not seek *new* friends, not being altogether sure that I should find them, but have unspeakable pleasure in being still beloved by an old one. I hope that now our correspondence has suffered its last interruption, and that we shall go down together to the grave, chatting and chirping as merrily as such a scene of things as this will permit.

I am happy that my poems have pleased you. My volume has afforded me no such pleasure at any time, either while I was writing it or since its publication, as I have derived from yours and my uncle's opinion of it. I make certain allowances for partiality, and for that peculiar quickness of taste with which you both relish what you like, and, after all drawbacks upon those accounts duly made, find myself rich in the measure of your approbation that still remains. But, above all, I honour "John Gilpin," since it was he who first encouraged you to write. I made him on purpose to laugh at, and he served his purpose well; but I am now in debt to him for a more valuable acquisition than all the laughter in the world amounts to, the recovery of my intercourse with you, which is to me inestimable.

My benevolent and generous cousin, when I was once asked if I wanted anything, and given delicately to understand that the inquirer was ready to supply all my occasions, I thankfully and civilly, but positively declined the favour. I neither suffer, nor have suffered any such inconveniences as I had not much rather endure than come under obligations of that sort to a person comparatively with yourself a stranger to me. But to you I answer otherwise. I know you thoroughly, and the liberality of your disposition; and have that consummate confidence in the sincerity of your wish to serve me that delivers me from all awkward constraint, and from all fear of trespassing by acceptance. To you therefore I reply, yes. Whensoever, and whatsoever, and in what manner soever you please; and add, moreover, that my affection for the giver is such as will increase to me tenfold the satisfaction that I shall have in receiving. It is necessary, however, that I should let you a little into the state of my finances, that you may not suppose them more narrowly circumscribed than they are. Since Mrs. Unwin and I have lived at Olney we have had but one purse, although during the whole of that time, till lately, her income was nearly double mine. Her revenues indeed are now in some measure reduced, and do not much exceed my own; the worst consequence of this is that we are forced to deny ourselves some things which hitherto we have been better able to afford, but they are such things as neither life, nor the well-being of life, depend upon. My own income has been better than it is, but when it was best it would not have enabled me to live as my connexions demanded that I should, had it not been combined with a better than itself, at least at this end of the kingdom. Of this I had full proof during three months that I spent in lodgings at Huntingdon, in which time, by the help of good management, and a clear notion of economical matters, I contrived to spend the income of a twelvemonth. Now, my beloved cousin, you are in possession of the whole case as it stands. Strain no points to your own inconvenience or hurt, for there is no need of it, but indulge yourself in communicating (no matter what) that you can spare without missing it, since by so doing you will be sure to add to the comforts of my life one of the sweetest that I can enjoy,—a token and proof of your affection.

In the affair of my next publication, toward which you also offer me so kindly your assistance, there will be no need that you should help me in the manner that you propose. It will be a large work, consisting, I should imagine, of six volumes at least. The twelfth of this month I shall have spent a year upon it, and it will cost me more than another. I do not love the booksellers well enough to make them a present of such a labour, but intend to publish by subscription. Your vote and interest, my dear cousin, upon the occasion, if you please, but nothing more. I will trouble you with some papers of proposals when the time shall come, and am sure that you will circulate as many for me as you can. Now, my dear, I am going to tell you a secret. It is a great secret, that you must not whisper even to your cat. No creature is at this moment apprised of it but Mrs. Unwin and her son. I am making a new translation of Homer, and am on the point of finishing the twenty-first book of the *Iliad*. The reasons upon which I undertake this Herculean labour, and by which I justify an enterprise in which I seem so effectually anticipated by Pope, although in fact he has not anticipated me at all, I may possibly give you, if you wish for them, when I can find nothing more interesting to say, a period which I do not conceive to be very near! I have not answered many things in your letter, nor can do it at present for want of room. I cannot believe but that I should know you, notwithstanding all that time may have done. There is not a feature of your face, could I meet it upon the road by itself, that I should not instantly recollect. I should say, that is my cousin's nose, or those are her lips and her chin, and no woman upon earth can claim them but herself. As for me, I am a very smart youth of my years. I am not indeed grown gray so much as I am grown bald. No matter. There was more hair in the world than ever had the honour to belong to me. Accordingly, having found just enough to curl a little at my ears, and to intermix with a little of my own that still hangs behind, I appear, if you see me in an afternoon, to have a very decent head-dress, not easily distinguished from my natural growth; which being worn with a small bag, and a black ribbon about my neck, continues to me the charms of my youth, even on the verge of age. Away with the fear of writing too often.—Yours, my dearest cousin,

W. C.

*P.S.*—That the view I give you of myself may be complete, I add the two following items,—that I am in debt to nobody, and that I grow fat.

TO THE SAME.

OLNEY, *February* 9, 1786.

MY DEAREST COUSIN—I have been impatient to tell you that I am impatient to see you again. Mrs. Unwin partakes with me in all my feelings upon this subject, and longs also to see you. I should have told you so by the last post, but have been so completely occupied by this tormenting specimen that it was impossible to do it. I sent the General a letter on Monday that would distress and alarm him; I sent him another yesterday, that will, I hope, quiet him again. Johnson has apologised very civilly for the multitude of his friend's strictures; and his friend has promised to confine himself in future to a comparison of me with the original, so that, I doubt not, we shall jog on merrily together. And now, my dear, let me tell you once more that your kindness in promising us a visit has charmed us both. I shall see you again. I shall hear your voice. We shall take walks together. I will show you my prospects, the hovel, the alcove, the Ouse and its banks, everything that I have described. I anticipate the pleasure of those days not very far distant, and I feel a part of it at this moment. Talk not of an inn! Mention it not for your life! We have never had so many visitors but we could easily accommodate them all; though we have received Unwin, and his wife, and his sister, and his son, all at once. My dear, I will not let you come till the end of May, or beginning of June, because before that time my greenhouse will not be ready to receive us, and it is the only pleasant room belonging to us. When the plants go out we go in. I line it with mats, and spread the floor with mats; and there you shall sit with a bed of mignonette at your side, and a hedge of honeysuckles, roses, and jasmine; and I will make you a bouquet of myrtle every day. Sooner than the time I mention, the country will not be in complete beauty. And I will tell you what you shall find at your first entrance. Imprimis, as soon as you have entered the vestibule, if you cast a look on either side of you, you shall see on the right hand a box of my making. It is the box in which have been lodged all my hares, and in which lodges Puss at present. But he, poor fellow, is worn out with age, and promises to die before you can see him. On the right hand stands a cupboard, the work of the same author; it was once a dove-cage, but I transformed it. Opposite to you stands a table, which I also made. But a merciless servant having scrubbed it until it became paralytic, it serves no purpose now but of ornament; and all my clean shoes stand under it. On the left hand, at the farther end of this superb vestibule, you will find the door of the parlour, into which I will conduct you, and where I will introduce you to Mrs. Unwin, unless we should meet her before, and where we will be as happy as the day is long. Order yourself, my cousin, to the "Swan" at Newport, and there you shall find me ready to conduct you to Olney.

My dear, I have told Homer what you say about casks and urns, and have asked him whether he is sure that it is a cask in which Jupiter keeps his wine. He swears that it is a cask, and that it will never be anything better than a cask to eternity. So if the god is content with it, we must even wonder at his taste, and be so to.—Adieu ! my dearest, dearest cousin, W. C.

TO THE SAME.

*Monday, April* 10, 1786.

THAT's my good cousin ! now I love you ! now I will think of June as you do, that it is the pleasantest of all months, unless you should happen to be here in November too, and make it equally delightful. Before I have finished my letter, Mrs. Unwin will have taken a view of the house concerning which you inquire, and I shall be able to give you a circumstantial account of it. The man who built it is lately dead. He had been a common sailor, and assisted under Wolfe and Amherst at the taking of Quebec. When we came hither he was almost penniless; but, climbing by degrees into the lace business, amassed money, and built the house in question. Just before he died, having an enterprising genius, he put almost his whole substance to hazard in sending a large cargo of lace to America, and the venture failing, he has left his widow in penury and distress. For this reason I conclude that she will have no objection to letting as much of her house as my cousin will have occasion for, and have therefore given you this short history of the matter. The bed is the best in the town, and the honest tar's folly was much laughed at, when it was known that he, who had so often swung in a hammock, had given twenty pounds for a bed. But now I begin to hope that he made a wiser bargain than once I thought it. She is no gentlewoman, as you may suppose, but she is nevertheless a very quiet, decent, sober body, and well respected among her neighbours.

But Hadley, my dearest cousin, what is to be said of

Hadley? Only this at present, that having such an inhabitant as Mr. Burrows, and the hope belonging to it of such another inhabitant as yourself, it has all charms, all possible recommendations. Yes, had I the wings that David wished for, I would surely stretch them to their utmost extent that I might reach any place where I should have you to converse with perhaps half the year. But, alas, my dear, instead of wings I have a chain and a collar, the history of which collar and chain Mrs. Unwin shall give you when you come; else would I fly, and she would fly also, with the utmost alacrity to Hadley, or whithersoever you should call us, for Olney has no hold upon us in particular. Here have we no family connexions, no neighbours with whom we can associate, no friendships. If the country is pleasant, so also are other countries; and so far as income is concerned, we should not, I suppose, find ourselves in a more expensive situation at Hadley, or anywhere, than here. But there are lets and hindrances which no power of man can remove, which will make your poor heart ache, my dear, when you come to know them. I will not say that they can never be removed, because I will not set bounds to that which has no bounds —the mercy of God; but of the removal of them there is no present apparent probability. I knew a Mr. Burrows once; it was when I lived in the Temple; so far knew him that we simpered at each other when we met, and on opposite sides of the way touched hats. This Mr. Burrows, though at that time a young man, was rather remarkable for corpulence, and yet tall. He was at the bar. On a sudden I missed him, and was informed soon after that he had taken orders. Is it possible that your Mr. Burrows and mine can be the same? The imagination is not famous for taking good likenesses of persons and faces that we never saw. In general the picture that we draw in our minds of an *inconnu* is of all possible pictures the most unlike the original. So it has happened to me in this instance; my fancy assured me that Mr. Burrows was a slim, elegant, young man, dressed always to the very point of exactness, with a sharp face, a small voice, a delicate address, and the gentlest manners. Such was my dream of Mr. Burrows, and how my dream of him came to be such I know not, unless it arose from what I seemed to have collected out of the several letters in which you have mentioned him. From them I learned that he has wit, sense, taste, and genius, with which qualities I do not generally connect the ideas of bulk and rotundity; and from them I also learned that he has numerous connexions at your end of the town, where the company of those who have anything rough in their exterior is least likely to be coveted. So it must have come to pass that I made to myself such a very unsuitable representation of him. But I am not sorry that he is such as he is. He is no loser by the bargain in my account. I am not the less delighted with his high approbation, and wish for no better fortune as a poet than always so to please such men as Mr. Burrows. I will not say, my dear, that you yourself gain any advantage in my opinion by the difference; for to seat you higher there than you were always seated is not possible. I will only observe in this instance, as always in all instances, I discover a proof of your own good sense and discernment, who, finding in Mr. Burrows a mind so deserving of your esteem and regard, have not suffered your eye to prejudice you against it; a *faux pas* into which I have known ladies of very good understanding betrayed ere now, I assure you. Had there been a question last year of our meeting at Olney, I should have felt myself particularly interested in this inattention of yours to the figure, for the sake of its contents, for at that time I had rather more body than it became a man who pretends to public approbation as a poet to carry about him. But, thanks to Dr. Kerr, I do not at present measure an inch more in the girth than is perfectly consistent with the highest pretensions that way. Apollo himself is hardly more chargeable with prominence about the waist than I am.

I by no means insist upon making ladies of the Trojan women, unless I can reconcile you to the term. But I must observe, in the first place, that though in our language the word be of modern use, it is likewise very ancient. We read in our oldest Bibles of the elect *Lady*, and of Babylon the *Lady* of kingdoms. In the next place, the Grecians,—Homer, at least,—when a woman of rank is accosted, takes care in many instances that she shall be addressed in a style suited to her condition, for which purpose he employs a word more magnificent in its amount than even *lady*, and which literally signifies very little less than a goddess. The word that I mean—that I may make it legible to you, is *Daimonie*. There were, no doubt, in Troy,—but I will say no more of it. I have that to write about to my English lady that makes all the ladies of antiquity nothing worth to me.

We are this moment returned from the house above mentioned. The parlour is small and neat, not a mere cupboard, but very passable; the chamber is better, and quite smart. There is a little room close to your own for Mrs. Eaton, and there is a room for Cookie and Samuel. The terms are half a guinea a week; but it seems as if we were never to take a step without a stumble. The kitchen is bad,—it has, indeed, never been used except as a wash-house; for people at Olney do not eat and drink as they do in other places. I do not mean, my dear, that they quaff nectar or feed on ambrosia, but *tout au contraire*. So what must be done about this abominable kitchen? It is out of doors: that is not amiss. It has neither range nor jack: that is terrible. But then range and jack are not unattainables; they may be easily supplied. And if it were not,—abominable kitchen that it is, —no bigger than half an egg-shell, shift might be made. The good woman is content that your servants should eat and drink in her parlour, but expects that they shall disperse themselves when they have done. But whither, who can say? unless into the arbour in the garden, for that they should solace themselves in the said kitchen were hardly to be expected. While I write this, Mrs. U. is gone to attempt a treaty with the linen-draper over the way, which, if she succeeds, will be best of all, because the rooms are better, and it is just at hand. I must halt till she returns.—She returns;—nothing done.—She is gone again to another place. Once more I halt. Again she returns and opens the parlour door with these tidings: —" I have succeeded beyond my utmost hopes. I went to Maurice Smith's " (he, you must know, my dear, is a Jack-of-all-trades). " I said, ' Do you know if Mr. Brightman could and would let lodgings ready furnished to a lady with three servants?' Maurice's wife calls out " (she is a Quaker) "' Why dost thee not take the vicarage?' I replied, 'There is no furniture.' 'Phsaw!' quoth Maurice's wife; 'we will furnish it for thee, and at the lowest rate: —from a bed to a platter we find all!'" "And what do you intend now?" said I to Mrs. Unwin, "Why, now," quoth she, "I am going to the curate to see what *he* says." So away she goes, and in about twenty minutes returns.—"Well, now, it is all settled. Lady H. is to have all the vicarage, except two rooms, at the rate of ten guineas a year; and Maurice will furnish it for five guineas from June to November, inclusive." So, my dear, you and your train are provided for to my heart's content. They are Lady Austen's lodgings, only with more room, and at the same price. You have a parlour sixteen feet by fourteen; chamber ditto; a room for your

own maid, near to your own, that I have occupied many a good time; an exceedingly good garret for Cookie, and another ditto, at a convenient distance, for Samuel; a cellar, a good kitchen, the use of the garden;—in short, all that you can want. Give us our commission in your next, and all shall be ready by the first of June. You will observe, my beloved cousin, that it is not in all above eight shillings a week in the whole year or but a trifle more. And the furniture is really smart, and the beds good. But you must find your own linen. Come, then, my beloved cousin, for I am determined that, whatsoever king shall reign, you shall be *Vicar* of Olney. Come and cheer my heart. I have left many things unsaid, but shall note them another time. Adieu!—Ever yours,
W. C.

I am so charmed with the subject that concludes my letter that I grudge every inch of paper to any other. Yet, must I allow myself space to say that Lord Dartmouth's behaviour to you at the concert has won my heart to him more than ever. It was such a well-timed kindness to me, and so evidently performed with an equal design of giving pleasure to you, that I love him for it at my heart. I have never, indeed, at any time, had occasion to charge him, as I know that many have done, with want of warmth in his friendship.—I honour you, my dear, for your constellation of nobles. I rejoice that the contents of my box have pleased you; may I never write anything that does not! My friend Bull brought me to-day the last *Gentleman's Magazine*. There your cousin is held up again. Oh rare Coz!

## TO THE REV. JOHN NEWTON.

OLNEY, *May* 20, 1786.

MY DEAR FRIEND—Within this hour arrived three sets of your new publication, for which we sincerely thank you. We have breakfasted since they came, and consequently, as you may suppose, have neither of us had yet an opportunity to make ourselves acquainted with the contents. I shall be happy (and, when I say that, I mean it to be understood in the fullest and most emphatical sense of the word) if my frame of mind shall be such as may permit me to study them. But Adam's approach to the tree of life, after he had sinned, was not more effectually prohibited by the flaming sword that turned every way, than mine to its great Antitype has been now almost these thirteen years, a short interval of three or four days, which passed about this time twelvemonth, alone excepted. For what reason it is that I am thus long excluded, if I am ever again to be admitted, is known to God only. I can say but this, that if He is still my Father, this paternal severity has towards me been such as that I have reason to account it unexampled. For though others have suffered desertion, yet few, I believe, for so long a time, and perhaps none a desertion accompanied with such experiences. But they have this belonging to them, that, as they are not fit for recital, being made up merely of infernal ingredients, so neither are they susceptible of it; for I know no language in which they could be expressed. They are as truly things which it is not possible for man to utter as those were which Paul heard and saw in the third heaven. If the ladder of Christian experience reaches, as I suppose it does, to the very presence of God, it has nevertheless its foot in the abyss. And if Paul stood, as no doubt he did, in that experience of his to which I have just alluded, on the topmost round of it, I have been standing and still stand on the lowest, in this thirteenth year that has passed since I descended. In such a situation of mind, encompassed by the midnight of absolute despair, and a thousand times filled with unspeakable horror, I first commenced an author. Distress drove me to it, and the impossibility of subsisting without some employment still recommends it. I am not, indeed, so perfectly hopeless as I was; but I am equally in need of an occupation, being often as much, and sometimes even more, worried than ever. I cannot amuse myself as I once could, with carpenters' or with gardeners' tools, or with squirrels and guinea-pigs. At that time I was a child. But since it has pleased God, whatever else He withholds, to restore to me a man's mind, I have put away childish things. Thus far, therefore, it is plain that I have not chosen or prescribed to myself my own way, but have been providentially led to it; perhaps I might say, with equal propriety, compelled and scourged into it: for, certainly, could I have made my choice, or were I permitted to make it even now, those hours which I spend in poetry I would spend with God. But it is evidently His will that I should spend them as I do, because every other way of employing them He himself continues to make impossible. If, in the course of such an occupation, or by inevitable consequence of it, either my former connexions of it are revived or new ones occur, these things are as much a part of the dispensations, as the leading points of it themselves; the effect as much as the cause. If His purposes in thus directing me are gracious, He will take care to prove them such in the issue, and in the meantime will preserve me (for He is able to do that in one condition as in another) from all mistakes in conduct that might prove pernicious to myself, or give reasonable offence to others.

I can say it as truly as it was ever spoken.—Here I am; let Him do with me as seemeth Him good.

At present, however, I have no connexions at which either you, I trust, or any who love me and wish me well, have occasion to conceive alarm. Much kindness indeed I have experienced at the hands of several, some of them near relations, others not related to me at all; but I do not know that there is among them a single person from whom I am likely to catch contamination. I can say of them all with more truth than Jacob uttered when he called kid venison, "The Lord thy God brought them unto me." I could show you among them two men whose lives, though they have but little of what we call evangelical light, are ornaments to a Christian country; men who fear God more than some who even profess to love Him. But I will not particularise farther on such a subject. Be they what they may, our situations are so distant, and we are likely to meet so seldom, that, were they, as they are not, persons of even exceptionable manners, their manners would have little to do with me. We correspond at present only on the subject of what passed at Troy three thousand years ago; and they are matters that, if they can do no good, will at least hurt nobody.

Your friendship for me, and the proof that I see of it in your friendly concern for my welfare on this occasion, demanded that I should be explicit. Assure yourself that I love and honour you, as upon all accounts, so especially for the interest that you take and have ever taken in my welfare, most sincerely. I wish you all happiness in your new abode, all possible success in your ministry, and much fruit of your newly-published labours, and am—with Mrs. Unwin's love to yourself and Mrs. Newton—most affectionately yours, my dear friend,

W C.

## TO LADY HESKETH.

*OLNEY, May 25, 1786.*

I HAVE at length, my cousin, found my way into my summer abode. I believe that I described it to you some time since, and will therefore now leave it undescribed. I will only say that I am writing in a bandbox, situated, at least in my account, delightfully, because it has a window in one side that opens into that orchard through which, as I am sitting here, I shall see you often pass, and which therefore I already prefer to all the orchards in the world. You do well to prepare me for all possible delays, because in this life all sorts of disappointments are possible; and I shall do well, if any such delay of your journey should happen, to practise that lesson of patience which you inculcate. But it is a lesson which, even with you for my teacher, I shall be slow to learn. Being sure, however, that you will not procrastinate without cause, I will make myself as easy as I can about it, and hope the best. To convince you how much I am under discipline and good advice, I will lay aside a favourite measure, influenced in doing so by nothing but the good sense of your contrary opinion. I had set my heart on meeting you at Newport. In my haste to see you once again I was willing to overlook many awkwardnesses I could not but foresee would attend it. I put them aside so long as I only foresaw them myself, but since I find that you foresee them too, I can no longer deal so slightly with them. It is therefore determined that we meet at Olney. Much I shall feel, but I will not die if I can help it, and I beg that you will take all possible care to outlive it likewise, for I know what it is to be balked in the moment of acquisition, and should be loath to know it again.

Last Monday, in the evening, we walked to Weston, according to our usual custom. It happened, owing to a mistake of time, that we set out half an hour sooner than usual. This mistake we discovered while we were in the Wilderness. So, finding that we had time before us, as they say, Mrs. Unwin proposed that we should go into the village and take a view of the house that I had just mentioned to you. We did so, and found it such a one as in most respects would suit you well. But Moses Brown, our vicar, who, as I told you, is in his eighty-sixth year, is not bound to die for that reason. He said himself when he was here last summer that he should live ten years longer, and for aught that appears so he may. In which case, for the sake of its near neighbourhood to us, the vicarage has charms for me that no other place can rival. But this, and a thousand things more, shall be talked over when you come.

We have been industriously cultivating our acquaintance with our Weston neighbours since I wrote last, and they on their part have been equally diligent in the same cause. I have a notion that we shall all suit well. I see much in them both that I admire. You know, perhaps, that they are Catholics.

It is a delightful bundle of praise, my cousin, that you have sent me. All jasmine and lavender. Whoever the lady is, she has evidently an admirable pen and a cultivated mind. If a person reads, it is no matter in what language, and if the mind be informed, it is no matter whether that mind belongs to a man or a woman. The taste and the judgment will receive the benefit alike in both. Long before the *Task* was published I made an experiment one day, being in a frolicsome mood, upon my friend. We were walking in the garden, and conversing on a subject similar to these lines :—

> The few that pray at all, pray oft amiss,
> And seeking grace t' improve the present good,
> Would urge a wiser suit than asking more.

I repeated them, and said to him, with an air of *nonchalance*, "Do you recollect those lines? I have seen them somewhere; where are they?" He put on a considering face, and after some deliberation replied, "Oh, I will tell you where they must be—in the *Night Thoughts*." I was glad my trial turned out so well, and did not undeceive him. I mention this occurrence only in confirmation of the letter-writer's opinion, but at the same time I do assure you, on the faith of an honest man, that I never in my life designed an imitation of Young or of any other writer; for mimicry is my abhorrence, at least in poetry.

Assure yourself, my dearest cousin, that both for your sake, since you make a point of it, and for my own, I will be as philosophically careful as possible that these fine nerves of mine shall not be beyond measure agitated when you arrive. In truth, there is much greater probability that they will be benefited, and greatly too. Joy of heart, from whatever occasion it may arise, is the best of all nervous medicines; and I should not wonder if such a turn given to my spirits should have even a lasting effect of the most advantageous kind upon them. You must not imagine, neither, that I am, on the whole, in any great degree subject to nervous affections; occasionally I am, and have been these many years, much liable to dejection. But at intervals, and sometimes for an interval of weeks, no creature would suspect it. For I have not that which commonly is a symptom of such a case belonging to me,— I mean extraordinary elevation in the absence of Mr. Bluedevil. When I am in the best health my tide of animal sprightliness flows with great equality, so that I am never at any time exalted in proportion as I am sometimes depressed. My depression has a cause, and if that cause were to cease I should be as cheerful thenceforth, and perhaps for ever, as any man need be. But, as I have often said, Mrs. Unwin shall be my expositor.

Adieu, my beloved cousin. God grant that our friendship, which, while we could see each other, never suffered a moment's interruption, and which so long a separation has not in the least abated, may glow in us to our last hour, and be renewed in a better world, there to be perpetuated for ever! For you must know that I should not love you half so well if I did not believe you would be my friend to eternity. There is not room enough for friendship to unfold itself in full bloom in such a nook of life as this. Therefore I am, and must, and will be, yours for ever, W. C.

TO THE SAME.

OLNEY, *May* 29, 1786.

THOU dear, comfortable cousin, whose letters among all that I receive have this property peculiarly their own, that I expect them without trembling, and never find anything in them that does not give me pleasure; for which, therefore, I would take nothing in exchange that the world could give me, save and except that for which I must exchange them soon—and happy shall I be to do so —your own company. That indeed is delayed a little too long; to my impatience at least it seems so, who find the spring, backward as it is, too forward, because many of its beauties will have faded before you will have an opportunity to see them. We took our customary walk yesterday in the Wilderness at Weston, and saw with regret the laburnums, syringas, and guelder-roses, some of them blown, and others just upon the point of blowing, and could not help observing—all these will be gone before Lady Hesketh comes. Still, however, there will be roses, and jasmine, and honeysuckle, and shady walks, and cool alcoves, and you will partake them with us. But I want you to have a share of everything that is delightful here, and cannot bear that the advance of the season should steal away a single pleasure before you can come to enjoy it.

Every day I think of you, and almost all the day long; I will venture to say that even *you* were never so expected in your life. I called last week at the Quaker's to see the furniture of your bed, the fame of which had reached me. It is, I assure you, superb, of printed cotton, and the subject classical. Every morning you will open your eyes on Phaeton kneeling to Apollo, and imploring his father to grant him the conduct of his chariot for a day. May your sleep be as sound as your bed will be sumptuous, and your nights at least will be well provided for.

I shall send up the sixth and seventh books of the *Iliad* shortly, and shall address them to you. You will forward them to the General. I long to show you my workshop, and to see you sitting on the opposite side of my table. We shall be as close packed as two wax figures in an old-fashioned picture frame. I am writing in it now. It is the place in which I fabricate all my verse in summer time. I rose an hour sooner than usual this morning, that I might finish my sheet before breakfast, for I must write this day to the General.

The grass under my windows is all bespangled with dewdrops, and the birds are singing in the apple trees, among the blossoms. Never poet had a more commodious oratory in which to invoke his muse.

I have made your heart ache too often, my poor dear cousin, with talking about my fits of dejection. Something has happened that has led me to the subject, or I would have mentioned them more sparingly. Do not suppose or suspect that I treat you with reserve; there is nothing in which I am concerned that you shall not be made acquainted with. But the tale is too long for a letter. I will only add, for your present satisfaction, that the cause is not exterior, that it is not within the reach of human aid, and that yet I have a hope myself, and Mrs. Unwin a strong persuasion, of its removal. I am indeed even now, and have been for a considerable time, sensible of a change for the better, and expect, with good reason, a comfortable lift from you. Guess then, my beloved cousin, with what wishes I look forward to the time of your arrival, from whose coming I promise myself not only pleasure, but peace of mind, at least an additional share of it. At present it is an uncertain and transient guest with me, but the joy with which I shall see and converse with you at Olney may perhaps make it an abiding one.

W. C.

TO JOSEPH HILL, ESQ.

OLNEY, *June* 9, 1786.

MY DEAR FRIEND—The little time that I can devote to any other purpose than that of poetry is, as you may suppose, stolen. Homer is urgent. Much is done, but much remains undone, and no schoolboy is more attentive to the performance of his daily task than I am. You will therefore excuse me if at present I am both unfrequent and short.

The paper tells me that the Chancellor has relapsed, and I am truly sorry to hear it. The first attack was dangerous, but a second must be more formidable still. It is not probable that I should ever hear from him again if he survive; yet of the much that I should have felt for him had our connexion never been interrupted, I still feel much. Everybody will feel the loss of a man whose abilities have made him of such general importance.

I correspond again with Colman, and upon the most friendly footing, and find in his instance, and in some others, that an intimate intercourse, which has been only

casually suspended, not forfeited on either side by outrage,
is capable not only of revival, but improvement.

I had a letter some time since from your sister Fanny
that gave me great pleasure. Such notices from old friends
are always pleasant, and of such pleasures I have received
many lately. They refresh the remembrance of early days,
and make me young again. The noble institution of the
Nonsense Club will be forgotten when we are gone who
composed it; but I often think of your most heroic line,
written at one of our meetings, and especially of it when
I am translating Homer—

"'To whom replied the Devil, yard-long tail'd.'"

There never was anything more truly Grecian than that
triple epithet, and were it possible to introduce it into
either *Iliad* or *Odyssey*, I should certainly steal it. I am
now flushed with expectation of Lady Hesketh, who
spends the summer with us. We hope to see her next
week. We have found admirable lodgings both for her
and her suite, and a Quaker in this town, still more
admirable than they, who, as if he loved her as much as
I do, furnishes them for her with real elegance.

W. C.


TO LADY HESKETH.

*June* 12, 1786.

I AM neither young nor superannuated, yet am I a
child. When I had read your letter I grumbled, not at
you, my dearest cousin, for you are in no fault, but at the
whole generation of coachmakers, as you may suppose,
and at yours in particular. I foresaw and foreknew that
he would fail in his promise, and yet was disappointed;
was in truth no more prepared for what I expected with
so much reason than if I had not at all expected it. I

grumbled till we went to dinner, and at intervals till we had dined; and when dinner was over, with very little encouragement, I could actually have cried. And if I had, I should in truth have thought them tears as well bestowed as most that I have shed for many years. At first I numbered months, then weeks, and then days, and was just beginning to number hours, and now I am thrown back to days again. My first speech was, after folding up your letter (for I will honestly tell you all), "I am crazed with Mondays, Tuesdays, and Wednesdays, and St. Albans, and Totteridges, and Hadley. When is she set out? When is she to be here? Do tell me, for perhaps you understand it better than I." "Why," says Mrs. Unwin (with much more composure in her air than properly belonged to her, for she also had her feelings on the occasion), "she sets out to-morrow se'nnight, and will be here on the Wednesday after." "And who knows that?" replied I; "will the coachmaker be at all more punctual in repairing the old carriage than in making the new one? For my part, I have no hope of seeing her this month, and if it be possible, I will not think of it, lest I should be again disappointed." And to say the truth, my dear, though hours have passed since thus I said, and I have had time for cooler consideration, the suspicion still sticks close to me that more delays may happen. A philosopher would prepare himself for such an event, but I am no philosopher, at least when the comfort of seeing you is in question. I believe in my heart that there have been just as many true philosophers upon earth as there have been men that have had little or no feeling, and not one more. Swift truly says:—

> "Indifference clad in reason's guise,
> All want of fortitude supplies."

When I wake in the night I feel my spirits the lighter because you are coming. When I am not in Troy I am either occupied in the recollection of a thousand passages of my past life, in which you were a partaker with me, or conversing about you with Mrs. Unwin. Thus my days and nights have been spent principally ever since you determined upon this journey, and especially, and almost without interruption from any other subject, since the time of your journey has seemed near at hand. While I despaired, as I did for many years, that I should ever see you more, I thought of you, indeed and often, but with less solicitude. I used to say to myself, Providence has so ordered it, and it is my duty to submit. He has cast me at a distance from her, and from all whom I once knew. He did it, and not I; it is He who has chosen my situation for me. Have I not reason to be thankful that, since He designed me to pass a part of my life, and no inconsiderable one neither, in a state of the deepest melancholy, he appointed me a friend in Mrs. Unwin, who should share all my sorrows with me, and watch over me in my helpless condition night and day? What and where had I been without her? Such considerations were sufficient to reconcile me at that time to perpetual separation even from you, because perpetual I supposed it must be, and without remedy. But now every hour of your absence seems long, for this very natural reason, because the same Providence has given me a hope that you will be present with me soon. A good that seems at an immeasurable distance, and that we cannot hope to reach, has therefore the less influence on our affections. But the same good brought nearer, made to appear practicable, promised to our hopes, and almost in possession, engages all our faculties and desires. All this is according to the natural and necessary course of things in the human heart; and the philosophy that would interfere with it is folly at least, if not frenzy. A throne has at present but little sensible attraction for me. And why? Perhaps only because I know that should I break my heart with wishes for a throne I should never reach one. But did I know assuredly that I should put on a crown to-morrow, perhaps I too should feel ambition and account the interposing night tedious. The sum of the whole matter, my dear, is this, that this villainous coach-maker has mortified me monstrously, and that I tremble lest he should do so again. From you I have no fears. I see in your letter, and all the way through it, what pains you take to assure me and give me comfort. I am and will be comforted for that very reason, and will wait still other ten days with all the patience that I can muster. You, I know, will be punctual if you can, and that, at least, is matter of real consolation.

I approve altogether, my cousin beloved, of your sending your goods by the waggon on Saturday, and Cookie by the coach on Tuesday. She will be here perhaps by four in the afternoon, at the latest, by five, and will have quite time enough to find out all the cupboards and shelves in her department before you arrive. But I declare and protest that Cookie shall sleep that night at our house, and get her breakfast here next morning. You will break her heart, child, if you send her into a strange house where she will find nothing that has life but the curate, who has not much neither. Servant, he keeps none. A woman makes his bed, and, after a fashion, as they say, dresses his dinner, and then leaves him to his lucubrations. I do therefore insist on it, and so does Mrs. Unwin, that Cookie shall be our guest for that time, and from this we will not depart. I tell thee, besides, that I shall be more glad to see her, than ever I was in my life to see one whom I never saw before. Guess why, if you can.

You must number your miles—fifty-six instead of fifty-four. The fifty-sixth mile ends but a few yards beyond the vicarage. Soon after you shall have entered Olney, you will find an opening on your right hand. It is a lane that leads to our dwelling. There your coach may stop and set down Mrs. Eaton; when she has walked about forty yards she will spy a green gate and rails on her left hand; and when she has opened the gate and reached the house-door, she will find herself at home. But we have another manœuvre to play off upon you, and in which we positively will not be opposed, or if we are, it shall be to no purpose. I have an honest fellow that works in my garden: his name is Kitchener, and we called him Kitch for brevity. He is sober and trusty as the day. He has a smart blue coat, that, when I had worn it some years, I gave him, and now he has worn it some years himself. I shall set him on horseback and order him to the "Swan" at Newport, there to await your arrival, and if you should not stop at that place, as perhaps you may not, immediately to throw himself into your suite and to officiate as your guide. For though the way from Newport hither is short, there are turnings that might puzzle your coachman, and he will be of use too in conducting you to your house, which otherwise you might not easily find, partly though the stupidity of those of whom you might inquire, and partly from its out-of-the-way situation. My brother drove up and down Olney in quest of us, almost as often as you up and down Chancery Lane in quest of the Madans, with fifty boys and girls at his tail, before he could find us. The first man, therefore, you shall see in a blue coat with white buttons, in the famous town of Newport, cry, Kitch! He will immediately answer, My Lady! and from that moment you are sure not to be lost.

Your house shall be as clean as scrubbing and dry-rubbing can make it, and in all respects fit to receive you. My friend the Quaker, in all that I have seen of his doings, has acquitted himself much to my satisfaction. Some little things, he says, will perhaps be missing at first, in such a multiplicity, but they shall be produced as soon as called for. Mrs. U. has bought you six ducks, and is fatting them for you. She has also rummaged up a coop that will hold six chickens, and designs to people it for you by the first opportunity; for these things are not to be got fit for table at Olney. Thus, my dear, are all things in the best train possible, and nothing remains but that you come and show yourself. Oh that moment! Shall we not both enjoy it?—That we shall.

I have received an anomymous complimentary Pindaric ode from a little poet who calls himself a schoolboy. I send you the first stanza by way of specimen. You shall see it all soon.

"To WILLIAM COWPER, OF THE INNER TEMPLE, ESQ., OF HIS POEMS IN THE SECOND VOLUME.

> " In what high strains, my Muse, wilt thou
>    Attempt great Cowper's worth to show?
> Pindaric strains shall tune the lyre,
>    And 't would require
>    A Pindar's fire
> To sing great Cowper's worth,
> The lofty bard, delightful sage,
> Ever the wonder of the age,
> And blessing to the earth."

Adieu, my precious cousin, your lofty bard and delightful sage expects you with all possible affection. — Ever yours,                                  WM. COWPER.

I am truly sorry for your friend Burrows!

Our dinner-hour is four o'clock. We will not surfeit you with delicacies; of that be assured. I know your palate, and am glad to know that it is easily pleased. Were it other than it is, it would stand but a poor chance to be gratified at Olney. I undertake for lettuce and cucumber, and Mrs. U. for all the rest. If she feeds you too well you must humble her.

### TO THE REV. WILLIAM UNWIN.

MY DEAR WILLIAM—How apt we are to deceive ourselves where self-interest is in question! You say I am in your debt, and I accounted you in mine,—a mistake to which you must attribute my arrears, if indeed I owe you any, for I am not backward to write where the uppermost thought is welcome.

I am obliged to you for all the books you have occasionally furnished me with. I did not indeed read many of Johnson's Classics—those of established reputation are so fresh in my memory, though many years have intervened since I made them my companions, that it was like reading what I read yesterday over again: and as to the minor Classics, I did not think them worth reading at all—I tasted most of them, and did not like them. It is a great thing to be indeed a poet, and does not happen to more than one man in a century. Churchill, the great Churchill, deserved the name of poet. Such natural unformed effusions of genius, the world, I believe, has never seen since the days of Shakspeare. I have read him twice, and some of his pieces three times over, and the last time with more pleasure than the first. The pitiful scribbler of his life seems to have undertaken that task, for which he was entirely unqualified, merely because it afforded him an opportunity to traduce him. He has inserted in it but one anecdote of consequence, for which he refers you to a novel, and introduces the story with doubts about the truth of it. But his barrenness as a biographer I could forgive, if the simpleton had not thought himself a judge of his writings, and, under the erroneous influence of that thought, informed his reader that "Gotham," "Independence," and the "Times" were catch-pennies. "Gotham," unless I am a greater blockhead than he, which I am far from believing, is a noble and beautiful poem, and a poem with which I make no doubt the author took as much pains as with any he ever wrote. Making allowance (and Dryden, perhaps, in his *Absolam and Achitophel* stands in need of the same indulgence) for an unwarrantable use of Scripture, it appears to me to be a masterly performance. "Independence" is a most animated piece, full of strength and spirit, and marked with that bold masculine character which I think is the great peculiarity of this writer. And the "Times" (except that the subject is disgusting to the last degree) stands equally high in my opinion. He is indeed a careless writer for the most part; but where shall we find in any of those authors who finish their works with the exactness of a Flemish pencil, those bold and daring strokes of fancy, those numbers so hazardously ventured upon, and so happily finished, the matter so compressed and yet so clear, and the colouring so sparingly laid on, and yet with such a beautiful effect? In short, it is not his least praise that he is never guilty of those faults as a writer, which he lays to the charge of others; a proof that he did not judge by a borrowed standard, or from rules laid down by critics, but that he was qualified to do it by his own native powers, and his great superiority of genius. For he that wrote so much, and so fast, would through inadvertence and hurry unavoidably have departed from rules which he might have found in books, but his own truly poetical talent was a guide which could not suffer him to err. A race-horse is graceful in his swiftest pace, and never makes an awkward motion though he is pushed to his utmost speed. A cart-horse might perhaps be taught to play tricks in the riding-school, and might prance and curvet like his betters, but at some unlucky time would be sure to betray the baseness of his original. It is an affair of very little consequence perhaps to the well-being of mankind, but I cannot help regretting that he died so soon. Those words of Virgil, upon the immature death of Marcellus, might serve for his epitaph :

> " Ostendent terris hunc tantum fata, neque ultra
> Esse sinent ———."

—Yours, W. C.

TO THE SAME.

OLNEY, *September* 24, 1786.

MY DEAR WILLIAM—So interesting a concern as your tutorship of the young gentleman in question cannot have been so long in a state of indecision without costing you much anxiety. We have sympathised with you under it all, but are glad to be informed that the long delay is not chargeable upon Mr. Hornby. Bishops are κακα θηρια, γαστερες αργοι. You have heard, I know, from Lady Hesketh, and she has exculpated me from all imputation of wilful silence, from which, indeed, of yourself you are so good as to discharge me in consideration of my present almost endless labour. I have nothing to say in particular on the subject of Homer, except that I am daily advancing in the work with all the despatch that a due concern for my own credit in the result will allow.

You have had your troubles, and we ours. This day three weeks your mother received a letter from Mr. Newton, which she has not yet answered, nor is likely to answer hereafter. It gave us both much concern, but her more than me; I suppose because my mind being necessarily occupied in my work, I had not so much leisure to

browse upon the wormwood that it contained. The
purport of it is a direct accusation of me, and of her an
accusation implied, that we have both deviated into for-
bidden paths, and lead a life unbecoming the Gospel; that
many of my friends in London are grieved, and the simple
people of Olney astonished; that he never so much doubted
of my restoration to Christian privileges as now;—in short,
that I converse too much with people of the world, and
find too much pleasure in doing so. He concludes with
putting your mother in mind that there is still an intercourse between London and Olney; by which he means
to insinuate that we cannot offend against the decorum
that we are bound to observe but the news of it will most
certainly be conveyed to him. We do not at all doubt it;
we never knew a lie hatched at Olney that waited long
for a bearer; and though we do not wonder to find ourselves made the subjects of false accusation in a place ever
fruitful of such productions, we do and must wonder a
little that he should listen to them with so much credulity.
I say this because if he had heard only the truth, or had
believed no more than the truth, he would not, I think,
have found either me censurable or your mother. And
that she should be suspected of irregularities is the more
wonderful (for wonderful it would be at any rate), because
she sent him not long before a letter conceived in such
strains of piety and spirituality as ought to have convinced
him that she at least was no wanderer. But what is the
fact, and how do we spend our [time] in reality? What
are the deeds for which we have been represented as thus
criminal? Our present course of life differs in nothing
from that which we have both held these thirteen years,
except that after great civilities shown us, and many
advances made on the part of the Throcks, we visit them.
That we visit also at Gayhurst; that we have frequently
taken airings with my cousin in her carriage; and that I

have sometimes taken a walk with her on a Sunday evening, and sometimes by myself, which, however, your mother has never done. These are the only novelties in our practice; and if by these procedures, so inoffensive in themselves, we yet give offence, offence must needs be given. God and our own consciences acquit us, and we acknowledge no other judges.

The two families with whom we have picked up this astonishing intercourse are as harmless in their conversation and manners as can be found anywhere. And as to my poor cousin, the only crime that she is guilty of against the people of Olney is, that she has fed the hungry, clothed the naked, and administered comfort to the sick; except indeed that, by her great kindness, she has given us a little lift in point of condition and circumstances, and has thereby excited envy in some who have not the knack of rejoicing in the prosperity of others. And this I take to be the root of the matter.

My dear William, I do not know that I should have teased your nerves and spirits with this disagreeable theme had not Mr. Newton talked of applying to you for particulars. He would have done it, he says, when he saw you last, but had not time. You are now qualified to inform him as minutely as we ourselves could of all our enormities. Adieu!

Our sincerest love to yourself and yours,     WM. C.

# LETTERS FROM WESTON UNDERWOOD.
## 1786-1793.

### TO LADY HESKETH.

WESTON LODGE, *November* 26, 1786.

IT is my birthday, my beloved cousin, and I determine to employ a part of it, that it may not be destitute of festivity, in writing to you. The dark, thick fog that has obscured it would have been a burden to me at Olney, but here I have hardly attended to it. The neatness and snugness of our abode compensate all the dreariness of the season, and whether the ways are wet or dry, our house at least is always warm and commodious. O for you, my cousin, to partake these comforts with us! I will not begin already to tease you upon that subject, but Mrs. Unwin remembers to have heard from your own lips that you hate London in the spring. Perhaps, therefore, by that time you may be glad to escape from a scene which will be every day growing more disagreeable, that you may enjoy the comforts of the Lodge. You well know that the best house has a desolate appearance unfurnished. This house accordingly, since it has been occupied by us and our *meubles*, is as much superior to what it was when you saw it, as you can imagine. The parlour is even elegant. When I say that the parlour is elegant, I do not mean to insinuate that the study is not so. It is neat, warm, and silent, and a much better study than I deserve if I do not produce in it an incomparable translation of Homer. I think every day of those lines of Milton, and congratulate myself on having obtained before I am quite superannuated what he seems not to have hoped for sooner :

> " And may at length my weary age
> Find out the peaceful hermitage."

For if it is not a hermitage, at least it is a much better thing ; and you must always understand, my dear, that when poets talk of cottages, hermitages, and such like things, they mean a house with six sashes in front, two comfortable parlours, a smart staircase, and three bedchambers of convenient dimensions ; in short, exactly such a house as this.

The Throckmortons continue the most obliging neighbours in the world. One morning last week they both went with me to the Cliff—a scene, my dear, in which you would delight beyond measure, but which you cannot visit except in the spring or autumn. The heat of summer and the clinging dirt of winter would destroy you. What is called the Cliff is no cliff, nor at all like one, but a beautiful terrace, sloping gently down to the Ouse, and from the brow of which, though not lofty, you have a view of such a valley as makes that which you see from the hills near Olney, and which I have had the honour to celebrate, an affair of no consideration.

Wintry as the weather is, do not suspect that it confines me. I ramble daily, and every day change my ramble. Wherever I go I find short grass under my feet, and when I have travelled perhaps five miles, come home with shoes not at all too dirty for a drawing-room. I was pacing yesterday under the elms that surround the field in which stands the great alcove, when, lifting my eyes, I saw two black genteel figures bolt through a hedge into the path where I was walking. You guess already who they were, and that they could be nobody but our neighbours. They had seen me from a hill at a distance, and had traversed a great turnip-field to get to me. You see, therefore, my dear, that I am in some request. Alas! in too much request with some people. The verses of Cadwallader have found me at last.

I am charmed with your account of our little cousin[1] at Kensington. If the world does not spoil him hereafter, he will be a valuable man.—Good-night, and may God bless thee! W. C.

TO THE SAME.

THE LODGE, *December* 4, 1786.

I SENT you, my dear, a melancholy letter, and I do not know that I shall now send you one very unlike it. Not that anything occurs in consequence of our late loss more afflictive than was to be expected, but the mind does not perfectly recover its tone after a shock like that which has been felt so lately. This I observe, that though my experience has long since taught me that this world is a world of shadows, and that it is the more prudent as well as the more Christian course to possess the comforts that we find in it as if we possessed them not, it is no easy matter to reduce this doctrine into practice. We forget that that God who gave them may, when he pleases, take them away; and that perhaps it may please him to take them at a time when we least expect or are least disposed to part from them. Thus it has happened in the present case. There never was a moment in Unwin's life when there seemed to be more urgent want of him than the moment in which he died. He had attained to an age

[1] Lord Cowper.

when, if they are at any time useful, men become more useful to their families, their friends, and the world. His parish began to feel, and to be sensible of, the advantages of his ministry. The clergy around him were many of them awed by his example. His children were thriving under his own tuition and management, and his eldest boy is likely to feel his loss severely, being by his years in some respect qualified to understand the value of such a parent; by his literary proficiency too clever for a schoolboy, and too young at the same time for the university. The removal of a man in the prime of life, of such a character, and with such connexions, seems to make a void in society that can never be filled. God seemed to have made him just what he was that he might be a blessing to others, and when the influence of his character and abilities began to be felt, removed him. These are mysteries, my dear, that we cannot contemplate without astonishment, but which will nevertheless be explained hereafter, and must in the meantime be revered in silence. It is well for his mother that she has spent her life in the practice of an habitual acquiescence in the dispensations of Providence, else I know that this stroke would have been heavier, after all that she has suffered upon another account, than she could have borne. She derives, as she well may, great consolation from the thought that he lived the life and died the death of a Christian. The consequence is, if possible, more unavoidable than the most mathematical conclusion, that therefore he is happy. So farewell, my friend Unwin! The first man for whom I conceived a friendship after my removal from St. Albans, and for whom I cannot but still continue to feel a friendship though I shall see thee with these eyes no more.

W. C.

### TO JOSEPH HILL, ESQ.

WESTON, *December* 9, 1786.

MY DEAR FRIEND—We had just begun to enjoy the pleasantness of our new situation, to find at least as much comfort in it as the season of the year would permit, when affliction found us out in our retreat, and the news reached us of the death of Mr. Unwin. He had taken a western tour with Mr. Henry Thornton, and, in his return, at Winchester was seized with a putrid fever, which sent him to his grave. He is gone to it, however, though young, as fit for it as age itself could have made him. Regretted, indeed, and always to be regretted by those who knew him, for he had everything that makes a man valuable both in his principles and in his manners, but leaving still this consolation to his surviving friends, that he was desirable in this world chiefly because he was so well prepared for a better.

I find myself here situated exactly to my mind. Weston is one of the prettiest villages in England, and the walks about it at all seasons of the year delightful. I know that you will rejoice with me in the change that we have made, and for which I am altogether indebted to Lady Hesketh. It is a change as great as (to compare metropolitan things with rural) from St. Giles' to Grosvenor Square. Our house is in all respects commodious, and in some degree elegant; and I cannot give you a better idea of that which we have left than by telling you the present candidates for it are a publican and a shoemaker. W. C.

### TO LADY HESKETH.

THE LODGE. *December* 11, 1786.

SHENSTONE, my dearest cousin, in his commentary on

the vulgar adage which says, Second thoughts are best, observes that the *third* thought generally resolves itself into the *first*. Thus it has happened to me. My first thought was to effect a transposition of the old glasses into the new frame; my second, that perhaps both the old glasses and the new frame might be broken in the experiment; and my third, nevertheless, to make the trial. Accordingly I walked down to Olney this day, referred the matter to the watchmaker's consideration, and he has succeeded in the attempt to a wonder. I am at this moment peering through the same medium as usual, but with the advantage of a more ornamental mounting. I conjecture, by the way, from a passage in your note that accompanied the parcel, that I am indebted not *only* to you for this new accession to my elegant accommodations, but to some kind Incognito likewise; I beg that you will present my thanks accordingly. The clerk of the parish has made me a new pair of straps to my buckles; and the gingerbread, by its genial warmth, has delivered me since dinner from a distention of stomach that was immoderately troublesome, so that I am the better for you, my dear, from head to foot. Long time I in vain endeavoured to make myself master of the lamp, and was obliged at last to call in William to my assistance. Now there are certain things which great geniuses miss, and which men born without any understanding at all hit immediately. In justification of the truth of this remark, William, who is a lump of dough, who never can be more dead than he is till he has been buried a month, explained it to *me* in a moment; accordingly we have used it twice to my great satisfaction.

I sent Fuseli a hare by the coach that went up this morning, and certainly no man could better deserve it, though it was one of the largest that ever was seen. I could not resist the impulse that I felt to acknowledge my obligations to his critical exertions; and yet shall be sorry that I complied with it, if in consequence of my civility he should become at all less rigorous in his demands, or less severe in his animadversions. I am on the point of finishing the correction of the ninth book, which I have now adjusted to two sheets filled with his strictures. He observes at the close of them, that to execute a translation of this book in particular, with felicity, appears to him a prodigious task. He considers it, and I think justly, as one of the most consummate efforts of genius, handed down to us from antiquity, and calls upon me for my utmost exertions. I have not failed to make them, with what success will be seen hereafter; but of this I am sure, that I have much improved it. The good-natured Padre of the Hall has offered me, in Mrs. Throckmorton's absence, his transcribing assistance, of which I shall avail myself, and deliver over to him the book in question in a day or two.

Mr. Chester paid me a morning visit about the middle of last week. He was, though a man naturally reserved, chatty and good-humoured on the occasion, and when he took leave begged that I would not put myself to inconvenience for the sake of returning his visit with a punctilious alacrity in this wet and dirty season; an allowance for which I was much obliged to him, for since we now live five miles asunder, and I never ride, it does not at present occur to me by what means I could possibly get at him.

Our old house is not yet tenanted, but there are candidates for it. They are two who would divide the building between them, a shoemaker and the alemonger at the Horse and Groom. The carpenter in the meantime has assured Mr. Smith, the landlord, that unless it be well propped, and speedily, it will infallibly fall. Thank you, my dear, for saving our poor noddles from such imminent danger.

I learned to-day, at the "Bull," that the liquors which the General has sent me I may expect to see here to-morrow: there are four hampers of sherry, and one of brandy and rum. The looking-glass which you destined to the study,—that, I mean, which came out of your chamber at the vicarage,—we have ventured to put up in the parlour. It is quite large enough, and makes a very smart appearance. The other, which you may remember to have seen in my chamber at Olney, we have transferred to Nibbs, who, being paid for the new frame, is to furnish us with a new glass for it.

What course have you taken with our friend Arnott? Has Lord Cowper discovered any intentions to perform the part of a Mecænas toward me, or did he leave England forgetful that there was so important a character in it as myself? His little boy, I hope, has recovered. It would grieve me if the family should lose so much generosity as seems to be included in that small bosom.

The cloud that I mentioned to you, my cousin, has passed away, or perhaps the skirts of it may still hang over me. I feel myself, however, tolerably brisk, and tell you so because I know you will be glad to hear it. The grinners at "John Gilpin" little dream what the author suffers sometimes.—How I hated myself yesterday for having wrote it! May God bless thee, my dear. Adieu!—Ever yours, W. C.

Soon after this reaches you we hope that you will receive a turkey. It was Mrs. Throckmorton's legacy to us when she went. It never had the honour to be crammed, for she crams none, but perhaps may not be the worse in flavour on that account. She fed it daily with her own hand.

### TO THE SAME.

*Weston, December* 21, 1786.

Your welcome letter, my beloved cousin, which ought by the date to have arrived on Sunday, being by some untoward accident delayed, came not till yesterday. It came, however, and has relieved me from a thousand distressing apprehensions on your account.

The dew of your intelligence has refreshed my poetical laurels. A little praise now and then is very good for your hard-working poet, who is apt to grow languid and perhaps careless without it. Praise, I find, affects us as money does. The more a man gets of it, with the more vigilance he watches over and preserves it. Such, at least is its effect on me, and you may assure yourself that I will never lose a mite of it for want of care.

I have already invited the good Padre in general terms, and he shall positively dine here next week, whether he will or not. I do not at all suspect that his kindness to Protestants has anything insidious in it, any more than I suspect that he transcribes Homer for me with a view for my conversion. He would find me a tough piece of business I can tell him; for when I had no religion at all, I had yet a terrible dread of the Pope. How much more now!

I should have sent you a longer letter, but was obliged to devote my last evening to the melancholy employment of composing a Latin inscription for the tombstone of poor William, two copies of which I wrote out and enclosed, one to Henry Thornton, and one to Mr. Newton. Homer stands by me biting his thumbs, and swears that if I do not leave off directly, he will choke me with bristly Greek, that shall stick in my throat for ever.

W. C.

TO THE SAME.

THE LODGE, *December* 24, 1786.

You must by no means, my dearest Coz, pursue the plan that has suggested itself to you on the supposed loss of your letter. In the first place, I choose that my Sundays, like the Sundays of other people, shall be distinguished by something that shall make me look forward to them with agreeable expectation, and for that reason desire that they may always bring me a letter from you. In the next place, if I know when to *expect* a letter, I know likewise when to *inquire after* a letter if it happens not to come; a circumstance of some importance considering how excessively careless they are at the "Swan," where letters are sometimes overlooked, and do not arrive at their destination, if no inquiry be made, till some days have passed after their arrival at Olney. It has happened frequently to me to receive a letter long after all the rest have been delivered, and the Padre assured me that Mr. Throckmorton has sent notes three several times to Mrs. Marriott complaining of this neglect. For these reasons, my dear, thou must write still on Saturdays, and as often on other days as thou pleasest.

The screens came safe, and one of them is at this moment interposed between me and the fire, much to the comfort of my peepers. The other of them being fitted up with a screw that was useless, I have consigned to proper hands, that it may be made as serviceable as its brother. They are very neat, and I account them a great acquisition. Our carpenter assures me that the lameness of the chairs was not owing to any injury received in their journey, but that the maker never properly finished them. They were not high when they came, and in order to reduce them to a level we have lowered them an inch. Thou knowest, child, that the short foot could not be lengthened, for which reason we shortened the long ones. The box containing the plate and the brooms reached us yesterday, and nothing had suffered the least damages by the way. Everything is smart, and everything is elegant, and we admire them all. The short candlesticks are short enough. I am now writing with those upon the table; Mrs. U. is reading opposite, and they suit us both exactly. With the money that you have in hand you may purchase, my dear, at your most convenient time, a tea-urn; that which we have at present having never been handsome, and being now old and patched. A parson once, as he walked across the parlour, pushed it down with his belly, and it never perfectly recovered itself. We want likewise a tea-waiter, meaning, if you please, such a one as you may remember to have seen at the Hall—a wooden one. To which you may add, from the same fund, three or four yards of yard-wide muslin, wherewithal to make neckcloths for my worship. If after all these disbursements anything should be left in the bottom of the purse, we shall be obliged to you if you will expend it in the purchase of silk pocket-handkerchiefs. There, my precious, I think I have charged thee with commissions in plenty.

You neither must nor shall deny us the pleasure of sending to you such small matters as we do. As to the partridges, you may recollect possibly, when I remind you of it, that I never eat them, and Mrs. Unwin rejoiced in receiving them only because she could pack them away to you; therefore never lay us under any embargoes of this kind, for I tell you beforehand that we are both incorrigible. My beloved cousin, the first thing I open my eyes upon in a morning, is it not the bed in which you have laid me? Did you not in our old dismal parlour at Olney give me the tea on which I breakfast, the chocolate that I drink at noon, and the table at which I dine? the everything, in short, that I possess in the shape of convenience, is it not all from you? and is it possible, think you, that we should either of us overlook an opportunity of making such a tiny acknowledgment of your kindness? Assure yourself that never, while my name is Giles Gingerbread, will I dishonour my glorious ancestry, and my illustrious appellation, by so unworthy a conduct. I love you at my heart, and so does Mrs. U., and we must say thank you, and send you a peppercorn when we can. So thank you, my dear, for the brawn and the chine, and for all the good things you announce, and at present I will, for your sake, say no more of thanksgiving.

I have answered the Welshman's letter, and have a hope that I shall hear no more of him. He desired my advice whether to publish or not. In answer I congratulated him on the possession of a poetical talent with which he might always amuse himself when fatigued with the weightier matters of the law. As to publication, I recommended it to him by all means as the principal incentive to exertion. And with regard to his probability of success, I told him that as he had, I understood, already made the experiment by appearing in print, he could judge how that matter stood better than I or any man could do it for him. What could I say, my dear? I was really unwilling to mortify a brother bard, and yet could not avoid it but at the expense of common honesty.

The Padre is to dine with us on Thursday next. I am highly pleased with him, and intend to make all possible advances to a nearer acquaintance. Why he is so silent in company I know not. Perhaps he is reserved like some other people; or perhaps he holds it unsuitable to his function to be forward in mixed conversation. Certain it is, that he has enough to say when he and I are together. He has transcribed the ninth book for me, and is now transcribing the twelfth, which Mrs. Throckmorton left unfinished. Poor Teedon has dined with us once, and it did me good to stuff him.

We have heard from the poor widow after whom you so kindly inquire. She answered a letter of Mrs. Unwin's about a week since. Her answer was affectionate, tender, and melancholy to a great degree, but not without expressions of hope and confidence in God. We understand that she has suffered much in her health, as well as in her mind. It could not be otherwise, for she was attached to her husband in the extreme. We have learned by a side-wind since I mentioned her last, that Billy left everything, or almost everything, to the children. But she has at present one hundred pounds a year, and will have another hundred hereafter, if she outlives Mrs. U., being jointured in her estate. In the meantime her sister lives with her, who has, I believe, determined never to marry, from which circumstance she must doubtless derive advantage. She spent some time at Clapham after her return from Winchester, is now with Mr. John Unwin at Croydon, and goes soon to her gloomy mansion, as she calls it, in Essex. We asked her hither, in hope that a little time spent at Weston might be of use to her; but her affairs would not suffer her to come. She is greatly to be pitied, and whether she will ever recover the stroke is, I think, very uncertain.

I had some time since a very clever letter from Henry C., which I answered as well as I could, but not in kind. I seem to myself immoderately stupid on epistolary occasions, and especially when I wish to shine. Such I seem now, and such to have been ever since I began. So much the worse for you. Pray, my dear, send me a bit of Indian glue, and an almanack.

It gives me true pleasure to learn that the General at least says he is better; but it would give me much more to hear others say the same. Thank your sister for her instructions concerning the lamp, which shall be exactly followed.—I am, my dearest, your most Gingerbread Giles, etc.  WM. COWPER.

TO SAMUEL ROSE, ESQ.

WESTON, *July* 24, 1787.

DEAR SIR—This is the first time I have written these six months, and nothing but the constraint of obligation could induce me to write now. I cannot be so wanting to myself as not to endeavour, at least, to thank you both for the visits with which you have favoured me, and the poems that you sent me. In my present state of mind I taste nothing; nevertheless I read, partly from habit, and partly because it is the only thing that I am capable of.

I have therefore read Burns's *Poems*, and have read them twice; and, though they be written in a language that is new to me, and many of them on subjects much inferior to the author's ability, I think them, on the whole, a very extraordinary production. He is, I believe, the only poet these kingdoms have produced in the lower rank of life, since Shakspeare (I should rather say since Prior), who need not be indebted for any part of his praise to a charitable consideration of his origin, and the disadvantages under which he has laboured. It will be a pity if he should not hereafter divest himself of barbarism, and content himself with writing pure English, in which he appears perfectly qualified to excel. He who can command admiration dishonours himself if he aims no higher than to raise a laugh.—I am, dear sir, with my best wishes for your prosperity, and with Mrs. Unwin's respects, your obliged and affectionate humble servant,

W. C.

### TO LADY HESKETH.

THE LODGE, *September* 15, 1787.

MY DEAREST COUSIN—On Monday last I was invited to meet your friend Miss Jekyll at the Hall, and there we found her. Her good-nature, her humorous manner, and her good sense, are charming; insomuch that even I, who was never much addicted to speech-making, and who at present find myself particularly indisposed to it, could not help saying at parting,—"I am glad that I have seen you, and sorry that I have seen so little of you." We were sometimes many in company; on Thursday we were fifteen, but we had not altogether so much vivacity and cleverness as Miss Jekyll, whose talent at mirth-making has this rare property to recommend it, that nobody suffers by it.

I am making a gravel walk for winter use, under a warm hedge in the orchard. It shall be furnished with a low seat for your accommodation, and if you do but like it, I shall be satisfied. In wet weather, or rather after wet weather, when the street is dirty, it will suit you well, for, lying on an easy declivity through its whole length, it must of course be immediately dry.

You are very much wished for by our friends at the Hall—how much by me I will not tell you till the second week in October.—Yours, W. C.

### TO THE SAME.

THE LODGE, *October* 5, 1787.

MY DEAREST COUSIN—My uncle's recommendation of my handwriting was the more agreeable to me as I have seldom received any on that subject. I write generally in the helter-skelter way, concerning myself about nothing more than to be legible. I am sorry for his deafness, which I hope, however, by this time, the doctor and the doctor's engine have removed. It is well if he is cheerful under that malady, which oppresses the spirits of most men more than any other disorder that is not accompanied with pain. We have but few senses, and can spare none of them without much inconvenience. But I know that when my uncle's spirits are good, they are proof against all oppression.

Mrs. Throck has not written to me, and now will not. Mr. Gregson had a letter from one of them to-day, in which they send compliments to us, and tell us they will be at home on Tuesday. How should she find time to write to me, who has been visiting her brother, one of the gayest young men in the world, who is building a great house, and has one of the finest pieces of water in England, with thirty boats on it? I am sorry to hear that his youth and his riches together bid fair to ruin him,—that he is a prey to his neighbours, plays deep, and consequently cannot be rich long. Excessive good-nature is a quality attended with so much danger to a young man, that, amiable as it is, one cannot help pitying the man that owns it.

Mrs. Chester paid her first visit here last Saturday, a prelude, no doubt, to the visit that she intends to you. I was angry with her for her omission of a civility to which you are so highly entitled; but, now that she discovers symptoms of repentance, feel myself inclined to pardon her. She is one of those women, indeed, to whom one pardons everything the moment they appear, not handsome, but showing a gentleness in her countenance, voice, and manner, that speaks irresistibly in her favour.

Your newspaper, for which I thank you, my cousin, pleases me more than any that I have seen lately. The pertness of the *Herall* is my detestation, yet I always read it; and why? because it is a newspaper, and should therefore doubtless read it were it ten times more disgusting than it is. Fielding was the only man who ever attempted to be witty with success in a newspaper, and even he could not support it long. But he led the way in his *Convent Garden Journal*, and a thousand blockheads have followed him. I am not pleased, however, with that furious attack upon the poor Abbé Mann. The zealous Protestant who makes it discovers too much of that spirit which he charges upon the Papists. The poor Abbé's narrative was in a manner extorted from him; and when I read it, instead of finding it insidious and hostile to the interests of the Church of England, I was foolish enough to think it discreet, modest, and temperate. The gentleman, therefore, has either more zeal, or a better nose at a plot, than I have.

The bedstead, my dear, suffered nothing by the long delay and the bad lodging that it met with: it could not have looked better than it does had it arrived at the time intended. It lost a screw indeed; but our neighbour, the tailor, happening to have an odd one of exactly the right size, supplied the deficiency. It will have its furniture to-morrow.

Poor Teedon, whom I daresay you remember, has never missed calling here once, and generally twice a week since January last. The poor man has gratitude if he has not wit, and in the possession of that one good quality has a sufficient recommendation. I blame myself often for finding him tiresome, but cannot help it. My only comfort is that I should be more weary of thousands who have all the cleverness that has been denied to Teedon.

I have been reading Hanway's *Travels*, and of course "The History of Nadir Shah, *alias* Kouli Khan"—a hero!

my dear,—and I am old enough to remember the time when he was accounted one. He built up pyramids of human heads, and had consequently many admirers. But he has found few, I imagine, in the world to which he is gone to give an account of his building. I have now just entered upon Baker's *Chronicle*, having never seen it in my life till I found it in the Hall library. It is a book at which you and I should have laughed immoderately some years ago. It is equally wise and foolish, which makes the most ridiculous mixture in the world.—With Mrs. U.'s affectionate respects, my dearest cousin, I am, ever yours, WM. COWPER.

TO THE SAME.

THE LODGE, *November* 27, 1787.

IT is the part of wisdom, my dearest cousin, to sit down contented under the demands of necessity, because they are such. I am sensible that you cannot, in my uncle's present infirm state, and of which it is not possible to expect any considerable amendment, indulge either of us, or yourself, with a journey to Weston. Yourself I say, both because I know it will give you pleasure to see *Causidice mi* once more, especially in the comfortable abode where you have placed him, and because, after so long an imprisonment in London, you, who love the country, and have a taste for it, would, of course, be glad to return to it. For my own part, to me it is ever new, and though I have now been an inhabitant of this village a twelvemonth, and have during the half of that time been at liberty to expatiate, and to make discoveries, I am daily finding out fresh scenes and walks, which you would never be satisfied with enjoying—some of them are unapproachable by you either on foot or in your carriage.

Had you twenty toes—whereas, I suppose, you have but ten—you could not reach them; and coach-wheels have never been seen there since the flood. Before it, indeed (as Burnet says that the earth was then perfectly free from all inequalities in its surface), they might have been seen there every day. We have other walks both upon hill-tops, and in valleys beneath, some of which, by the help of your carriage, and many of them without its help, would be always at your command.

On Monday morning last Sam brought me word that there was a man in the kitchen who desired to speak with me. I ordered him in. A plain, decent, elderly figure made its appearance, and being desired to sit, spoke as follows: "Sir, I am clerk of the parish of All-Saints in Northampton; brother of Mr. Cox the upholsterer. It is customary for the person in my office to annex to a bill of mortality, which he publishes at Christmas, a copy of verses. You would do me a great favour, sir, if you would furnish me with one." To this I replied, "Mr. Cox, you have several men of genius in your town, why have you not applied to some of them? There is a namesake of yours in particular, Cox, the statuary, who, everybody knows, is a first-rate maker of verses. He surely is the man of all the world for your purpose."—"Alas! sir, I have heretofore borrowed help from him, but he is a gentleman of so much reading, that the people of our town cannot understand him." I confess to you, my dear, I felt all the force of the compliment implied in this speech, and was almost ready to answer, Perhaps, my good friend, they may find me unintelligible too for the same reason. But on asking him whether he had walked over to Weston on purpose to implore the assistance of my muse, and on his replying in the affirmative, I felt my mortified vanity a little consoled, and pitying the poor man's distress, which appeared to be considerable, promised to supply him. The waggon accordingly has gone this day to Northampton loaded in part with my effusions in the mortuary style. A fig for poets who write epitaphs upon individuals! I have written *one* that serves *two hundred* persons.

A few days since I received a second very obliging letter from Mr. Mackenzie. He tells me that his own papers, which are by far, he is sorry to say it, the most numerous, are marked V. I. Z. Accordingly, my dear, I am happy to find that I am engaged in a correspondence with Mr. Viz, a gentleman for whom I have always entertained the profoundest veneration. But the serious fact is, that the papers distinguished by those signatures have ever pleased me most, and struck me as the work of a sensible man, who knows the world well, and has more of Addison's delicate humour than anybody.

A poor man begged food at the Hall lately. The cook gave him some vermicelli soup. He ladled it about some time with the spoon, and then returned it to her saying, "I am a poor man, it is true, and I am very hungry; but yet I cannot eat broth with maggots in it." Once more, my dear, a thousand thanks for your box full of good things, useful things, and beautiful things.—Yours ever, W. C.

TO THE REV. WALTER BAGOT.

WESTON, *December* 6, 1787.

MY DEAR FRIEND—A short time since, by the help of Mrs. Throckmorton's chaise, Mrs. Unwin and I reached Chicheley. "Now," said I to Mrs. Chester, "I shall write boldly to your brother Walter, and will do it immediately. I have passed the gulf that parted us, and he will be glad to hear it." But let not the man who translates Homer be so presumptuous as to have a will of his own, or to promise anything. A fortnight has, I suppose, elapsed since I paid this visit, and I am only now beginning to fulfil what I then undertook to accomplish without delay. The old Grecian must answer for it.

I spent my morning there so agreeably that I have ever since regretted more sensibly that there are five miles of a dirty country interposed between us. For the increase of my pleasure, I had the good fortune to find your brother the Bishop there. We had much talk about many things, but most, I believe, about Homer; and great satisfaction it gave me to find, that on the most important points of that subject his Lordship and I were exactly of one mind. In the course of our conversation he produced from his pocket-book a translation of the first ten or twelve lines of the *Iliad*, and in order to leave my judgment free, imformed me kindly at the same time that they were not his own. I read them, and, according to the best of my recollection of the original, found them well executed. The Bishop, indeed, acknowleged that they were not faultless; neither did I find them so. Had they been such, I should have felt their perfection as a discouragement hardly to be surmounted; for at that passage I have laboured more abundantly than at any other, and hitherto with the least success. I am convinced that Homer placed it at the threshold of his work as a scarecrow to all translators. Now, Walter, if thou knowest the author of this version, and it be not treason against thy brother's confidence in thy secrecy, declare him to me. Had I been so happy as to have seen the Bishop again before he left this country, I should certainly have asked him the question, having a curiosity upon the matter that is extremely troublesome.

The awkward situation in which you found yourself on receiving a visit from an authoress, whose works, though presented to you long before, you had never read, made me laugh, and it was no sin against my friendship for you to do so. It was a ridiculous distress, and I can laugh at it even now. I hope she catechised you well. How did you extricate yourself?—Now laugh at me. The clerk of the parish of All-Saints, in the town of Northampton, having occasion for a poet, has appointed me to the office. I found myself obliged to comply. The bellman comes next, and then, I think, though even borne upon your swan's quill, I can soar no higher!—I am, my dear friend, faithfully yours, W. C.

TO LADY HESKETH.

*The Lodge, December 10, 1787.*

I THANK you for the snip of cloth, commonly called a pattern. At present I have two coats, and but one back. If at any time hereafter I should find myself possessed of fewer coats, or more backs, it will be of use to me.

Even as you suspect, my dear, so it proved. The ball was prepared for, the ball was held, and the ball passed, and we had nothing to do with it. Mrs. Throckmorton, knowing our trim, did not give us the pain of an invitation, for a pain it would have been. And why? as Sternhold says—Because, as Hopkins answers, we must have refused it. But it fell out singularly enough that this ball was held, of all the days in the year, on my birthday—and so I told them—but not till it was all over.

Though I have thought proper never to take any notice of the arrival of my MSS. together with the *other good things* in the box, yet certain it is, that I received them. I have furbished up the tenth book till it is as bright as silver, and am now occupied in bestowing the same labour upon the eleventh. The twelfth and thirteenth are in the hands of ·———, and the fourteenth and fifteenth are ready to succeed them. This notable job is the delight of my heart, and how sorry shall I be when it is ended.

The smith and the carpenter, my dear, are both in the room, hanging a bell; if I therefore make a thousand blunders, let the said intruders answer for them all.

I thank you, my dear, for your history of the G———s. What changes in that family! And how many thousand families have in the same time experienced changes as violent as theirs! The course of a rapid river is the justest of all emblems, to express the variableness of our scene below. Shakespeare says none ever bathed himself twice in the same stream, and it is equally true that the world upon which we close our eyes at night is never the same with that on which we open them in the morning.

I do not always say, give my love to my uncle, because he knows that I always love him. I do not always present Mrs. Unwin's love to you, partly for the same reason—Deuce take the smith and the carpenter!—and partly because I forget it. But to present my own I forget never, for I always have to finish my letter, which I know not how to do, my dearest Coz, without telling you that I am ever yours, W. C.

TO THE SAME.

*December* 19, 1787.

SATURDAY, my dearest cousin, was a day of receipts. In the morning I received a box filled with an abundant variety of stationery ware, containing, in particular, a quantity of paper sufficient, well-covered with good writing, to immortalise any man. I have nothing to do therefore but to cover it as aforesaid, and my name will never die. In the evening I received a smaller box, but still more welcome on account of its contents. It contained an almanac in red morocco, a pencil of a new invention, called an everlasting pencil, and a noble purse, with a noble gift in it, called a bank-note for twenty-five pounds. I need use no arguments to assure you, my cousin, that by the help of ditto note, we shall be able to fadge very comfortably till Christmas is turned, without having the least occasion to draw upon you. By the post yesterday —that is, Sunday morning—I received also a letter from Anonymous giving me advice of the kind present which I have just particularised, in which letter allusion is made to a certain piece by me composed, entitled, I believe, "A drop of Ink." The only copy I ever gave of that piece I gave to yourself. It is *possible* therefore that between you and *Anonymous* there may be some communication. If that should be the case, I will beg you just to signify to him, as opportunity may occur, the safe arrival of his most acceptable present, and my most grateful sense of it.

My toothache is in a great measure, that is to say, almost entirely removed: not by snipping my ears, as poor Lady Strange's ears were snipped, nor by any other chirurgical operation, except such as I could perform myself. The manner of it was as follows: We dined last Thursday at the Hall; I sat down to table, trembling lest the tooth, of which I told you in my last, should not only refuse its own office, but hinder all the rest. Accordingly, in less than five minutes, by a hideous dislocation of it, I found myself not only in great pain, but under an absolute prohibition not only to eat, but to speak another word. Great emergencies sometimes meet the most effectual remedies. I resolved, if it were possible, then and there to draw it. This I effected so dexterously by a sudden twitch, and afterwards so dexterously conveyed it into my pocket, that no creature present, not even Mrs. Unwin, who sat facing me, was sensible either of my distress, or of the manner of my deliverance from it. I am poorer by one tooth than I was, but richer by the unimpeded use of all the rest.

When I lived in the Temple I was rather intimate with the son of the late Admiral Rowley and a younger brother of the present Admiral. Since I wrote to you last I received a letter from him, in a very friendly and affectionate style. It accompanied half a dozen books, which I had lent him five-and-twenty years ago, and which he apologised for having kept so long, telling me that they had been sent to him at Dublin by mistake; for at Dublin, it seems, he now resides. Reading my poems, he felt, he said, his friendship for me revive, and wrote accordingly. I have now, therefore, a correspondent in Ireland, another in Scotland, and a third in Wales. All this would be very diverting had I a little more time to spare them.

My dog, my dear, is a spaniel. Till Miss Gunning begged him, he was the property of a farmer, and while he was their property had been accustomed to lie in the chimney corner, among the embers, till the hair was singed from his back, and till nothing was left of his tail but the gristle. Allowing for these disadvantages, he is really handsome; and when nature shall have furnished him with a new coat,—a gift which, in consideration of the ragged condition of his old one, it is hoped she will not long delay,—he will then be unrivalled in personal endowments by any dog in this country. He and my cat are excessively fond of each other, and play a thousand gambols together that it is impossible not to admire.

Know thou that from this time forth, the post comes

daily to Weston. This improvement is effected by an annual subscription of ten shillings. The Throcks invited us to the measure, and we have acceded to it. Their servant will manage this concern for us at the Olney post-office, and the subscription is to pay a man for stumping three times a week from Olney to Newport Pagnel, and back again.

Returning from my walk to-day, while I was passing by some small closes at the back of the town, I heard the voices of some persons extremely merry at the top of the hill. Advancing into the large field behind our house, I there met Mr. Throck, wife, and brother George. Combine in your imagination as large proportions as you can of earth and water intermingled so as to constitute what is commonly called mud, and you will have but an imperfect conception of the quantity that had attached itself to her petticoats; but she had half-boots, and laughed at her own figure. She told me that she had this morning transcribed sixteen pages of my Homer. I observed in reply, that to write so much, and to gather all that dirt, was no bad morning's work, considering the shortness of the days at this season.—Yours, my dear, W. C.

TO THE SAME.

THE LODGE, *February* 7, 1788.

MY DEAREST COUSIN—Thanks beforehand for the books which you give me to expect. They will all be welcome. Of the two editions of Shakspeare I prefer that which is printed in the largest type, independent of all other considerations. Don Quixote by any hand must needs be welcome, and by Smollett's especially, because I have never seen it. He had a drollery of his own, which, for aught I know, may suit an English taste as well as that of Cervantes; perhaps better, because to us somewhat more intelligible.

It is pretty well known (the clerk took care it should be so), both at Northampton and in this county, who wrote the "Mortuary Verses." All that I know of their success is, that he sent a bundle of them to Maurice Smith at Olney, who sold them for threepence a piece, a high price for a *Memento Mori*, a commodity not generally in great request. The other small poem, addressed to Mrs. Throck, has given, as I understand, great satisfaction at Buckland. The old baronet and his lady, having heard that such a piece existed (Mrs. Bromley Chester, I suppose, must have been their informant), wrote to desire a copy. A copy was sent, and they answered it with warm encomiums.

Mr. Bull, the lame curate, having been lately preferred to a living, another was of course wanted to supply his place. By the recommendation of Mr. Romaine, a Mr. C—— came down. He lodges at Mr. Socket's in this village, and Mr. Socket lives in the small house to which you had once conceived a liking. Our lacquey is also clerk of the parish. C——, a day or two after his arrival, had a corpse to bury at Weston. Having occasion to consult with the clerk concerning this matter, he sought him in our kitchen. Samuel entered the study to inform us that there was a clergyman without; he was accordingly invited in, and in he came. We had but lately dined; the wine was on the table, and he drank three glasses while the corpse in question was getting ready for its last journey. The moment he entered the room I felt myself incurably prejudiced against him; his features, his figure, his address, and all that he uttered, confirmed that prejudice, and I determined, having once seen him, to see him no more. Two days after he overtook me in the village. "Your humble servant, Mr. Cowper! a fine morning, sir, for a walk.

I had liked to have called on you yesterday morning to tell you that I had become your near neighbour. I live at Mr. Socket's." I answered, without looking at him, as drily as possible, "Are you come to stay any time in the country?" He believed he was. "Which way," I replied, "are you going? to Olney?" "Yes." "I am going to Mr. Throckmorton's garden, and I wish you a good-day, sir." I was in fact going to Olney myself, but this *rencontre* give me such a violent twist another way that I found it impossible to recover that direction, and accordingly there we parted. All this I related at the Hall the next time we dined there, describing also my apprehensions and distress lest, whether I would or not, I should be obliged to have intercourse with a man to me so perfectly disagreeable. A good deal of laugh and merriment ensued, and there for that time it ended. The following Sunday, in the evening, I received a note to this purport: "Mr. C——'s compliments," etc. Understanding that my friends at the Hall were to dine with me the next day, he took the liberty to invite himself to eat a bit of mutton with me, being sure that I should be happy to introduce him. Having read the note, I threw it to Mrs. Unwin. "There," said I, "take that and read it; then tell me if it be not an effort of impudence the most extraordinary you ever heard of." I expected some such push from the man; I knew he was equal to it. She read it, and we were both of a mind. I sat down to my desk, and with a good deal of emotion gave it just such an answer as it would have deserved had it been genuine. But having heard by accident in the morning that he spells his name with a C, and observing in the note that it was spelt with a K, a suspicion struck me that it was a fiction. I looked at it more attentively, and perceived that it was directed by Mrs. Throck. The inside I found afterwards was written by her brother

George. This served us with another laugh on the subject, and I have hardly seen, and never spoken to Mr. C—— since. So, my dear, *that's the little story I promised you.* Mr. Bull called here this morning; from him I learn what follows concerning P——. He waited on the Bishop of London, like a blundering ignoramus as he is, without his canonicals. The Bishop was highly displeased, as he had cause to be; and, having pretty significantly given him to know it, addressed himself to his chaplain with tokens of equal displeasure, enjoining him never more to admit a clergyman to him in such attire. To pay this visit he made a journey from Clapham to town on horseback. His horse he left at an inn on the Lambeth side of Westminster Bridge. Thence he proceeded to the Bishop's, and from the Bishop's to Mr. Scott. Having finished this last visit, he begged Mr. Scott's company to the inn where he had left his horse, which he said was at the foot of *London* Bridge. Thither they went, but neither the inn nor the horse were there. "Then," says P——, "it must be at Blackfriar's Bridge that I left it." Thither also they went, but to as little purpose. Luckily for him there was but one more bridge, and there they found it. To make the poor youth amends for all these misadventures, it so happened that the incumbent, his predecessor, died before the crops of last year were reaped. The whole profits of that year, by consequence, go into P——'s pocket, which was never so stuffed before.

Good-night, my dearest Coz. Mrs. Unwin's love attends you.—Affectionately yours,     WM. COWPER.

### TO THE SAME.

THE LODGE, *March* 3, 1788

ONE day last week, Mrs. Unwin and I, having taken our morning walk, and returning homeward through the

Wilderness, met the Throckmortons. A minute after we had met them we heard the cry of hounds at no great distance, and mounting the broad stump of an elm which had been felled, and by the aid of which we were enabled to look over the wall, we saw them. They were all that time in our orchard; presently we heard a terrier, belonging to Mrs. Throckmorton, which you may remember by the name of Fury, yelping with much vehemence, and saw her running through the thickets, within a few yards of us, at her utmost speed, as if in pursuit of something which we doubted not was the fox. Before we could reach the other end of the Wilderness the hounds entered also; and when we arrived at the gate which opens into the grove, there we found the whole weary cavalcade assembled. The huntsman dismounting begged leave to follow his hounds on foot, for he was sure, he said, that they had killed him,—a conclusion which, I suppose, he drew from their profound silence. He was accordingly admitted, and with a sagacity that would not have dishonoured the best hound in the world, pursuing precisely the same track which the fox and the dogs had taken, though he had never had a glimpse of either after their first entrance through the rails, arrived where he found the slaughtered prey. He soon produced dead reynard, and rejoined us in the grove with all his dogs about him. Having an opportunity to see a ceremony, which I was pretty sure would never fall in my way again, I determined to stay, and to notice all that passed with the most minute attention. The huntsman having by the aid of a pitchfork lodged reynard on the arm of an elm, at the height of about nine feet from the ground, there left him for a considerable time. The gentlemen sat on their horses contemplating the fox for which they had toiled so hard; and the hounds assembled at the foot of the tree, with faces not less expressive of the most rational delight, contemplated the same object. The huntsman remounted, cut off a foot, and threw it to the hounds—one of them swallowed it whole like a bolus. He then once more alighted, and drawing down the fox by the hinder legs, desired the people, who were by this time rather numerous, to open a lane for him to the right and left. He was instantly obeyed, when, throwing the fox to a distance of some yards and screaming like a fiend, "tear him to pieces" at least six times repeatedly, he consigned him over absolutely to the pack, who in a few minutes devoured him completely. Thus, my dear, as Virgil says, what none of the gods could have ventured to promise me, time itself, pursuing its accustomed course, has of its own accord presented me with. I have been in at the death of a fox, and you now know as much of the matter as I, who am as well informed as any sportsman in England.—Yours,

W. C.

### TO THE SAME.

THE LODGE, *July* 28, 1788.

IT is in vain that you tell me that you have no talent at description, while in fact you describe better than anybody. You have given me a most complete idea of your mansion and its situation; and I doubt not that with your letter in my hand by way of map, could I be set down on the spot in a moment, I should find myself qualified to take my walks and my pastime in whatever quarter of your paradise it should please me the most to visit. We also, as you know, have scenes at Weston worthy of description; but because you know them well, I will only say that one of them has, within these few days, been much improved,—I mean the Lime Walk. By the help of the axe and the woodbill, which have of late been constantly employed in cutting out all straggling branches that intercepted the arch, Mr. Throckmorton has now defined it with such exactness that no cathedral in the world can show one of more magnificence or beauty. I bless myself that I live so near it; for were it distant several miles, it would be well worth while to visit it, merely as an object of taste; not to mention the refreshment of such a gloom both to the eyes and spirits. And these are the things which our modern improvers of parks and pleasure-grounds have displaced without mercy; because, forsooth, they are rectilinear. It is a wonder that they do not quarrel with the sunbeams for the same reason.

Have you seen the account of five hundred celebrated authors now living? I am one of them; but stand charged with the high crime and misdemeanour of totally neglecting method; an accusation which, if the gentleman would take the pains to read me, he would find sufficiently refuted. I am conscious at least myself of having laboured much in the arrangement of my matter, and of having given to the several parts of every book of the *Task*, as well as to each poem in the first volume, that sort of slight connexion which poetry demands; for in poetry (except professedly of the didactic kind) a logical precision would be stiff, pedantic, and ridiculous. But there is no pleasing some critics; the comfort is, that I am contented, whether they be pleased or not. At the same time, to my honour be it spoken, the chronicler of us five hundred prodigies bestows on me, for aught I know, more commendations than on any other of my confraternity. May he live to write the histories of as many thousand poets, and find me the very best among them! Amen!

I join with you, my dearest Coz, in wishing that I owned the fee-simple of all the beautiful scenes around you, but such emoluments were never designed for poets. Am I not happier than ever poet was, in having thee for my cousin, and in the expectation of thy arrival here whenever Strawberry Hill shall lose thee?—Ever thine,

W. C.

TO MRS. KING.

WESTON UNDERWOOD, *August* 28, 1788.

MY DEAR MADAM—Should you discard me from the number of your correspondents, you would treat me as I seem to deserve, though I do not actually deserve it. I have lately been engaged with company at our house, who resided with us five weeks, and have had much of the rheumatism into the bargain. Not in my fingers, you will say;—true. But you know as well as I, that pain, be it where it may, indisposes us to writing.

You express some degree of wonder that I found you out to be sedentary, at least much a stayer within doors, without any sufficient data for my direction. Now, if I should guess your figure and stature with equal success, you will deem me not only a poet but a conjurer. Yet in fact I have no pretensions of that sort. I have only formed a picture of you in my own imagination, as we ever do of a person of whom we think much, though we have never seen that person. Your height I conceive to be about five feet five inches, which, though it would make a short man, is yet height enough for a woman. If you insist on an inch or two more, I have no objection. You are not very fat, but somewhat inclined to be fat, and unless you allow yourself a little more air and exercise, will incur some danger of exceeding in your dimensions before you die. Let me, therefore, once more recommend to you to walk a little more, at least in your garden, and to amuse yourself occasionally with pulling up here and there a weed, for it will be an inconvenience to you to be much fatter than you are, at a time of life when your strength will be naturally on the decline. I have given you a fair complexion, a slight tinge of the rose in your cheeks, dark brown hair, and, if the fashion would give you leave to show it, an open and well-formed forehead. To all this I add a pair of eyes, not quite black but nearly approaching to that hue, and very animated. I have not absolutely determined on the shape of your nose, or the form of your mouth; but should you tell me that I have in all other respects drawn a tolerable likeness, I have no doubt but I can describe them too. I assure you that though I have a great desire to read him, I have never seen Lavater, nor have availed myself in the least of any of his rules on this occasion. Ah, madam! if with all that sensibility of yours, which exposes you to so much sorrow, and necessarily must expose you to it, in a world like this, I have had the good fortune to make you smile, I have then painted, whether with a strong resemblance or with none at all, to very good purpose.

I had intended to have sent you a little poem which I have lately finished, but have no room to transcribe it. You shall have it by another opportunity. Breakfast is on the table, and my time also fails as well as my paper. I rejoice that a cousin of yours found my volumes agreeable to him, for, being your cousin, I will be answerable for his good taste and judgment.

When I wrote last, I was in mourning for a dear and much-valued uncle, Ashley Cowper. He died at the age of eighty-six. My best respects attend Mr. King; and I am, dear madam, most truly yours, W. C.

TO THE SAME.

WESTON UNDERWOOD, *October* 11, 1788.

MY DEAR MADAM—You are perfectly secure from all danger of being overwhelmed with presents from me. It is not much that a poet can possibly have it in his power to give. When he has presented his own works, he may be supposed to have exhausted all means of donation. They are his only superfluity. There was a time, but that time was before I commenced writer for the press, when I amused myself in a way somewhat similar to yours; allowing, I mean, for the difference between masculine and feminine operations. The scissors and the needle are your chief implements; mine were the chisel and the saw. In those days you might have been in some danger of too plentiful a return for your favours. Tables, such as they were, and joint-stools such as never were, might have travelled to Pertenhall in most convenient abundance. But I have long since discontinued this practice, and many others which I found it necessary to adopt, that I might escape the worst of all evils, both in itself and in its consequences—an idle life. Many arts I have exercised with this view for which nature never designed me; though among them were some in which I arrived at considerable proficiency by mere dint of the most heroic perseverance. There is not a squire in all this country who can boast of having made better squirrel-houses, hutches for rabbits, or bird-cages, than myself; and in the article of cabbage-nets I had no superior. I even had the hardiness to take in hand the pencil, and studied a whole year the art of drawing. Many figures were the fruit of my labours, which had, at least, the merit of being unparalleled by any production either of art or nature. But before the year was ended I had occasion to wonder at the progress that may be made, in despite of natural deficiency, by dint alone of practice; for I actually produced three landscapes, which a lady thought worthy to be framed and glazed. I then judged it high time to exchange this occupation for another, lest, by any subsequent productions of inferior merit, I should forfeit the honour I had so fortunately acquired. But gardening was, of all employments, that in which I succeeded best, though even in this I did not suddenly attain perfection. I began with lettuces and cauliflowers; from them I proceeded to cucumbers; next to melons. I then purchased an orange-tree, to which, in due time, I added two or three myrtles. These served me day and night with employment during a whole severe winter. To defend them from the frost, in a situation that exposed them to its severity, cost me much ingenuity and much attendance. I contrived to give them a fire heat; and have waded night after night through the snow, with the bellows under my arm, just before going to bed, to give the latest possible puff to the embers, lest the frost should seize them before morning. Very minute beginnings have sometimes important consequences. From nursing two or three little evergreens I became ambitious of a greenhouse, and accordingly built one; which, verse excepted, afforded me amusement for a longer time than any expedient of all the many to which I have fled for refuge from the misery of having nothing to do. When I left Olney for Weston I could no longer have a greenhouse of my own; but in a neighbour's garden I find a better, of which the sole management is consigned to me.

I had need take care, when I begin a letter, that the subject with which I set off be of some importance; for, before I can exhaust it, be it what it may, I have generally filled my paper. But self is a subject inexhaustible, which is the reason, that though I have said little, and nothing, I am afraid, worth your hearing, I have only room to add that I am, my dear madam, most truly yours, W. C.

Mrs. Unwin bids me present her best compliments, and say how much she shall be obliged to you for the receipt to make that most excellent cake which came hither in its native pan. There is no production of yours that will not be always most welcome at Weston.

TO THE REV. WALTER BAGOT.

WESTON, *October* 30, 1788.

MY DEAR FRIEND—The good fortune that you wished me I have actually enjoyed, having had an opportunity, by means of Lady Hesketh's carriage, to see your brother Howard at Chicheley. I had the pleasure of spending near an hour with him in the study, for the consequences of his unfortunate fall which he got in Norfolk did not permit him to join the ladies in the saloon. It gave me much concern that not having seen him so many years, I should at last find him with a broken bone. He was, however, otherwise in good health, and, as I told him, had suffered less in his looks by the lapse of time that has passed since we were all at school together than any of us.

I was truly happy to be the instrument of bringing the Chesters and my cousin to an acquaintance. She and your sister would love each other more than people generally do in this neighbourhood, could they often come together. Another year perhaps may afford more frequent opportunities than they are likely to find in the present, which is now far spent, and threatens us with foul weather soon and dirty roads, which makes Chicheley unapproachable by mortal wight who is subject to fear in a carriage. Menelaus tells Telemachus that had Ulysses returned safe from Troy it was his intention to have built him a city and a house in Argos, that he and his people, transferring themselves hither from Ithaca, might have become his neighbours. Had I the thousands with which some people are favoured I would gladly build for the Chesters, not a city, which they would not want, but a house at least as good as that which Menelaus had designed for Ulysses, in the precincts of Weston Underwood, their non-residence here being the only defect in the situation. But I ought to account myself in my present circumstances here, if not so happy as in that case I should be, at least as happy as a world which I do not hold, as the saying is, in a string, is ever likely to make me. We are but one remove from brother and sister, and that distance has long since been absorbed by a more than sisterly affection.

The Northampton clerk has been with me again, and I have again promised him my assistance. You may depend on my sending you a printed copy of this my second meditation upon churchyard subjects as soon as I have received the impression. It is likely, indeed, to be an annual remittance; for said clerk will, I daresay, resort to me for poetical aid till either he or I shall want an epitaph for ourselves. I am not sorry to be employed by him, considering the task, in respect of the occasion of it, as even more important than *Iliad* and *Odyssey* together. To put others in mind of their latter end is at least as proper an occupation for a man whose own latter end is nearer by almost sixty years than it once was, as to write about gods and heroes. Let me once get well out of these two long stories, and if I ever meddle with such matters more call me, as Fluellen says, a fool and an ass and a prating coxcomb.

It gives me much pleasure to hear that Lord Bagot is so well, and I sincerely wish that he may find the Naiads of Buxton as propitious to him as those of Cheltenham. The Peerage can ill spare such Peers as he.

With Mrs. Unwin's best respects, I remain, my dear friend, most truly yours,           Wm. Cowper.

TO SAMUEL ROSE, ESQ.

The Lodge, *January* 19, 1789.

My dear Sir—I have taken, since you went away, many of the walks which we have taken together; and none of them, I believe, without thoughts of you. I have, though not a good memory in general, yet a good local memory, and can recollect, by the help of a tree or stile, what you said on that particular spot. For this reason I purpose, when the summer is come, to walk with a book in my pocket; what I read at my fireside I forget, but what I read under a hedge, or at the side of a pond, that pond and that hedge will always bring to my remembrance; and this is a sort of *memoria technica* which I would recommend to you if I did not know that you have no occasion for it.

I am reading Sir John Hawkins, and still hold the same opinion of his book as when you were here. There are in it, undoubtedly, some awkwardnesses of phrase, and, which is worse, here and there some unequivocal indications of a vanity not easily pardonable in a man of his years; but on the whole I find it amusing; and to me at least, to whom everything that has passed in the literary world within these five and twenty years is new, sufficiently replete with information. Mr. Throckmorton told me about three days since that it was lately recommended to him by a sensible man as a book that would give him great insight into the history of modern literature and modern men of letters—a commendation which I really think it merits. Fifty years hence, perhaps, the world will feel itself obliged to him. W. C.

TO THE SAME.

THE LODGE, *January* 24, 1789.

MY DEAR SIR—We have heard from my cousin in Norfolk Street; she reached home safely, and in good time. An observation suggests itself which, though I have but little time for observation-making, I must allow myself time to mention. Accidents, as we call them, generally occur when there seems least reason to expect them; if a friend of ours travels far in different roads, and at an unfavourable season, we are reasonably alarmed for the safety of one in whom we take so much interest; yet how seldom do we hear a tragical account of such a journey! It is, on the contrary, at home, in our yard or garden, perhaps in our parlour, that disaster finds us; in any place, in short, where we seem perfectly out of the reach of danger. The lesson inculcated by such a procedure on the part of Providence towards us seems to be that of perpetual dependence.

Having preached this sermon I must hasten to a close; you know that I am not idle, nor can I afford to be so; I would gladly spend more time with you, but by some means or other this day has hitherto proved a day of hindrance and confusion. W. C.

TO THE REV. WALTER BAGOT.

WESTON, *January* 29, 1789.

MY DEAR FRIEND—I shall be a better, at least a more

frequent correspondent, when I have done with Homer. I am not forgetful of any letters that I owe, and least of all forgetful of my debts in that way to you; on the contrary, I live in a continual state of self-reproach for not writing more punctually; but the old Grecian, whom I charge myself never to neglect, lest I should never finish him, has at present a voice that seems to drown all other demands, and many to which I could listen with more pleasure than even to his *Os rotundum*. I am now in the eleventh book of the *Odyssey*, conversing with the dead. Invoke the muse in my behalf, that I may roll the stone of Sisyphus with some success. To do it as Homer has done it is, I suppose, in our verse and language, impossible; but I will hope not to labour altogether to as little purpose as Sisyphus himself did.

Though I meddle little with politics, and can find but little leisure to do so, the present state of things unavoidably engages a share of my attention. But as they say, Archimedes, when Syracuse was taken, was found busied in the solution of a problem, so, come what may, I shall be found translating Homer.—Sincerely yours,

W. C.

TO SAMUEL ROSE, ESQ.

THE LODGE, *June* 5, 1789.

MY DEAR FRIEND—I am going to give you a deal of trouble; but London folks must be content to be troubled by country folks; for in London only can our strange necessities be supplied. You must buy for me, if you please, a cuckoo clock; and now I will tell you where they are sold, which, Londoner as you are, it is possible you may not know. They are sold, I am informed, at more houses than one in that narrow part of Holborn which leads into broad St. Giles'. It seems they are well-going clocks, and cheap, which are the two best recommendations of any clock. They are made in Germany, and such numbers of them are annually imported that they are become even a considerable article of commerce.

I return you many thanks for Boswell's *Tour*. I read it to Mrs. Unwin after supper, and we find it amusing. There is much trash in it, as there must always be in every narrative that relates indiscriminately all that passed. But now and then the Doctor speaks like an oracle, and that makes amends for all. Sir John was a coxcomb, and Boswell is not less a coxcomb, though of another kind. I fancy Johnson made coxcombs of all his friends, and they in return made him a coxcomb; for, with reverence be it spoken, such he certainly was, and, flattered as he was, he was sure to be so.

Thanks for your invitation to London, but unless London can come to me, I fear we shall never meet. I was sure that you would love my friend when you should once be well acquainted with him; and equally sure that he would take kindly to you.

Now for Homer.     W. C.


TO MRS. THROCKMORTON.

*July* 18, 1789.

MANY thanks, my dear madam, for your extract from George's letter. I retain but little Italian, yet that little was so forcibly mustered by the consciousness that I was myself the subject, that I presently became màster of it. I have always said that George is a poet, and I am never in his company but I discover proofs of it; and the delicate address by which he has managed his complimentary mention of me, convinces me of it still more than ever.

Here are a thousand poets of us, who have impudence enough to write for the public; but amongst the modest men who are by diffidence restrained from such an enterprise are those who would eclipse us all. I wish that George would make the experiment; I would bind on his laurels with my own hand.

Your gardener has gone after his wife, but having neglected to take his lyre, *alias* fiddle, with him, has not yet brought home his Eurydice. Your clock in the hall has stopped, and (strange to tell!) it stopped at sight of the watchmaker. For he only looked at it, and it has been motionless ever since. Mr. Gregson is gone, and the Hall is a desolation. Pray don't think any place pleasant that you may find in your rambles, that we may see you the sooner. Your aviary is all in good health. I pass it every day, and often inquire at the lattice; the inhabitants of it send their duty, and wish for your return. I took notice of the inscription on your seal, and had we an artist here capable of furnishing me with another, you should read on mine, *Encore une lettre.*—Adieu.

W. C.

TO SAMUEL ROSE, ESQ.

WESTON, *August* 8, 1789.

MY DEAR FRIEND—Come when you will, or when you can, you cannot come at a wrong time, but we shall expect you on the day mentioned.

If you have any book that you think will make pleasant evening reading, bring it with you. I now read Mrs. Piozzi's *Travels* to the ladies after supper, and shall probably have finished them before we shall have the pleasure of seeing you. It is the fashion, I understand, to condemn them. But we who make books ourselves are more merciful to book-makers. I would that every fastidious judge of authors were himself obliged to write; there goes more to the composition of a volume than many critics imagine. I have often wondered that the same poet who wrote the *Dunciad* should have written these lines:

"The mercy I to others show,
That mercy show to me."

Alas for Pope! if the mercy he showed to others was the measure of the mercy he received! He was the less pardonable, too, because experienced in all the difficulties of composition.

I scratch this between dinner and tea; a time when I cannot write much without disordering my noddle, and bringing a flush into my face. You will excuse me therefore if, through respect for the two important considerations of health and beauty, I conclude myself ever yours,

W. C.

TO JOSEPH HILL, ESQ.

*August* 12, 1789.

MY DEAR FRIEND—I rejoice that you and Mrs. Hill are so agreeably occupied in your retreat. August, I hope, will make us amends for the gloom of its many wintry predecessors. We are now gathering from our meadows not hay, but muck, such stuff as deserves not the carriage, which yet it must have that the after-crop may have leave to grow. The Ouse has hardly deigned to run in his channel since the summer began.

My muse were a vixen if she were not always ready to fly in obedience to your commands. But what can be done? I can write nothing in the few hours that remain to me of this day that will be fit for your purpose; and, unless I could despatch what I write by to-morrow's post, it would not reach you in time. I must add, too, that my friend, the vicar of the next parish, engaged me, the day before yesterday, to furnish him by next Sunday with a hymn, to be sung on the occasion of his preaching to the children of the Sunday School, of which hymn I have not yet produced a syllable. I am somewhat in the case of Lawyer Dowling in *Tom Jones*, and could I split myself into as many poets as there are muses, could find employment for them all. Adieu, my dear friend.—I am ever yours, WM. COWPER.

TO MRS. BODHAM.

WESTON, *February* 27, 1790.

MY DEAREST ROSE—Whom I thought withered and fallen from the stalk, but whom I find still alive: nothing could give me greater pleasure than to know it, and to learn it from yourself. I loved you dearly when you were a child, and love you not a jot the less for having ceased to be so. Every creature that bears any affinity to my mother is dear to me, and you, the daughter of her brother, are but one remove distant from her: I love you, therefore, and love you much, both for her sake and for your own. The world could not have furnished you with a present so acceptable to me as the picture which you have so kindly sent me. I received it the night before last, and viewed it with a trepidation of nerves and spirits somewhat akin to what I should have felt had the dear original presented herself to my embraces. I kissed it, and hung it where it is the last object that I see at night, and of course the first on which I open my eyes in the morning. She died when I had completed my sixth year; yet I remember her well, and am an ocular witness of the great fidelity of the copy. I remember, too, a multitude of the maternal tendernesses which I received from her, and which have endeared her memory to me beyond expression. There is in me, I believe, more of the

Donne than of the Cowper; and though I love all of both names, and have a thousand reasons to love those of my own name, yet I feel the bond of nature draw me vehemently to your side. I was thought in the days of my childhood much to resemble my mother, and in my natural temper, of which at the age of fifty-eight I must be supposed a competent judge, can trace both her, and my late uncle, your father. Somewhat of his irritability, and a little I would hope both of his and of her ——, I know not what to call it without seeming to praise myself, which is not my intention, but speaking to *you*, I will even speak out, and say *good nature*. Add to all this, I deal much in poetry, as did our venerable ancestor, the Dean of St. Paul's, and I think I shall have proved myself a Donne at all points. The truth is, that whatever I am, I love you all.

I account it a happy event that brought the dear boy, your nephew, to my knowledge, and that, breaking through all the restraints which his natural bashfulness imposed on him, he determined to find me out. He is amiable to a degree that I have seldom seen, and I often long with impatience to see him again.

My dearest cousin, what shall I say in answer to your affectionate invitation? I *must* say this : I cannot come now, nor soon, and I wish with all my heart I could. But I will tell you what may be done perhaps, and it will answer to us just as well: you and Mr. Bodham can come to Weston, can you not? The summer is at hand, there are roads and wheels to bring you, and you are neither of you translating Homer. I am crazed that I cannot ask you all together for want of house-room; but for Mr. Bodham and yourself we have good room, and equally good for any third, in the shape of a Donne, whether named Hewitt, Bodham, Balls, or Johnson, or by whatever name distinguished. Mrs. Hewitt has particular claims upon me; she was my playfellow at Berkhampstead, and has a share in my warmest affections. Pray tell her so. Neither do I at all forget my cousin Harriet. She and I have been many a time merry at Catfield, and have made the parsonage ring with laughter. Give my love to her. Assure yourself, my dearest cousin, that I shall receive you as if you were my sister; and Mrs. Unwin is, for my sake, prepared to do the same. When she has seen you she will love you for your own.

I am much obliged to Mr. Bodham for his kindness to my Homer, and with my love to you all, and with Mrs. Unwin's kind respects, am, my dear, dear Rose, ever yours,                                       W. C.

*P.S.*—I mourn the death of your poor brother Castres, whom I should have seen had he lived, and should have seen with the greatest pleasure. He was an amiable boy, and I was very fond of him.

*Still another P.S.*—I find, on consulting Mrs. Unwin, that I have underrated our capabilities, and that we have not only room for you and Mr. Bodham, but for two of your sex, and even for your nephew into the bargain. We shall be happy to have it all so occupied.

Your nephew tells me that his sister, in the qualities of the mind, resembles you; that is enough to make her dear to me, and I beg you will assure her that she is so. Let it not be long before I hear from you.


TO JOHN JOHNSON, ESQ.

WESTON, *February* 28, 1790.

MY DEAR COUSIN JOHN—I have much wished to hear from you; and though you are welcome to write to Mrs.

Unwin as often as you please, I wish myself to be numbered among your correspondents.

I shall find time to answer you, doubt it not. Be as busy as we may, we can always find time to do what is agreeable to us. By the way, had you a letter from Mrs. Unwin? I am witness that she addressed one to you before you went into Norfolk; but your mathematico-poetical head forgot to acknowledge the receipt of it.

I was never more pleased in my life than to learn, and to learn from herself, that my dearest Rose is still alive. Had she not engaged me to love her by the sweetness of her character when a child, she would have done it effectually now, by making me the most acceptable present in the world, my own dear mother's picture. I am perhaps the only person living who remembers her, but I remember her well, and can attest, on my own knowledge, the truth of the resemblance. Amiable and elegant as the countenance is, such exactly was her own; she was one of the tenderest parents, and so just a copy of her is therefore to me invaluable.

I wrote yesterday to my Rose to tell her all this, and to thank her for her kindness in sending it. Neither do I forget your kindness, who intimated to her that I should be happy to possess it.

She invites me into Norfolk, but, alas! she might as well invite the house in which I dwell; for all other considerations and impediments apart, how is it possible that a translator of Homer should lumber to such a distance? But though I cannot comply with her kind invitation, I have made myself the best amends in my power, by inviting her and all the family of Donnes to Weston. Perhaps we could not accommodate them all at once, but in succession we could; and can at any time find room for five, three of them being females, and one a married one. You are a mathematician; tell me, then, how five persons can by lodged in three beds (two males and three females), and I shall have good hope that you will proceed a senior optime. It would make me happy to see our house so furnished. As to yourself, whom I know to be a *subscalarian*, or a man that sleeps under the stairs, I should have no objection at all, neither could you possibly have any yourself, to the garret, as a place in which you might be disposed of with great felicity of accommodation.

I thank you much for your services in the transcribing way, and would by no means have you despair of an opportunity to serve me in the same way yet again. Write to me soon, and tell me when I shall see you.

I have not said the half that I have to say, but breakfast is at hand, which always terminates my epistles.

What have you done with your poem? The trimming that it procured you here has not, I hope, put you out of conceit with it entirely: you are more than equal to the alteration that it needs. Only remember that, in writing, perspicuity is always more than half the battle. The want of it is the ruin of more than half the poetry that is published. A meaning that does not stare you in the face is as bad as no meaning, because nobody will take the pains to poke for it. So now adieu for the present. Beware of killing yourself with problems; for if you do you will never live to be another Sir Isaac.

Mrs. Unwin's affectionate remembrances attend you; Lady Hesketh is much disposed to love you; perhaps most who know you have some little tendency the same way.

TO LADY HESKETH.

THE LODGE, *March* 22, 1790.

I REJOICE, my dearest cousin, that my MSS. have

roamed the earth so successfully, and have met with no disaster. The single book excepted that went to the bottom of the Thames and rose again, they have been fortunate without exception. I am not superstitious, but have nevertheless as good a right to believe that adventure an omen, and a favourable one, as Swift had to interpret, as he did, the loss of a fine fish, which he had no sooner laid on the bank than it flounced into the water again. This, he tells us himself, he always considered as a type of his future disappointments; and why may not I as well consider the marvellous recovery of my lost book from the bottom of the Thames as typical of its future prosperity? To say the truth, I have no fears now about the success of my Translation, though in time past I have had many. I knew there was a style somewhere, could I but find it, in which Homer ought to be rendered, and which alone would suit him. Long time I blundered about it ere I could attain to any decided judgment on the matter; at first I was betrayed, by a desire of accommodating my language to the simplicity of his, into much of the quaintness that belonged to our writers of the fifteenth century. In the course of many revisals I have delivered myself from this evil, I believe, entirely; but I have done it slowly, and as a man separates himself from his mistress when he is going to marry. I had so strong a predilection in favour of this style at first that I was crazed to find that others were not as much enamoured with it as myself. At every passage of that sort which I obliterated, I groaned bitterly, and said to myself, I am spoiling my work to please those who have no taste for the simple graces of antiquity. But in measure as I adopted a more modern phraseology, I became a convert to their opinion, and in the last revisal, which I am now making, am not sensible of having spared a single expression of the obsolete kind. - I see my work so much improved by this alteration that I am filled with wonder at my own backwardness to assent to the necessity of it; and the more when I consider that Milton, with whose manner I account myself intimately acquainted, is never quaint, never twangs through the nose, but is everywhere grand and elegant, without resorting to musty antiquity for his beauties. On the contrary, he took a long stride forward, left the language of his own day far behind him, and anticipated the expressions of a century yet to come.

I have now, as I said, no longer any doubt of the event, but I will give thee a shilling if thou wilt tell me what I shall say in my Preface. It is an affair of much delicacy, and I have as many opinions about it as there are whims in a weathercock.

Send my MSS. and thine when thou wilt. In a day or two I shall enter on the last *Iliad*. When I have finished it I shall give the *Odyssey* one more reading, and shall therefore shortly have occasion for the copy in thy possession; but you see that there is no need to hurry.

I leave the little space for Mrs. Unwin's use, who means, I believe, to occupy it, and am evermore thine most truly, W. C.

*Postscript in the hand of Mrs. Unwin.*

You cannot imagine how much your ladyship would oblige your unworthy servant if you would be so good to let me know in what point I differ from you. All that at present I can say is, that I will readily sacrifice my own opinion, unless I can give you a substantial reason for adhering to it.

TO JOHN JOHNSON, ESQ.

WESTON, *March* 23, 1790.

YOUR MSS. arrived safe in New Norfolk Street, and I

am much obliged to you for your labours. Were you now at Weston I could furnish you with employment for some weeks, and shall perhaps be equally able to do it in summer, for I have lost my best amanuensis in this place, Mr. George Throckmorton, who is gone to Bath.

You are a man to be envied, who have never read the *Odyssey*, which is one of the most amusing story-books in the world. There is also much of the finest poetry in the world to be found in it, notwithstanding all that Longinus has insinuated to the contrary. His comparison of the *Iliad* and *Odyssey* to the meridian and to the declining sun is pretty, but I am persuaded not just. The prettiness of it seduced him; he was otherwise too judicious a reader of Homer to have made it. I can find in the latter no symptoms of impaired ability, none of the effects of age; on the contrary, it seems to me a certainty that Homer, had he written the *Odyssey* in his youth, could not have written it better; and if the *Iliad* in his old age, that he would have written it just as well. A critic would tell me that instead of *written* I should have said *composed*. Very likely; but I am not writing to one of that snarling generation.

My boy, I long to see thee again. It has happened some way or other that Mrs. Unwin and I have conceived a great affection for thee. That I should is the less to be wondered at, because thou art a shred of my own mother; neither is the wonder great that she should fall into the same predicament, for she loves everything that I love. You will observe that your own personal right to be beloved makes no part of the consideration. There is nothing that I touch with so much tenderness as the vanity of a young man; because I know how extremely susceptible he is of impressions that might hurt him in that particular part of his composition. If you should ever prove a coxcomb, from which character you stand just now at a greater distance than any young man I know, it shall never be said that I have made you one; no, you will gain nothing by me but the honour of being much valued by a poor poet, who can do you no good while he lives, and has nothing to leave you when he dies. If you can be contented to be dear to me on these conditions, so you shall; but other terms more advantageous than these, or more inviting, none have I to propose.

Farewell. Puzzle not yourself about a subject when you write to either of us; everything is subject enough from those we love.   W. C.


TO THE SAME.

WESTON, *April* 17, 1790.

YOUR letter that now lies before me is almost three weeks old, and therefore of full age to receive an answer, which it shall have without delay, if the interval between the present moment and that of breakfast should prove sufficient for the purpose.

Yours to Mrs. Unwin was received yesterday, for which she will thank you in due time. I have also seen, and have now in my desk, your letter to Lady Hesketh; she sent it thinking that it would divert me; in which she was not mistaken. I shall tell her when I write to her next that you long to receive a line from her. Give yourself no trouble on the subject of the politic device you saw good to recur to when you presented me with your manuscript; it was an innocent deception, at least it could harm nobody save yourself—an effect which it did not fail to produce; and since the punishment followed it so closely, by me at least it may very well be forgiven. You ask how I can tell that you are not addicted to practices of the deceptive kind? And certainly, if the little time that I have had to study you were alone to be considered, the question would not be unreasonable; but in general, a man who reaches my years finds

> " That long experience does attain
> To something like prophetic strain."

I am very much of Lavater's opinion, and persuaded that faces are as legible as books, only with these circumstances to recommend them to our perusal, that they are read in much less time, and are much less likely to deceive us. Yours gave me a favourable impression of you the moment I beheld it, and though I shall not tell you in particular what I saw in it, for reasons mentioned in my last, I will add that I have observed in you nothing since that has not confirmed the opinion I then formed in your favour. In fact, I cannot recollect that my skill in physiognomy has ever deceived me, and I should add more on this subject had I room.

When you have shut up your mathematical book, you must give yourself to the study of Greek; not merely that you may be able to read Homer and the other Greek classics with ease, but the Greek Testament and the Greek Fathers also. Thus qualified, and by the aid of your fiddle into the bargain, together with some portion of the grace of God (without which nothing can be done) to enable you to look well to your flock, when you shall get one, you will be well set up for a parson; in which character, if I live to see you in it, I shall expect and hope that you will make a very different figure from most of your fraternity.—Ever yours, W. C.

TO MRS. THROCKMORTON.

THE LODGE, *May* 10, 1790.

MY DEAR MRS. FROG—You have by this time (I presume) heard from the Doctor, whom I desired to present to you our best affections, and to tell you that we are well. He sent an urchin (I do not mean a hedgehog, commonly called an urchin in old times, but a boy, commonly so called at present), expecting that he would find you at Buckland's, whither he supposed you gone on Thursday. He sent him charged with divers articles, and among others with letters, or, at least, with a letter; which I mention, that if the boy should be lost, together with his despatches, past all possibility of recovery, you may yet know that the Doctor stands acquitted of not writing. That he is utterly lost (that is to say, the boy, for the Doctor being the last antecedent, as the grammarians say, you might otherwise suppose that he was intended) is the more probable, because he was never four miles from his home before, having only travelled at the side of a plough-team; and when the Doctor gave him his direction to Buckland's, he asked, very naturally, if that place was in England. So what has become of him Heaven knows!

I do not know that any adventures have presented themselves since your departure worth mentioning, except that the rabbit that infested your Wilderness has been shot for devouring your carnations; and that I myself have been in some danger of being devoured in like manner by a great dog, namely, Pearson's. But I wrote him a letter on Friday (I mean a letter to Pearson, not to his dog, which I mention to prevent mistakes; for the said last antecedent might occasion them in this place also), informing him, that unless he tied up his great mastiff in the day-time, I would send him a worse thing, commonly called and known by the name of an attorney. When I go forth to ramble in the fields I do not sally, like Don Quixote, with a purpose of encountering monsters, if any such can be found; but am a peaceable poor gentleman, and a poet, who mean nobody any harm, the fox-hunters and the two universities of this land excepted.

I cannot learn from any creature whether the Turnpike Bill is alive or dead; so ignorant am I, and by such ignoramuses surrounded. But if I know little else, this at least I know, that I love you and Mr. Frog; that I long for your return, and that I am, with Mrs. Unwin's best affections, ever yours, W. C.

### TO LADY HESKETH.

THE LODGE, *May* 28, 1790.

MY DEAREST COZ—I thank thee for the offer of thy best services on this occasion. But Heaven guard my brows from the wreath you mention, whatever wreath beside may hereafter adorn them! It would be a leaden extinguisher clapped on all the fire of my genius, and I should never more produce a line worth reading. To speak seriously, it would make me miserable, and therefore I am sure that thou, of all my friends, wouldst least wish me to wear it. Adieu! Ever thine—in Homer-hurry, W. C.

### TO THE SAME.

WESTON, *June* 3, 1790.

YOU will wonder when I tell you that I, even I, am considered by people, who live at a great distance, as having interest and influence sufficient to procure a place at Court for those who may happen to want one. I have accordingly been applied to within these few days by a Welshman, with a wife and many children, to get him made Poet-laureate as fast as possible. If thou wouldst wish to make the world merry twice a-year, thou canst not do better than procure the office for him. I will promise thee that he shall afford thee a hearty laugh in return, every birthday, and every new year. He is an honest man. Adieu! W. C.

### TO THE REV. WALTER BAGOT.

*Weston, June 22, 1790.*

MY DEAR FRIEND—I rejoice with you in the good Bishop's removal to St. Asaph, and especially because the Norfolk parsons much more resemble the ants above mentioned than he the serpent. He is neither of vast size, nor unwieldy, nor voracious; neither, I daresay, does he sleep after dinner, according to the practice of the said serpent. But harmless as he is, I am mistaken if his mutinous clergy did not sometimes disturb his rest, and if he did not find their bite, though they could not actually eat through him, in a degree resembling fire. Good men like him, and peaceable, should have good and peaceable folks to deal with, and I heartily wish him such in his new diocese. But if he will keep the clergy to their business, he shall have trouble, let him go where he may; and this is boldly spoken, considering that I speak it to one of that reverend body. But ye are like Jeremiah's basket of figs. Some of you could not be better, and some of you are stark naught. Ask the Bishop himself if this be not true! W. C.

### TO JOHN JOHNSON, ESQ.

*Weston, July 31, 1790.*

YOU have by this time, I presume, answered Lady

Hesketh's letter? if not, answer it without delay; and this injunction I give you, judging that it may not be entirely unnecessary; for though I have seen you but once, and only for two or three days, I have found out that you are a scatter-brain. I made the discovery perhaps the sooner, because in this you very much resemble myself, who in the course of my life have, through mere carelessness and inattention, lost many advantages; an insuperable shyness has also deprived me of many. And here again there is a resemblance between us. You will do well to guard against both, for of both, I believe, you have a considerable share as well as myself.

We long to see you again, and are only concerned at the short stay you propose to make with us. If time should seem to you as short at Weston as it seems to us, your visit here will be gone "as a dream when one awaketh, or as a watch in the night."

It is a life of dreams; but the pleasantest one naturally wishes longest.

I shall find employment for you, having made already some part of the fair copy of the *Odyssey* a foul one. I am revising it for the last time, and spare nothing that I can mend. The *Iliad* is finished.

If you have Donne's Poems bring them with you, for I have not seen them many years, and should like to look them over.

You may treat us too, if you please, with a little of your music, for I seldom hear any, and delight much in it. You need not fear a rival, for we have but two fiddles in the neighbourhood,—one a gardener's, the other a tailor's; terrible performers both!     W. C.

### TO MRS. BODHAM.

*Weston, September* 9, 1790.

My dearest Cousin—I am truly sorry to be forced after all to resign the hope of seeing you and Mr. Bodham at Weston this year; the next may possibly be more propitious, and I heartily wish it may. Poor Catharine's unseasonable indisposition has also cost us a disappointment, which we much regret; and were it not that Johnny has made shift to reach us, we should think ourselves completely unfortunate. But him we have, and him we will hold, as long as we can; so expect not very soon to see him in Norfolk. He is so harmless, cheerful, gentle, and good-tempered, and I am so entirely at my ease with him, that I cannot surrender him without a *needs must*, even to those who have a superior claim upon him. He left us yesterday morning, and whither do you think he is gone, and on what errand? Gone, as sure as you are alive, to London, and to convey my Homer to the bookseller's. But he will return the day after to-morrow, and I mean to part with him no more, till necessity shall force us asunder. Suspect me not, my cousin, of being such a monster as to have imposed this task myself on your kind nephew, or even to have thought of doing it. It happened that one day, as we chatted by the fireside, I expressed a wish that I could hear of some trusty body going to London, to whose care I might consign my voluminous labours, the work of five years; for I purpose never to visit that city again myself, and should have been uneasy to have left a charge of so much importance to me altogether to the care of a stage-coachman. Johnny had no sooner heard my wish than, offering himself to the service, he fulfilled it; and his offer was made in such terms, and accompanied with a countenance and manner expressive of so much alacrity, that unreasonable as I thought it at first to give him so much trouble, I soon found that I should mortify him by a refusal. He is gone, therefore, with a box full of poetry, of which I think nobody will plunder him. He has only to say what it is, and there is no commodity I think a freebooter would covet less.         W. C.


TO SAMUEL ROSE, ESQ.

THE LODGE, *September* 13, 1790.

MY DEAR FRIEND—Your letter was particularly welcome to me, not only because it came after a long silence, but because it brought me good news—news of your marriage, and consequently, I trust, of your happiness. May that happiness be durable as your lives, and may you be the *Felices ter et amplius* of whom Horace sings so sweetly! This is my sincere wish, and, though expressed in prose, shall serve as your epithalamium. You comfort me when you say that your marriage will not deprive us of the sight of you hereafter. If you do not wish that I should regret your union, you must make that assurance good as often as you have opportunity.

After perpetual versification during five years, I find myself at last a vacant man, and reduced to read for my amusement. My Homer is gone to the press, and you will imagine that I feel a void in consequence. The proofs, however, will be coming soon, and I shall avail myself, with all my force, of this last opportunity to make my work as perfect as I wish it. I shall not, therefore, be long time destitute of employment, but shall have sufficient to keep me occupied all the winter, and part of the ensuing spring, for Johnson purposes to publish either in March, April, or May. My very Preface is finished; it did not cost me much trouble, being neither long nor learned. I have spoken my mind as freely as decency would permit on the subject of Pope's version, allowing him at the same time, all the merit to which I think him entitled. I have given my reasons for translating in blank verse, and hold some discourse on the mechanism of it, chiefly with a view to obviate the prejudices of some people against it. I expatiate a little on the manner in which I think Homer ought to be rendered, and in which I have endeavoured to render him myself, and anticipated two or three cavils, to which I foresee that I shall be liable from the ignorant or uncandid, in order, if possible, to prevent them. These are the chief heads of my Preface, and the whole consists of about twelve pages.

It is possible, when I come to treat with Johnson about the copy, I may want some person to negotiate for me; and knowing no one so intelligent as yourself in books, or so well qualified to estimate their just value, I shall beg leave to resort to and rely on you as my negotiator. But I will not trouble you unless I should see occasion. My cousin was the bearer of my MSS. to London: he went on purpose, and returns to-morrow. Mrs. Unwin's affectionate felicitations, added to my own, conclude me, my dear friend, sincerely yours, W. C.


TO JOSEPH HILL, ESQ.

*September* 17, 1790.

MY DEAR FRIEND—I received last night a copy of my subscribers' names from Johnson, in which I see how much I have been indebted to yours and to Mrs. Hill's solicitations. Accept my best thanks, so justly due to you both. It is an illustrious catalogue, in respect of rank and title, but methinks I should have liked it as well had it been more numerous. The sum subscribed, however, will defray the expense of printing; which is as much as, in these unsubscribing days, I had any reason to promise myself. I devoutly second your droll wish, that the booksellers may contend about me. The more the better. Seven times seven, if they please; and let them fight with the fury of Achilles

> "Till every rubric-post be crimson'd over
> With blood of booksellers, in battle slain,
> For me, and not a periwig untorn."

—Most truly yours,         WM. COWPER.

TO JOHN JOHNSON, ESQ.

WESTON, *January* 21, 1791.

I KNOW that you have already been catechised by Lady Hesketh on the subject of your return hither before the winter shall be over, and shall therefore only say, that if you CAN COME, we shall be happy to receive you. Remember also that nothing can excuse the non-performance of a promise but absolute necessity! In the meantime, my faith in your veracity is such that I am persuaded you will suffer nothing less than necessity to prevent it. Were you not extremely pleasant to us, and just the sort of youth that suits us, we should neither of us have said half so much, or perhaps a word on the subject.

Yours, my dear Johnny, are vagaries that I shall never see practised by any other; and whether you slap your ancle, or reel as if you were fuddled, or dance in the path before me, all is characteristic of yourself, and therefore to me delightful. I have hinted to you indeed sometimes that you should be cautious of indulging antic habits and singularities of all sorts, and young men in general have need enough of such admonition. But yours are a sort of fairy habits, such as might belong to Puck or Robin Goodfellow, and therefore, good as the advice is, I should be half sorry should you take it.

This allowance at least I give you ;—continue to take your walks, if walks they may be called, exactly in their present fashion till you have taken orders! Then indeed, forasmuch as a skipping, curvetting, bounding divine might be a spectacle not altogether seemly, I shall consent to your adoption of a more grave demeanour.

W. C.

TO THE SAME.

*February* 27, 1791.

Now, my dearest Johnny, I must tell thee in few words how much I love and am obliged to thee for thy affectionate services.

My Cambridge honours are all to be ascribed to you, and to you only. Yet you are but a little man; and a little man into the bargain who have kicked the mathematics, their idol, out of your study. So important are the endings which Providence frequently connects with small beginnings. Had you been here, I could have furnished you with much employment; for I have so dealt with your fair manuscripts in the course of my polishing and improving, that I have almost blotted out the whole. Such, however, as it is, I must now send it to the printer, and he must be content with it, for there is not time to make a fresh copy. We are now printing the second book of the *Odyssey*.

Should the Oxonians bestow none of their notice on me on this occasion, it will happen singularly enough, that as Pope received all his university honours in the subscription way from Oxford, and none at all from Cambridge, so I shall have received all mine from Cambridge, and none from Oxford. This is the more likely to be the case, because I understand that on whatsoever occasion either of those learned bodies thinks fit to move, the other always makes it a point to sit still, thus proving its superiority.

I shall send up your letter to Lady Hesketh in a day or two, knowing that the intelligence contained in it will afford her the greatest pleasure. Know likewise, for your own gratification, that all the Scotch universities have subscribed, none excepted.

We are all as well as usual; that is to say, as well as reasonable folks expect to be on the crazy side of this frail existence.

I rejoice that we shall so soon have you again at our fireside. W. C.

TO THE REV. MR. HURDIS.

WESTON, *March* 6, 1791.

SIR—I have always entertained, and have occasionally avowed, a great degree of respect for the abilities of the unknown author of the "Village Curate," unknown at that time, but now well known, and not to me only, but to many. For before I was favoured with your obliging letter, I knew your name, your place of abode, your profession, and that you had four sisters—all which I learned neither from our bookseller, nor from any of his connexions; you will perceive, therefore, that you are no longer an author incognito. The writer, indeed, of many passages that have fallen from your pen could not long continue so. Let genius, true genius, conceal itself where it may, we may say of it, as the young man in Terence of his beautiful mistress, "*Diu latere non potest.*"

I am obliged to you for your kind offers of service, and

will not say that I shall not be troublesome to you hereafter; but at present I have no need to be so. I have within these two days given the very last stroke of my pen to my long translation, and what will be my next career I know not. At any rate we shall not, I hope, hereafter be known to each other as poets only, for your writings have made me ambitious of a nearer approach to you. Your door, however, will never be opened to me. My fate and fortune have combined with my natural disposition to draw a circle round me which I cannot pass; nor have I been more than thirteen miles from home these twenty years, and so far very seldom. But you are a younger man, and therefore may not be quite so immovable; in which case, should you choose at any time to move Weston-ward, you will always find me happy to receive you; and in the meantime I remain, with much respect, your most obedient servant, critic, and friend, W. C.

*P.S.*—I wish to know what you mean to do with Sir Thomas. For though I expressed doubts about his theatrical possibilities, I think him a very respectable person, and with some improvement well worthy of being introduced to the public.


### TO JOSEPH HILL, ESQ.

*March* 10, 1791.

GIVE my affectionate remembrances to your sisters, and tell them I am impatient to entertain them with my old story new dressed.

I have two French prints hanging in my study, both on *Iliad* subjects; and I have an English one in the parlour, on a subject from the same poem. In one of the former,

Agamemnon addresses Achilles exactly in the attitude of a dancing-master turning miss in a minuet; in the latter the figures are plain, and the attitudes plain also. This is, in some considerable measure, I believe, the difference between my translation and Pope's; and will serve as an exemplification of what I am going to lay before you and the public. W. C.

### TO THE REV. WALTER BAGOT.

WESTON, *March* 18, 1791.

MY DEAR FRIEND—I give you joy that you are about to receive some more of my elegant prose, and I feel myself in danger of attempting to make it even more elegant than usual, and thereby of spoiling it, under the influence of your commendations. But my old helter-skelter manner has already succeeded so well that I will not, even for the sake of entitling myself to a still greater portion of your praise, abandon it.

I did not call in question Johnson's true spirit of poetry, because he was not qualified to relish blank verse (though, to tell you the truth, I think that but an ugly symptom); but if I did not express it, I meant, however, to infer it from the perverse judgment that he has formed of our poets in general, depreciating some of the best, and making honourable mention of others, in my opinion, not undeservedly neglected. I will lay you sixpence, that, had he lived in the days of Milton, and by any accident had met with his *Paradise Lost*, he would neither have directed the attention of others to it, nor have much admired it himself. Good sense, in short, and strength of intellect, seem to me, rather than a fine taste, to have been his distinguishing characteristics. But should you still think otherwise, you have my free permission; for so long as you have yourself a taste for the beauties of Cowper, I care not a fig whether Johnson had a taste or not.

I wonder where you find all your quotations, pat as they are to the present condition of France. Do you make them yourself, or do you actually find them? I am apt to suspect sometimes that you impose them only on a poor man who has but twenty books in the world, and two of them are your brother Chester's. They are, however, much to the purpose, be the author of them who he may.

I was very sorry to learn lately that my friend at Chicheley has been some time indisposed, either with gout or rheumatism (for it seems to be uncertain which), and attended by Dr. Kerr. I am at a loss to conceive how so temperate a man should acquire the gout, and am resolved therefore to conclude that it must be the rheumatism, which, bad as it is, is in my judgment the best of the two; and will afford me besides some opportunity to sympathise with him, for I am not perfectly exempt from it myself. Distant as you are in situation, you are yet, perhaps, nearer to him in point of intelligence than I; and if you can send me any particular news of him, pray do it in your next.

I love and thank you for your benediction. If God forgive me my sins, surely I shall love Him much, for I have much to be forgiven. But .the quantum need not discourage me, since there is One whose atonement can suffice for all.

Τοῦ δὲ καθ' αἷμα ῥέεν, καὶ σοὶ, καὶ ἐμοὶ, καὶ ἀδελφοῖς
'Ημετέροις, αὐτοῦ σωζομένοις θανάτῳ.

Accept our joint remembrances, and believe me affectionately yours, W. C.

## TO MRS. THROCKMORTON.

*April* 1, 1791.

MY DEAR MRS. FROG—A word or two before breakfast, which is all that I shall have time to send you. You have not, I hope, forgot to tell Mr. Frog how much I am obliged to him for his kind, though unsuccessful, attempt in my favour at Oxford. It seems not a little extraordinary that persons so nobly patronised themselves, on the score of literature, should resolve to give no encouragement to it in return. Should I find a fair opportunity to thank them hereafter, I will not neglect it.

> " Could Homer come himself, distress'd and poor,
> And tune his harp at Rhedycina's door,
> The rich old vixen would exclaim, I fear,
> ' Begone ! no tramper gets a farthing here.' "

I have read your husband's pamphlet through and through. You may think, perhaps, and so may he, that a question so remote from all concern of mine could not interest me ; but if you think so, you are both mistaken. He can write nothing that will not interest me ; in the first place, for the writer's sake ; and in the next place, because he writes better and reasons better than anybody, with more candour, and with more sufficiency, and, consequently, with more satisfaction to all his readers, save only his opponents. They, I think, by this time wish that they had let him alone.

Tom is delighted past measure with his wooden nag, and gallops at a rate that would kill any horse that had a life to loose. Adieu !  W. C.

## TO THE REV. MR. BUCHANAN.

WESTON, *May* 11, 1791.

MY DEAR SIR—You have sent me a beautiful poem,

wanting nothing but metre. I would to Heaven that you would give it that requisite yourself; for he who could make the sketch cannot but be well qualified to finish it. But if you will not, I will; provided always, nevertheless, that God gives me ability; for it will require no common share to do justice to your conceptions.—I am much yours,
W. C.

Your little messenger vanished before I could catch him.

### TO JOHN JOHNSON, ESQ.

WESTON, *June* 1, 1791.

MY DEAREST JOHNNY—Now you may rest.—Now I can give you joy of the period, of which I gave you hope in my last; the period of all your labours in my service. But this I can foretell you also, that if you persevere in serving your friends at this rate, your life is likely to be a life of labour. Yet persevere! your rest will be the sweeter hereafter! In the meantime I wish you, if at any time you should find occasion for him, just such a friend as you have proved to me! W. C.

### TO LADY HESKETH.

THE LODGE, *June* 23, 1791.

SEND me a draft, my dearest Coz, for as much money as I hope thou hast by this time received on my account, viz. from Anonymous, and viz. from William Cowper, for we are driven to our last guinea. Let me have it by Sunday's post, lest we become absolutely insolvent.

> We have received beef, tongues, and tea,
> And certainly from none but thee;
> Therefore with all our power of songs,
> Thanks for the beef, and tea, and tongues!

As I said, so it proves. I told you that I should like our guests when they had been here a day or two, and accordingly I like them so well now that it is impossible to like them better. Mrs. Balls is an unaffected, plain-dressing, good-tempered, cheerful, motherly sort of a body, and has the affection of a parent for her niece and nephew. Her niece is an amiable young woman in all respects, a handsome likeness of Johnny, and with a smile so like my mother's, that in this cousin of mine she seems almost restored to me again. I would that she had better health, but she has suffered sadly in her constitution by divers causes, and especially by nursing her father in his last illness, from whose side she stirred not till he expired. Johnny, with whom I have been always delighted, is also so much in love with me that no place in the world will suit him to live in at present except Weston. Where he lives his sister will live likewise, and their aunt is under promise to live with them, at least till Catharine shall have attained under her tuition some competent share of skill in the art of housekeeping. They have looked at a house, the next but one to ours, and like it. You may perhaps remember it; it is an old house with *girt* casement windows, and has a fir tree in the little court in front of it. Here they purpose to settle, if Aunt Bodham, who is most affectionately attached to them all, can be persuaded not to break her heart about it. Of this there are some hopes, because, did they live in Norfolk, they would neither live with her nor even in her neighbourhood, but at thirty miles distance. Johnny is writing to her now, with a view to reconcile her with the measure, and should he succeed, the house will be hired immediately. It will please thee, I think, to know that we are likely to have our solitary situation a little enlivened, and therefore I have given thee this detail of the matter.

I told thee, I believe, that my work is to be published

on the first of July. So Johnson purposed when I heard from him last; but whether he will so perform or not must be left to time to discover. I see not what should hinder it. He has not yet made known on what terms he will treat with me for the copy. Perhaps he will stay till he has had an opportunity in some measure to learn the world's opinion of it, to which I have no objection. I do not wish more than a just price for it, but should be sorry to take less; and there will be danger of either too much or too little till the public shall have stamped its value.

My chief distress at present is that I cannot write, at least can write nothing that will satisfy myself. I have made once or twice a beginning, and, disgusted with what I have done, have dropped it. I have a subject, and a subject for a long work, a subject that I much like, and that will suggest much poetical matter. Mr. Buchanan gave it me, and it is called "The Four Ages of Man." But I had need to have many more ages before me unless I can write on it to better purpose.

With affectionate compliments from our guests, and with Mrs. Unwin's kindest remembrances, I remain, dearest Coz, ever thine, WM. COWPER.

TO THE SAME.

THE LODGE, *July* 11, 1791.

MY DEAREST COZ—Your draft is safe in our possession, and will soon be out of it,—that is to say, will soon be negotiated. Many thanks for that, and still more for your kindness in bidding me draw yet again, should I have occasion. None I hope will offer. I have a purse at Johnson's to which, if need should arise, I can recur at pleasure. The present is rather an expensive time with us, and will probably cause the consumption of some part of my loose cash in the hands of my bookseller.

I am not much better pleased with that dealer in authors than yourself. His first proposal, which was to pay me with my own money, or in other words to get my copy for nothing, not only dissatisfied but hurt me, implying, as I thought, the meanest opinion possible of my labours. For that for which an intelligent man will give nothing can be worth nothing. The consequence was that my spirits sank considerably below par, and have but just begun to recover themselves. His second offer, which is, to pay all expenses, and to give me a thousand pounds next mid-summer, leaving the copyright still in my hands, is more liberal. With this offer I have closed, and Mr. Rose will to-morrow clench the bargain. Josephus understands that Johnson will gain two hundred pounds by it, but I apprehend that he is mistaken, and that Mr. Rose is right who estimates his gains at one. Mr. Hill's mistake, if he be mistaken, arises from his rating the expenses of the press at only five hundred pounds, whereas Johnson rates them at six. Be that as it may, I am contented. If he gains two, I shall not grudge; and if he gains but one, considering all things, I think he will gain enough.

As to Sephus's scheme of signing the seven hundred copies in order to prevent a clandestine multiplication of them, at the same time that I feel the wisdom of it, I feel also an insurmountable dislike of it. It would be calling Johnson a knave, and telling the public that I think him one. Now though I do not perhaps think so highly of his liberality as some people do, and I was once myself disposed to think, yet I have no reason at present to charge him with dishonesty. I must even take my chance, as other poets do, and if I am wronged, must comfort myself with what somebody has said—that authors are the natural prey of booksellers.

You judge right in supposing that I pity the King and Queen of France. I can truly say, that, except the late melancholy circumstances of our own (when our sovereign had lost his senses, and his wife was almost worried out of hers), no royal distresses have ever moved me so much. And still I pity them, prisoners as they now are for life, and, since their late unsuccessful attempt, likely to be treated more scurvily than ever. Heaven help them, for in their case all other help seems vain.

The establishment of our guests at Weston is given up; not for any impediment thrown in the way by Mrs. Bodham, for she consented with the utmost disinterestedness, to the measure, but because on surveying accurately the house in which they must have dwelt, it was found to be so near a ruin that it would have cost its value to make it habitable. They could only take it from year to year, for which reason the landlord would do nothing.

Many thanks for the Mediterranean hint, but unless I were a better historian than I am, there would be no proportion between the theme and my ability. It seems indeed not so properly to be the subject for one poem as for a dozen.

I was pleased with Bouillie's letter, or, to say the truth, rather by the principles by which it was dictated. The letter itself seems too much the language of passion, and can only be cleared of the charge of extravagance by the accomplishment of its denunciations—an event, I apprehend, not much to be expected.

We are all well except poor Catharine, who yesterday consulted Dr. Kerr, and to-day is sick of his prescription. Our affectionate hearts all lay themselves at your pettitoes, and with Mrs. Unwin's best remembrances, I remain for my own peculiar, most entirely thine,   WM. COWPER.

The Frogs are expected here on Wednesday.

TO THE REV. WM. BULL, BRIGHTON, SUSSEX.

WESTON, *July* 27, 1791.

MY DEAR MR. BULL—Mindful of my promise I take the pen, though fearing, and with reason enough, that the performance will be hardly worth the postage. Such as it is, however, here it comes, and if you like it not, you must thank yourself for it.

I have blest myself on your account that you are at Brighton and not at Birmingham, where it seems they are so loyal and so pious that they show no mercy to dissenters. How can you continue in a persuasion so offensive to the wise and good ! Do you not yet perceive that the Bishops themselves hate you not more than the very blacksmith of the establishment, and will you not endeavour to get the better of your aversion to red-nosed singing men and organs ? Come—be received into the bosom of mother church, so shall you never want a jig for your amusement on Sundays, and shall save perhaps your academy from a conflagration.

As for me, I go on at the old rate, giving all my time to Homer, who I suppose was a Presbyterian too, for I understand that the Church of England will by no means acknowledge him as one of hers. He, I say, has all my time, except a little that I give every day to no very cheering promise of futurity. I would I were a Hottentot, or even a dissenter, so that my views of an hereafter were more comfortable. But such as I am, hope, if it please God, may visit even me ; and should we ever meet again, possibly we may part no more. Then if Presbyterians ever find the way to Heaven, you and I may know each other in that better world, and rejoice in the recital of the terrible things that we endured in this. I will wager sixpence with you now, that when that day comes, you shall acknowledge my story a more wonderful one than yours;—only order your executors to put sixpence in your mouth when they bury you, that you may have wherewithal to pay me.

I have received a long letter from an unknown somebody, filled with the highest eulogiums on my Homer. This has raised my spirits and is the true cause of all the merriment with which I have treated you this morning. Pardon me, as Vellum says in the comedy, for being jocular. Mrs. Unwin joins me in love to yourself and your very good son, and we both hope and both sincerely wish to hear of Mrs. Bull's recovery.—Yours affectionately, WM. COWPER.

TO JOHN JOHNSON, ESQ.

WESTON, *August* 9, 1791.

MY DEAREST JOHNNY—The little that I have heard about Homer myself has been equally, or more flattering than Dr. ——'s intelligence, so that I have good reason to hope, that I have not studied the old Grecian, and how to dress him, so long, and so intensely, to no purpose. At present I am idle, both on account of my eyes, and because I know not to what to attach myself in particular. Many different plans and projects are recommended to me. Some call aloud for original verse, others for more translation, and others for other things. Providence, I hope, will direct me in my choice; for other guide I have none, nor wish for another. God bless you, my dearest Johnny. W. C.

TO LADY HESKETH.

THE LODGE, *August* 30, 1791.

MY DEAREST COZ—The walls of Ogressa's chamber

shall be furnished as elegantly as they can be, and at little cost, and when you see them you shall cry, Bravo! Bedding we have, but two chairs will be wanting, the servants' hall having engaged all our supernumeraries. These you will either send or give us commission to buy them. Such as will suit may be found probably at Maurice Smith's, of house-furnishing memory, and this latter course I should think the best, because they are of all things most liable to fracture in a waggon.

I know not how it can have happened that Homer is such a secret at Tunbridge, for I can tell you that his fame is on the wing, and flies rapidly. Johnson, however, seems to be clear from blame; and when you recollect that the whole edition is his by purchase, and that he has no possible way to get his money again but by the sale of it, thou thyself will think so. A tradesman—an old stager too—may safely be trusted with his own interest.

I have spoken big words about Homer's fame, and bigger, perhaps, than my intelligence will justify, for I have not heard much, but what I have heard has been pretty much to the purpose. First, little Johnny going through Cambridge in his way home, learned from his tutor there that it had found many admirers amongst the best qualified judges of that university, and that they were very liberal of their praises. Secondly, Mr. Rye wrote me word lately that a certain candid fair critic and excellent judge, of the county of Northampton, gives it high encomiums. Thirdly, Mr. Rye came over himself from Gayhurst yesterday on purpose to tell me how much he was delighted with it. He had just been reading the sixth *Iliad*, and comparing it with Pope and with the original, and professed himself enchanted. Fourthly, Mr. Frog is much pleased with it; and fifthly, Henry Cowper is bewitched with it; and sixthly, so are —— you and I, —*ca suffit*.

But now if thou hast the faculty of erecting thy ears lift them into the air, first taking off thy cap, that they may have the highest possible elevation. Mrs. Unwin says, No, don't tell her ladyship all,—tell her only enough to raise her curiosity, that she may come the sooner to Weston to have it gratified. But I say, Yes, I will tell her all, lest she should be overcharged and burst by the way.

The Chancellor and I, my dear, have had a correspondence on the subject of Homer. He had doubts, it seems, about the propriety of translating him in blank verse, and wrote to Henry to tell him so, adding a translation of his own in rhyme of the speech of Achilles to Phœnix, in the ninth book, and referring him to me, who, he said, could elevate it, and polish it, and give it the tone of Homer. Henry sent this letter to me, and I answered it in one to his lordship, but not meddling with his verses, for I remembered what happened between Gil Blas and the Archbishop of Toledo. His lordship sent me two sheets in reply, filled with arguments in favour of rhyme, which I was to answer if I could; and containing another translation of the same passage, only in blank verse, leaving it to me to give it rhyme, to make it close, and faithful, and poetical. All this I performed as best I could, and yesterday I heard from him again. In his last letter he says, "I am clearly convinced that Homer may be best translated *without* rhyme, and that you have succeeded in the passages I have looked into."

Such is the candour of a wise man and a real scholar. I would to Heaven that all prejudiced persons were like him!—I answered this letter immediately; and here, I suppose, our correspondence ends. Have I not made a great convert? You shall see the letters, both his and mine, when you come.

My picture hangs in the study. I will not tell thee

what others think of it; but thou shalt judge for thyself. I altogether approve Mrs. Carter's sentiments upon the Birmingham riots, and admire her manner of expressing them. The Frogs come down to-day, bringing Catherina with them. Mrs. Frog has caught cold, as I hear, in her journey; therefore how she may be now I know not, but before she went she was well and in excellent spirits. I rejoice that thy poor lungs can play freely, and shall be happy when they can do the same at Weston. My eyes are weak and somewhat inflamed, and have never been well this month past.

Mrs. Unwin is tolerably well,—that is, much as usual. She joins me in best love, and in everything that you can wish us both to feel for you. Adieu, my dearest Coz. Ever thine, WM. COWPER.

TO SAMUEL ROSE, ESQ.

THE LODGE, *September* 14, 1791.

MY DEAR FRIEND—Whoever reviews me will in fact have a laborious task of it, in the performance of which he ought to move leisurely, and to exercise much critical discernment. In the meantime my courage is kept up by the arrival of such testimonies in my favour as give me the greatest pleasure, coming from quarters the most respectable. I have reason, therefore, to hope that our periodical judges will not be very averse to me, and that perhaps they may even favour me. If one man of taste and letters is pleased, another man so qualified can hardly be displeased; and if critics of a different description grumble, they will not, however, materially hurt me.

You, who know how necessary it is to me to be employed, will be glad to hear that I have been called to a new literary engagement, and that I have not refused it.

A Milton that is to rival, and if possible to exceed in splendour Boydell's Shakespeare, is in contemplation, and I am in the editor's office. Fuseli is the painter. My business will be to select notes from others, and to write original notes; to translate the Latin and Italian poems, and to give a correct text. I shall have years allowed me to do it in. W. C.

TO MRS. KING.

WESTON UNDERWOOD, *October* 21, 1791.

MY DEAR MADAM—You could not have sent me more agreeable news than that of your better health, and I am greatly obliged to you for making me the first of your correspondents to whom you have given that welcome intelligence. This is a favour which I should have acknowledged much sooner, had not a disorder in my eyes, to which I have always been extremely subject, required that I should make as little use of my pen as possible. I felt much for you when I read that part of your letter in which you mention your visitors, and the fatigue which, indisposed as you have been, they could not fail to occasion you. Agreeable as you would have found them at another time, and happy as you would have been in their company, you could not but feel the addition they necessarily made to your domestic attentions as a considerable inconvenience. But I have always said, and shall never say otherwise, that if patience under adversity, and submission to the afflicting hand of God, be true fortitude, which no reasonable person can deny, then your sex have ten times more fortitude to boast than ours; and I have not the least doubt that you carried yourself with infinitely more equanimity on that occasion than I should have done, or any he of my acquaintance. Why is it, since the first offender on earth was a woman, that the women are nevertheless in all the most important points superior to men? That they are so I will not allow to be disputed, having observed it ever since I was capable of making the observation. I believe, on recollection, that when I had the happiness to see you here, we agitated this question a little; but I do not remember that we arrived at any decision of it. The Scripture calls you the *weaker vessels;* and perhaps the best solution of the difficulty, therefore, may be found in those other words of Scripture, *My strength is perfected in weakness.* Unless you can furnish me with a better key than this, I shall be much inclined to believe that I have found the true one.

I am deep in a new literary engagement, being retained by my bookseller as editor of an intended most magnificent publication of Milton's Poetical Works. This will occupy me as much as Homer did for a year or two to come; and when I have finished it I shall have run through all the degrees of my profession, as author, translator, and editor. I know not that a fourth could be found; but if a fourth can be found, I daresay I shall find it.

Mrs. Unwin joins me in best compliments to yourself and Mr. King, who I hope by this time has entirely recovered from the cold he had when you wrote, and from all the effects of it. I shall be happy to learn from you that you have had no more attacks of your most painful disorder in the stomach, and remain in the meantime, my dear madam, your affectionate friend and humble servant, W. C.

TO JOSEPH HILL, ESQ.

*November* 14, 1791.

MY DEAR FRIEND—I have waited and wished for your opinion with the feelings that belong to the value I have for it, and am very happy to find it so favourable. In my table-drawer I treasure up a bundle of suffrages sent me by those of whose approbation I was most ambitious, and shall presently insert yours among them.

I know not why we should quarrel with compound epithets; it is certain at least they are as agreeable to the genius of our language as to that of the Greek, which is sufficiently proved by their being admitted into our common and colloquial dialect. Black-eyed, nut-brown, crook-shanked, hump-backed, are all compound epithets, and, together with a thousand other such, are used continually, even by those who profess a dislike to such combinations in poetry. Why, then, do they treat with so much familiarity a thing that they say disgusts them? I doubt if they could give this question a reasonable answer, unless they should answer it by confessing themselves unreasonable.

I have made a considerable progress in the translation of Milton's Latin poems. I give them, as opportunity offers, all the variety of measure that I can. Some I render in heroic rhyme, some in stanzas, some in seven, and some in eight-syllable measure, and some in blank verse. They will altogether, I hope, make an agreeable miscellany for the English reader. They are certainly good in themselves, and cannot fail to please but by the fault of their translator. W. C.

TO SAMUEL ROSE, ESQ.

THE LODGE, *December* 21, 1791.

MY DEAR FRIEND—It grieves me, after having indulged a little hope that I might see you in the holidays, to be obliged to disappoint myself. The occasion, too, is such as will ensure me your sympathy.

On Saturday last, while I was at my desk near the window, and Mrs. Unwin at the fireside opposite to it, I heard her suddenly exclaim, "Oh! Mr. Cowper, don't let me fall!" I turned and saw her actually falling, together with her chair, and started to her side just in time to prevent her. She was seized with a violent giddiness, which lasted, though with some abatement, the whole day, and was attended, too, with some other very very alarming symptoms. At present, however, she is relieved from the vertigo, and seems in all respects better.

She has been my faithful and affectionate nurse for many years, and consequently has a claim on all my attentions. She has them, and will have them as long as she wants them; which will probably be, at the best, a considerable time to come. I feel the shock, as you may suppose, in every nerve. God grant that there may be no repetition of it! Another such a stroke upon her would, I think, overset me completely; but at present I hold up bravely. W. C.

TO THE REV. JOHN NEWTON.

*February* 20, 1792.

MY DEAR FRIEND—When I wrote the words in question I was, as I almost always am, so pressed for time that I was obliged to put them down in a great hurry. Perhaps I printed them wrong. If a full stop be made at the end of the second line, the appearance of inconsistency perhaps will vanish; but should you still think them liable to that objection, they may be altered thus:—

"In vain to live from age to age,
We modern bards endeavour;
But write in Patty's book one page,
You gain your point for ever."

Trifling enough I readily confess they are; but I have always allowed myself to trifle occasionally; and on this occasion had not, nor have at present, time to do more. By the way, should you think this amended copy worthy to displace the former, I must wait for some future opportunity to send you them properly transcribed for the purpose.

It is rather singular that the same post which brought me yours, in which you express your disapprobation of this trifle, as such, brought me likewise a request from a very pious lady that I would write for her a copy of verses on a pen stolen by a niece of hers from the Prince of Wales' standish. I am obliged to comply, and consequently must trifle again; and thus it fares with poets by profession. Our wits are not at our own command, but must of necessity be sometimes directed to such subjects, not as we should choose for ourselves, but as our friends are pleased to choose for us.

Your demand of more original composition from me will, if I live, and it please God to afford me health, in all probability be sooner or later gratified. In the meantime you need not—and if you turn the matter in your thoughts a little, you will perceive that you need not—think me unworthily employed in preparing a new edition of Milton. His two principal are of a kind that call for an editor who believes the Gospel, and is well grounded in all evangelical doctrine. Such an editor they have never had yet, though only such a one can be qualified for the office.

We mourn for the mismanagement at Botany Bay, and foresee the issue. The Romans were, in their origin, banditti; and if they became in time masters of the world, it was not by drinking grog, and allowing themselves in all sorts of licentiousness. The African colonisation, and the manner of conducting it, has long been matter to us of pleasing speculation. God has highly honoured Mr. Thornton, and I doubt not that the subsequent history of the two settlements will strikingly evince the superior wisdom of his proceedings.

I write now in a hurry not to be easily conceived, and am at this moment called to breakfast. Mrs. Unwin, I thank God, is still recovering, though still slowly. She unites with me in affectionate remembrances to yourself and Miss Catlett, and Lady Hesketh adds her compliments. Adieu, my dear friend.—I am most truly yours,

WM. COWPER.

Many thanks for a barrel of oysters which came, notwithstanding the late warm weather, perfectly sweet and good.

*P.S.*—Lady Hesketh made the same objection to my verses as you; but she being a lady critic I did not heed her. As they stand at present, however, they are hers; and I believe you will think them much improved.

My heart bears me witness how glad I shall be to see you at the time you mention, and Mrs. Unwin says the same.

TO JOHN JOHNSON, ESQ.

WESTON, *March* 11, 1792.

MY DEAREST JOHNNY—You talk of primroses that you pulled on Candlemas Day; but what think you of me who heard a nightingale on New Year's Day? Perhaps I am the only man in England who can boast of such good fortune—good indeed, for if it was at all an omen it could not be an unfavourable one. The winter, however, is now making himself amends, and seems the more peevish for having been encroached on at so undue a season. Nothing less than a large slice out of the spring will satisfy him.

Lady Hesketh left us yesterday. She intended, indeed, to have left us four days sooner; but in the evening before the day fixed for her departure snow enough fell to occasion just so much delay of it.

We have faint hopes that in the month of May we shall see her again. I know that you have had a letter from her, and you will no doubt have the grace not to make her wait long for an answer.

We expect Mr. Rose on Tuesday, but he stays with us only till the Saturday following. With him I shall have some conferences on the subject of Homer,—respecting a new edition I mean, and some, perhaps, on the subject of Milton; on him I have not yet begun to comment, or even fix the time when I shall.—Forget not your promised visit! W. C.

TO THE REV. JOHN NEWTON.

*March* 18, 1792.

MY DEAR FRIEND—We are now once more reduced to our dual state, having lost our neighbours at the Hall, and our inmate Lady Hesketh. Mr. Rose, indeed, has spent two or three days here, and is still with us; but he leaves us in the afternoon. There are those in the world whom we love, and whom we are happy to see; but we are happy likewise in each other, and so far independent of our fellow mortals as to be able to pass our time comfortably without them; as comfortably at least as Mrs. Unwin's frequent indispositions, and my no less frequent troubles of mind, will permit. When I am much distressed any company but hers distresses me more, and makes me doubly sensible of my sufferings; though sometimes I confess it falls out otherwise, and by the help of more general conversation I recover that elasticity of mind which is able to resist the pressure. On the whole I believe I am situated exactly as I should wish to be were my situation to be determined by my own election; and am denied no comfort that is compatible with the total absence of the chief of all.

William Peace called on me, I forget when, but about a year ago. His errand was to obtain from me a certificate of his good behaviour during the time he had lived with us. His conduct in our service had been such for sobriety and integrity as entitled him to it, and I readily gave him one. At the same time I confess myself not at all surprised that the family to which you recommended him soon grew weary of him. He had a bad temper, that always sat astride on a runaway tongue, and ceased not to spur and to kick it into all the sin and mischief that such an ungovernable member, so ridden, was sure to fall into. He had no sooner quitted us, which he did when he married, than he made even us, who had always treated him with kindness, a mark for his slanderous humour. What he said we know not, because we chose not to know; but such things we are assured, and credibly too, as, had we known them, would have been extremely offensive to us. Whether he be a Christian or not is no business of mine to determine. There was a time when he seemed to have had Christian experience; and there has been a much longer time in which, his attention on ordinances excepted, he has manifested, I doubt, no one symptom of the Christian character. Prosperity did him harm; adversity, perhaps, may do him good. I wish it may; and if he be indeed a pupil of divine grace, it certainly will, when he has been sufficiently exercised with it, of which he seems at present to have a very promising prospect.

You judge well concerning the Prince, and better than I did. His seducers are certainly most to be blamed, and so I have been used both to say and to think; but when I wrote my last they happened not to occur to me. That he and all dissolute princes are entitled to compassion on account of the snares to which their situation exposes them, is likewise a remark which I have frequently made myself, but did not on that occasion advert to it. But the day is come when it behoves princes to be a little more cautious. These allowances will not be made by the many; especially they will be apt to censure their excesses with a good deal of severity if themselves should be called upon to play the piper. That our royal hopes are not a little more discreet in their management at such a time as this seems utterly unaccountable, unless on a supposition that their practices have brought them to a state of blind and frantic desperation that will not suffer them to regard the consequences. The ministers of sedition are busy—indefatigable, indeed, and the expense that attends a kingly government is an argument which millions begin to feel the force of. But I shall tire you with my politics, and the more, perhaps, because they are so gloomy. The sable cloud, however, has a luminous edge. The unmanageable prince, and the no less unmanageable multitude, have each a mouth into which God can thrust a curb when He pleases, and kings shall reign and the people obey to the last moment of His appointment.

Adieu! my dear friend, with our united love to yourself and Miss Catlett.—I remain, affectionately yours,

WM. COWPER.

Mr. Rose desires his respectful compliments.

TO THE REV. MR. HURDIS.

WESTON, *March* 23, 1792.

MY DEAR SIR—I have read your play carefully, and with great pleasure; it seems now to be a performance that cannot fail to do you much credit. Yet, unless my memory deceives me, the scene between Cecilia and Heron in the garden has lost something that pleased me much when I saw it first; and I am not sure that you have not likewise obliterated an account of Sir Thomas's execution that I found very pathetic. It would be strange if, in these two particulars, I should seem to miss what never existed; you will presently know whether I am as good at remembering what I never saw as I am at forgetting what I have seen. But if I am right, I cannot help recommending the omitted passages to your reconsideration. If the play were designed for representation, I should be apt to think Cecilia's first speech rather too long, and should prefer to have it broken into dialogue by an interposition now and then from one of her sisters. But since it is designed, as I understand, for the closet only, that objection seems of no importance; at no rate, however, would I expunge it, because it is both prettily imagined and elegantly written.

I have read your *cursory remarks*, and am much pleased both with the style and the argument. Whether the latter be new or not I am not competent to judge; if it be, you are entitled to much praise for the invention of it. Where other data are wanting to ascertain the time when an author of many pieces wrote each in particular, there can be no better criterion by which to determine the point than the more or less proficiency manifested in the composition. Of this proficiency, where it appears, and of those plays in which it appears not, you seem to me to have judged well and truly; and consequently I approve of your arrangement.

I attended, as you desired me, in reading the character of Cecilia, to the hint you gave me concerning your sister Sally, and give you joy of such a sister. This, however, not exclusively of the rest, for though they may not be all Cecilias, I have a strong persuasion that they are all very amiable. W. C.

TO LADY HESKETH.

The Lodge, *March* 25, 1792.

My dearest Coz—Mr. Rose's longer stay than he at first intended was the occasion of the longer delay of my answer to your note, as you may both have perceived by the date thereof, and learned from his information. It was a daily trouble to me to see it lying in the window-seat while I knew you were in expectation of its arrival. By this time, I presume, you have seen him, and have seen likewise Mr. Hayley's friendly letter and complimentary sonnet, as well as the letter of the honest Quaker; all of which, at least the two former, I shall be glad to receive again at a fair opportunity. Mr. Hayley's letter slept six weeks in Johnson's custody. It was necessary I should answer it without delay, and accordingly I answered it the very evening on which I received it, giving him to understand, among other things, how much vexation the bookseller's folly had cost me, who had detained it so long; especially on account of the distress that I knew it must have occasioned to him also. From his reply, which the return of the post brought me, I learn that in the long interval of my non-correspondence he had suffered anxiety and mortification enough; so much, that I daresay he made twenty vows never to hazard again either letter or compliment to an unknown author. What, indeed, could he imagine less than that I meant by such an obstinate silence to tell him that I valued neither him nor his praises, nor his proffered friendship—in short, that I considered him as a rival, and therefore, like a true author, hated and despised him? He is now, however, convinced that I love him, as indeed I do, and I account him the chief acquisition that my own verse has ever procured me. Brute should I be if I did not, for he promises me every assistance in his power.

I have likewise a very pleasing letter from Mr. Park, which I wish you were here to read; and a very pleasing poem that came enclosed in it for my revisal, written when he was only twenty years of age, yet wonderfully well written, though wanting some correction.

To Mr. Hurdis I return *Sir Thomas More* to-morrow, having revised it a second time. He is now a very respectable figure, and will do my friend, who gives him to the public this spring, considerable credit.   W. C.


### TO WILLIAM HAYLEY, ESQ.

WESTON, *April* 6, 1792.

MY DEAR FRIEND—God grant that this friendship of ours may be a comfort to us all the rest of our days, in a world where true friendships are rarities, and especially where, suddenly formed, they are apt soon to terminate! But as I said before, I feel a disposition of heart toward you that I never felt for one whom I had never seen; and that shall prove itself I trust in the event a propitious omen.

*   *   *   *   *   *

Horace says somewhere, though I may quote it amiss perhaps, for I have a terrible memory—

> " Utrumque nostrum incredibili modo
> Consentit astrum.―――"

\* \* \* Our *stars consent*, at least have had an influence somewhat similar, in another and more important article. \* \* \*

It gives me the sincerest pleasure that I may hope to see you at Weston; for as to any migrations of mine, they must, I fear, notwithstanding the joy I should feel in being a guest of yours, be still considered in the light of impossibilities. Come then, my friend, and be as welcome, as the country people say here, as the flowers in May! I am happy, as I say, in the expectation, but the fear, or rather the consciousness, that I shall not answer on a nearer view, makes it a trembling kind of happiness, and a doubtful.

After the privacy which I have mentioned above, I went to Huntingdon : soon after my arrival there, I took up my quarters at the house of the Rev. Mr. Unwin; I lived with him while he lived, and ever since his death have lived with his widow. Her, therefore, you will find mistress of the house; and I judge of you amiss, or you will find her just such as you would wish. To me she has been often a nurse, and invariably the kindest friend, through a thousand adversities that I have had to grapple with in the course of almost thirty years. I thought it better to introduce her to you thus, than to present her to you at your coming, quite a stranger.

Bring with you any books that you think may be useful to my commentatorship, for with you for an interpreter I shall be afraid of none of them. And in truth, if you think that you shall want them, you must bring books for your own use also, for they are an article with which I am *heinously unprovided;* being much in the condition of the man whose library Pope describes as

"—— no mighty store,
His own works neatly bound, and little more!"

You shall know how this has come to pass hereafter.

Tell me, my friend, are your letters in your own handwriting? If so I am in pain for your eyes, lest by such frequent demands upon them I should hurt them. I had rather write you three letters for one, much as I prize your letters, than *that* should happen. And now, for the present, adieu. I am going to accompany Milton into the lake of fire and brimstone, having just begun my annotations. W. C.

### TO THE SAME.

WESTON, *June* 5, 1792.

YESTERDAY was a noble day with us—speech almost perfect—eyes open almost the whole day, without any effort to keep them so—and the step wonderfully improved. But the night has been almost a sleepless one, owing partly, I believe to her having had as much sleep again as usual the night before; for even when she is in tolerable health she hardly ever sleeps well two nights together. I found her accordingly a little out of spirits this morning, but still insisting on it that she is better. Indeed, she always tells me so, and will probably die with those very words upon her lips. They will be true then at least, for then she will be best of all. She is now (the clock has just struck eleven) endeavouring, I believe, to get a little sleep; for which reason I do not yet let her know that I have received your letter.

Can I ever honour you enough for your zeal to serve me? Truly, I think not; I am, however, so sensible of the love I owe you on this account, that I every day regret the acuteness of your feelings for me, convinced that they expose you to much trouble, mortification, and disappointment. I have, in short, a poor opinion of my destiny, as I told you when you were here; and though I believe that if any man living can do me good, you will, I cannot yet persuade myself that even you will be successful in attempting it. But it is no matter: you are yourself a good which I can never value enough, and whether rich or poor in other respects, I shall always account myself better provided for than I deserve, with such a friend at my back as you. Let it please God to continue to me my William and Mary, and I will be more reasonable than to grumble.

I rose this morning wrapped round with a cloud of melancholy, and with a heart full of fears; but if I see Mary's amendment a little advanced, when she rises, I shall be better.

I have just been with her again. Except that she is fatigued for want of sleep, she seems as well as yesterday. The post brings me a letter from Hurdis, who is broken-hearted for a dying sister. Had we eyes sharp enough, we should see the arrows of Death flying in all directions, and account it a wonder that we and our friends escape them but a single day. W. C.

TO LADY HESKETH.

WESTON, *June* 11, 1792.

MY DEAREST COZ—Thou art ever in my thoughts, whether I am writing to thee or not; and my correspondence seems to grow upon me at such a rate, that I am not able to address thee so often as I would. In fact, I live only to write letters. Hayley is, as you see, added to the number, and to him I write almost as duly as I rise in the morning; nor is he only added, but his friend Carwardine also—Carwardine the generous, the disinterested, the friendly. I seem, in short, to have stumbled suddenly on a race of heroes, men who resolve to have no interests of their own till mine are served.

But I will proceed to other matters that concern me more intimately and more immediately than all that can be done for me either by the great or the small, or by both united. Since I wrote last, Mrs. Unwin has been continually improving in strength, but at so gradual a rate that I can only mark it by saying that she moves about every day with less support than the former. Her recovery is most of all retarded by want of sleep. On the whole, I believe she goes on as well as could be expected, though not quite well enough to satisfy me. And Dr. Austen, speaking from the reports I have made of her, says he has no doubt of her restoration.

During the last two months I seem to myself to have been in a dream. It has been a most eventful period, and fruitful to an uncommon degree, both in good and evil. I have been very ill, and suffered excruciating pain. I recovered, and became quite well again. I received within my doors a man, but lately an entire stranger, and who now loves me as his brother, and forgets himself to serve me. Mrs. Unwin has been seized with an illness that for many days threatened to deprive me of her, and to cast a gloom, an impenetrable one, on all my future prospects. She is now granted to me again. A few days since I should have thought the moon might have descended into my purse as likely as any emolument, and now it seems not impossible. All this has come to pass with such rapidity as events move with in romance indeed, but not often in real life. Events of all sorts creep or fly exactly as God pleases.

To the foregoing I have to add, in conclusion, the arrival of my Johnny, just when I wanted him most, and when only a few days before I had no expectation of him. He came to dinner on Saturday, and I hope I shall keep him long. What comes next I know not, but shall endeavour, as you exhort me, to look for good, and I know I shall have your prayers that I may not be disappointed.

Hayley tells me you begin to be jealous of him, lest I should love him more than I love you, and bids me say, "that should I do so, you in revenge must love him more than I do." Him I know you will love, and me, because you have such a habit of doing it that you cannot help it.

Adieu! my knuckles ache with letter-writing. With my poor patient's affectionate remembrances, and Johnny's, I am ever thine, W. C.

TO WILLIAM HAYLEY, ESQ.

WESTON, *June* 19, 1792.

MY Mary goes on well. Be it known to you that we have these four days discarded our sedan with two elbows. Here is no more carrying, or being carried, but she walks upstairs boldly, with one hand upon the balustrade, and the other under my arm, and in like manner she comes down in a morning. Still I confess she is feeble, and misses much of her former strength. The weather, too, is sadly against her; it deprives her of many a good turn in the orchard, and fifty times have I wished this very day that Dr. Darwin's scheme of giving rudders and sails to the Ice Islands, that spoil all our summers, were actually put into practice. So should we have gentle airs instead of churlish blasts; and those everlasting sources of bad weather being once navigated into the southern hemisphere, my Mary would recover as fast again. We are both of your mind respecting the journey to Eartham, and think that July, if by that time she have strength for the journey, will be better than August. We shall have more long days before us, and then we shall want as much for our return as for our going forth. This, however, must be left to the Giver of all good. If our visit to you be according to His will, He will smooth the way before us, and appoint the time of it; and I thus speak, not because I wish to seem a saint in your eyes, but because my poor Mary actually is one, and would not set her foot over the threshold unless she had, or thought she had, God's free permission. With that she would go through floods and fire, though without it she would be afraid of everything,—afraid even to visit you, dearly as she loves, and much as she longs to see you.

W. C.

TO THE SAME.

WESTON, *July* 15, 1792.

THE progress of the old nurse in Terence is very much like the progress of my poor patient in the road of recovery. I cannot, indeed, say that she moves but advances not, for advances are certainly made, but the progress of a week is hardly perceptible. I know not, therefore, at present, what to say about this long postponed journey. The utmost that it is safe for me to say at this moment is this: You know that you are dear to us both; true it is that you are so, and equally true that the very instant we feel ourselves at liberty, we will fly to Eartham. I have been but once within the Hall door since the

Courtenays came home, much as I have been pressed to dine there, and have hardly escaped giving a little offence by declining it; but though I should offend all the world by my obstinacy in this instance, I would not leave my poor Mary alone. Johnny serves me as a representative, and him I send without scruple. As to the affair of Milton, I know not what will become of it. I wrote to Johnson a week since to tell him that the interruption of Mrs. Unwin's illness still continuing, and being likely to continue, I knew not when I should be able to proceed. The translations, I said, were finished, except the revisal of a part.

God bless your dear little boy and poet! I thank him for exercising his dawning genius upon me, and shall be still happier to thank him in person.

> Abbot is painting me so true,
> That, trust me, you would stare,
> And hardly know, at the first view,
> If I were here, or there.

I have sat twice; and the few who have seen his copy of me are much struck with the resemblance. He is a sober, quiet man, which, considering that I must have him at least a week longer for an inmate, is a great comfort to me.

My Mary sends you her best love. She can walk now, leaning on my arm only, and her speech is certainly much improved. I long to see you. Why cannot you and dear Tom spend the remainder of the summer with us? We might all then set off for Eartham merrily together. But I retract this, conscious that I am unreasonable. It is a wretched world, and what we would is almost always what we cannot.

Adieu! Love me, and be sure of a return.     W. C.

TO THE SAME.

WESTON, *July* 22, 1792.

THIS important affair, my dear brother, is at last decided, and we are coming. Wednesday se'ennight, if nothing occur to make a later day necessary, is the day fixed for our journey. Our rate of travelling must depend on Mary's ability to bear it. Our mode of travelling will occupy three days unavoidably, for we shall come in a coach. Abbot finishes my picture to-morrow; on Wednesday he returns to town, and is commissioned to order one down for us, with four steeds to draw it;

>  ———Hollow pamper'd jades of Asia,
> That cannot go but forty miles a day.

Send us our route, for I am as ignorant of it almost as if I were in a strange country. We shall reach St. Alban's, I suppose, the first day; say where we must finish our second day's journey, and at what inn we may best repose? As to the end of the third day, we know where that will find us, namely, in the arms and under the roof of our beloved Hayley.

General Cowper, having heard a rumour of this intended migration, desires to meet me on the road, that we may once more see each other. He lives at Ham, near Kingston. Shall we go through Kingston, or near it? For I would give him as little trouble as possible, though he offers very kindly to come as far as Barnet for that purpose. Nor must I forget Carwardine, who so kindly desired to be informed what way we should go. On what point of the road will it be easiest for him to find us? On all these points you must be my oracle. My friend and brother, we shall overwhelm you with our numbers; this is all the trouble that I have left. My Johnny of Norfolk, happy in the thought of accompanying us, would be broken-hearted to be left behind.

In the midst of all these solicitudes I laugh to think what they are made of, and what an important thing it is for me to travel. Other men steal away from their homes silently, and make no disturbance; but when I move, houses are turned upside down, maids are turned out of their beds, all the counties through which I pass appear to be in an uproar; Surrey greets me by the mouth of the General, and Essex by that of Carwardine. How strange does all this seem to a man who has seen no bustle, and made none, for twenty years together. Adieu!                                                W. C.

### TO THE REV. WM. BULL.

*July* 25, 1792.

MY DEAR MR. BULL—Engaged as I have been ever since I saw you, it was not possible that I should write sooner; and busy as I am at present, it is not without difficulty that I can write even now; but I promised you a letter, and must endeavour at least to be as good as my word. How do you imagine I have been occupied these last ten days? In sitting—not on cockatrice eggs, nor yet to gratify a mere idle humour, nor because I was too sick to move; but because my cousin Johnson has an aunt who has a longing desire for my picture, and because he would, therefore, bring a painter from London to draw it. For this purpose I have been sitting, as I say, these ten days, and am heartily glad that my sitting-time is over. You have now, I know, a burning curiosity to learn two things, which I may choose whether I will tell you or not. First, who was the painter; and secondly, how he has succeeded. The painter's name is Abbot.

You never heard of him you say. It is very likely; but there is, nevertheless, such a painter, and an excellent one he is. *Multa sunt quæ bonus Bernadus nec vidit, nec audivit.* To your second inquiry I answer that he has succeeded to admiration. The likeness is so strong that when my friends enter the room where my picture is they start, astonished to see me where they know I am not. Miserable man that you are, to be at Brighton instead of being here to contemplate this prodigy of art, which therefore you can never see; for it goes to London next Monday, to be suspended awhile at Abbot's; and then proceeds into Norfolk, where it will be suspended for ever.

But the picture is not the only prodigy I have to tell you of. A greater belongs to me, and one that you will hardly credit, even on my own testimony. We are on the eve of a journey, and a long one. On this very day se'ennight we set out for Eartham, the seat of my brother bard, Mr. Hayley, on the other side of London, nobody knows where, a hundred and twenty miles off. Pray for us, my friend, that we may have a safe going and return. It is a tremendous exploit, and I feel a thousand anxieties when I think of it. But a promise, made to him when he was here, that we would go if we could, and a sort of persuasion that we can if we will oblige us to it. The journey and the change of air, together with the novelty to us of the scene to which we are going, may, I hope, be useful to us both, especially to Mrs. Unwin, who has most need of restoratives. She sends her love to you and to Thomas, in which she is sincerely joined by your affectionate                                               W. C.

TO WILLIAM HAYLEY, ESQ.

WESTON, *July* 29, 1792.

Through floods and flames, to your retreat,
I win my desp'rate way,
And when we meet, if e'er we meet,
Will echo your huzza !

You will wonder at the word *desp'rate* in the second line, and at the *if* in the third ; but could you have any conception of the fears I have had to battle with, of the dejection of spirits that I have suffered concerning this journey, you would wonder much more that I still courageously persevere in my resolution to undertake it. Fortunately for my intentions, it happens that as the day approaches my terrors abate ; for had they continued to be what they were a week since, I must after all have disappointed you, and was actually once on the verge of doing it. I have told you something of my nocturnal experiences, and assure you now that they were hardly ever more terrific than on this occasion. Prayer has, however, opened my passage at last, and obtained for me a degree of confidence that I trust will prove a comfortable viaticum to me all the way. On Wednesday, therefore, we set forth.

The terrors that I have spoken of would appear ridiculous to most ; but to you they will not, for you are a reasonable creature, and know well that to whatever cause it be owing (whether to constitution, or to God's express appointment), I am hunted by spiritual hounds in the night season. I cannot help it. You will pity me, and wish it were otherwise ; and though you may think there is much of the imaginary in it, will not deem it for that reason an evil less to be lamented. So much for fears and distresses. Soon I hope they shall all have a joyful termination, and I, my Mary, my Johnny, and my dog, be skipping with delight at Eartham !

Well, this picture is at last finished, and well finished, I can assure you. Every creature that has seen it has been astonished at the resemblance. Sam's boy bowed to it, and Beau walked up to it, wagging his tail as he went, and evidently showing that he acknowledged its likeness to his master. It is a half-length, as it is technically but absurdly called ; that is to say, it gives all but the foot and ancle. To-morrow it goes to town, and will hang some months at Abbot's, when it will be sent to its due destination in Norfolk.

I hope, or rather wish, that at Eartham I may recover that habit of study which, inveterate as it once seemed, I now seem to have lost—lost to such a degree that it is even painful to me to think of what it will cost me to acquire it again.

Adieu ! my dear, dear Hayley ; God give us a happy meeting. Mary sends her love. She is in pretty good plight this morning, having slept well, and, for her part, has no fears at all about the journey. Ever yours,

W. C.

# LETTERS FROM EARTHAM.

### TO THE REV. MR. GREATHEED.

*Eartham, August* 6, 1792.

MY DEAR SIR—Having first thanked you for your affectionate and acceptable letter, I will proceed, as well as I can, to answer your equally affectionate request that I would send you early news of our arrival at Eartham. Here we are in the most elegant mansion that I have ever inhabited, and surrounded by the most delightful pleasure-grounds that I have ever seen ; but which, dissipated as my powers of thought are at present, I will not undertake to describe. It shall suffice me to say that they occupy three sides of a hill, which in Buckinghamshire might well pass for a mountain, and from the summit of which is beheld a most magnificent landscape bounded by the sea, and in one part by the Isle of Wight, which may also be seen plainly from the window of the library in which I am writing.

It pleased God to carry us both through the journey with far less difficulty and inconvenience than I expected. I began it indeed with a thousand fears, and when we arrived the first evening at Barnet, found myself oppressed in spirit to a degree that could hardly be exceeded. I saw Mrs. Unwin weary, as she might well be, and heard such noises, both within the house and without, that I concluded she would get no rest. But I was mercifully disappointed. She rested, though not well, yet sufficiently; and when we finished our next day's journey at Ripley, we were both in better condition, both of body and mind, than on the day preceding. At Ripley we found a quiet inn, that housed, as it happened, that night no company but ourselves. There we slept well, and rose perfectly refreshed. And except some terrors that I felt at passing over the Sussex hills by moonlight, met with little to complain of till we arrived about ten o'clock at Eartham. Here we are as happy as it is in the power of terrestrial good to make us. It is almost a Paradise in which we dwell; and our reception has been the kindest that it was possible for friendship and hospitality to contrive. Our host mentions you with great respect, and bids me tell you that he esteems you highly. Mrs. Unwin, who is, I think, in some points already the better for her excursion, unites with mine her best compliments both to yourself and Mrs. Greatheed. I have much to see and enjoy before I can be perfectly apprised of all the delights of Eartham, and will therefore now subscribe myself yours, my dear sir, with great sincerity, W. C.

TO MRS. COURTENAY.

EARTHAM, *August* 12, 1792.

MY DEAREST CATHARINA—Though I have travelled far, nothing did I see in my travels that surprised me half so agreeably as your kind letter; for high as my opinion of your good nature is, I had no hopes of hearing from you till I should have written first,—a pleasure which I intended to allow myself the first opportunity.

After three days' confinement in a coach, and suffering

as we went all that could be suffered from excessive heat and dust, we found ourselves late in the evening at the door of our friend Hayley. In every other respect the journey was extremely pleasant. At the "Mitre," in Barnet, where we lodged the first evening, we found our friend Rose, who had walked thither from his house in Chancery Lane to meet us; and at Kingston, where we dined the second day, I found my old and much valued friend General Cowper, whom I had not seen in thirty years, and but for this journey should never have seen again. Mrs. Unwin, on whose account I had a thousand fears before we set out, suffered as little from fatigue as myself, and begins, I hope, already to feel some beneficial effects from the air of Eartham, and the exercise that she takes in one of the most delightful pleasure-grounds in the world. They occupy three sides of a hill, lofty enough to command a view of the sea, which skirts the horizon to a length of many miles, with the Isle of Wight at the end of it. The inland scene is equally beautiful, consisting of a large and deep valley well cultivated, and enclosed by magnificent hills all crowned with wood. I had, for my part, no conception that a poet could be the owner of such a Paradise; and his house is as elegant as his scenes are charming.

But think not, my dear Catharina, that amidst all these beauties I shall lose the remembrance of the peaceful but less splendid Weston. Your precincts will be as dear to me as ever when I return; though when that day will arrive I know not, our host being determined, as I plainly see, to keep us as long as possible. Give my best love to your husband. Thank him most kindly for his attention to the old bard of Greece, and pardon me that I do not send you now an epitaph for Fop. I am not sufficiently recollected to compose even a bagatelle at present; but in due time you shall receive it.

Hayley, who will some time or other, I hope, see you at Weston, is already prepared to love you both, and being passionately fond of music, longs much to hear you.—Adieu !  W. C.

TO LADY HESKETH.

EARTHAM, *August* 26, 1792.

I KNOW not how it is, my dearest Coz, but in a new scene, and surrounded by strange objects, I find my powers of thinking dissipated to a degree that makes it difficult to me even to write a letter, and even a letter to you; but such a letter as I can, I will, and have the fairest chance to succeed this morning, Hayley, Romney, Hayley's son, and Beau, being all gone together to the sea for bathing. The sea, you must know, is nine miles off, so that unless stupidity prevent, I shall have opportunity to write not only to you, but to poor Hurdis also, who is broken-hearted for the loss of his favourite sister, lately dead: and whose letter, giving an account of it, which I received yesterday, drew tears from the eyes of all our party. My only comfort respecting even yourself is, that you write in good spirits, and assure me that you are in a state of recovery; otherwise I should mourn not only for Hurdis, but for myself, lest a certain event should reduce me, and in a short time too, to a situation as distressing as his; for though nature designed you only for my cousin, you have had a sister's place in my affections ever since I knew you. The reason is, I suppose, that having no sister, the daughter of my own mother, I thought it proper to have one, the daughter of yours. Certain it is, that I can by no means afford to lose you; and that unless you will be upon honour with me, to give me always a true account of yourself, at least when we are not together, I shall always be unhappy, because always suspicious that you deceive me.

Now for ourselves. I am, without the least dissimulation, in good health; my spirits are about as good as you have ever seen them; and if increase of appetite and a double portion of sleep be advantageous, such are the advantages that I have received from this migration. As to that gloominess of mind which I have had these twenty years, it cleaves to me even here; and could I be translated to Paradise, unless I left my body behind me, would cleave to me even there also. It is my companion for life, and nothing will ever divorce us. So much for myself. Mrs. Unwin is evidently the better for her jaunt, though by no means as she was before this last attack; still wanting help when she would rise from her seat, and a support in walking; but she is able to use more exercise than she could at home, and moves with rather a less tottering step. God knows what He designs for me; but when I see those who are dearer to me than myself distempered and enfeebled, and myself as strong as in the days of my youth, I tremble for the solitude in which a few years may place me. I wish her and you to die before me, indeed, but not till I am more likely to follow immediately. Enough of this!

Romney has drawn me in crayons, and in the opinion of all here, with his best hand, and with the most exact resemblance possible.

The seventeenth of September is the day on which I intend to leave Eartham. We shall then have been six weeks resident here; a holiday time long enough for a man who has much to do. And now farewell!

W. C.

*P.S.*—Hayley, whose love for me seems to be truly that of a brother, has given me his picture, drawn by Romney about fifteen years ago—an admirable likeness.

TO THE REV. MR. HURDIS.

EARTHAM, *August* 26, 1792.

MY DEAR SIR—Your, kind but very affecting letter found me not at Weston, to which place it was directed, but in a bower of my friend Hayley's garden, at Eartham, where I was sitting with Mrs. Unwin. We both knew the moment we saw it from whom it came; and observing a red seal, both comforted ourselves that all was well at Burwash; but we soon felt that we were called not to rejoice, but to mourn with you. We do indeed sincerely mourn with you; and if it will afford you any consolation to know it, you may be assured that every eye here has testified what our hearts have suffered for you. Your loss is great, and your disposition I perceive such as exposes you to feel the whole weight of it. I will not add to your sorrow by a vain attempt to assuage it; your own good sense and the piety of your principles will, of course, suggest to you the most powerful motives of acquiescence in the will of God. You will be sure to recollect that the stroke, severe as it is, is not the stroke of an enemy, but of a Father; and will find I trust hereafter that like a father He has done you good by it. Thousands have been able to say, and myself as loud as any of them, it has been good for me that I was afflicted; but time is necessary to work us to this persuasion, and in due time it shall be yours. Mr. Hayley, who tenderly sympathises with you, has enjoined me to send you as pressing an invitation as I can frame, to join me at this place. I have every motive to wish your consent,—both your benefit and my own, which I believe would be abundantly answered by your coming, ought to make me eloquent in such a cause. Here you will find silence and retirement in perfection, when you would seek them; and here such company as I have no doubt would suit you,—all cheerful, but not noisy; and all alike disposed to love you: you and I seem to have here a fair opportunity of meeting. It were a pity we should be in the same county, and not come together. I am here till the seventeenth of September, an interval that will afford you time to make the necessary arrangements, and to gratify me at last with an interview which I have long desired. Let me hear from you soon, that I may have double pleasure,—the pleasure of expecting as well as that of seeing you.

Mrs. Unwin, I thank God, though still a sufferer by her last illness, is much better, and has received considerable benefit by the air of Eartham. She adds to mine her affectionate compliments, and joins me and Hayley in this invitation.

Mr. Romney is here, and a young man, a cousin of mine. I tell you who we are, that you may not be afraid of us.

Adieu! May the Comforter of all the afflicted who seek Him be yours! God bless you.      W. C.


### TO LADY HESKETH.

EARTHAM, *September* 9, 1792.

MY DEAREST COUSIN—I determine, if possible, to send you one more letter, or at least, if possible, once more to send you something like one, before we leave Eartham. But I am in truth so unaccountably local in the use of my pen that, like the man in the fable, who could leap well nowhere but at Rhodes, I seem incapable of writing at all except at Weston. This is, as I have already told you, a delightful place; more beautiful scenery

I have never beheld nor expect to behold; but the charms of it, uncommon as they are, have not in the least alienated my affections from Weston. The genius of that place suits me better; it has an air of snug concealment, in which a disposition like mine feels itself peculiarly gratified; whereas here I see from every window woods like forests, and hills like mountains—a wildness, in short, that rather increases my natural melancholy, and which, were it not for the agreeables I find within, would soon convince me that mere change of place can avail me little. Accordingly, I have not looked out for a house in Sussex, nor shall.

The intended day of our departure continues to be the seventeenth. I hope to reconduct Mrs. Unwin to the Lodge with her health considerably mended: but it is in the article of speech chiefly, and in her powers of walking, that she is sensible of much improvement. Her sight and her hand still fail her, so that she can neither read nor work; mortifying circumstances both to her, who is never willingly idle.

On the eighteenth I purpose to dine with the General, and to rest that night at Kingston; but the pleasure I shall have in the interview will hardly be greater than the pain I shall feel at the end of it, for we shall part probably to meet no more.

Johnny, I know, has told you that Mr. Hurdis is here. Distressed by the loss of his sister, he has renounced the place where she died for ever, and is about to enter on a new course of life at Oxford. You would admire him much. He is gentle in his manners, and delicate in his person, resembling our poor friend Unwin, both in face and figure, more than any one I have ever seen. But he has not, at least he has not at present, his vivacity.

I have corresponded since I came here with Mrs. Courtenay, and had yesterday a very kind letter from her.

T

Adieu, my dear! may God bless you! Write to me as soon as you can after the twentieth. I shall then be at Weston, and indulging myself in the hope that I shall ere long see you there also. W. C.

### TO MRS. COURTENAY, WESTON UNDERWOOD.

EARTHAM, *September* 10, 1792.

MY DEAR CATHARINA—I am not so uncourteous a knight as to leave your last kind letter, and the last I hope that I shall receive for a long time to come, without an attempt, at least, to acknowledge and to send you something in the shape of an answer to it; but having been obliged to dose myself last night with laudanum, on account of a little nervous fever, to which I am always subject, and for which I find it the best remedy, I feel myself this morning particularly under the influence of Lethean vapours, and consequently in danger of being uncommonly stupid.

You could hardly have sent me intelligence that would have gratified me more than that of my two dear friends, Sir John and Lady Throckmorton, having departed from Paris two days before the terrible 10th of August. I have had many anxious thoughts on their account, and am truly happy to learn that they have sought a more peaceful region, while it was yet permitted them to do so. They will not, I trust, revisit those scenes of tumult and horror while they shall continue to merit that description. We are here all of one mind respecting the cause in which the Parisians are engaged, wish them a free people, and as happy as they can wish themselves. But their conduct has not always pleased us. We are shocked at their sanguinary proceedings, and begin to fear, myself in particular, that they will prove themselves unworthy, because incapable of enjoying it, of the inestimable blessings of liberty. My daily toast is, Sobriety and Freedom to the French, for they seem as destitute of the former as they are eager to secure the latter.

We still hold our purpose of leaving Eartham on the 17th, and again my fears on Mrs. Unwin's account begin to trouble me, but they are now not quite so reasonable as in the first instance. If she could bear the fatigue of travelling then, she is more equal to it at present, and supposing that nothing happens to alarm her, which is very probable, may be expected to reach Weston in much better condition than when she left it. Her improvement, however, is chiefly in her looks and in the articles of speaking and walking, for she can neither rise from her chair without help, nor walk without support, nor read, nor use her needles. Give my love to the good Doctor, and make him acquainted with the state of his patient, since he, of all men, seems to have the best right to know it.

I am proud that you are pleased with the epitaph I sent you, and shall be still prouder to see it perpetuated by the chisel. It is all that I have done since here I came, and all that I have been able to do. I wished, indeed, to have requited Romney for his well-drawn copy of me, in rhyme, and have more than once or twice attempted it, but I find, like the man in the fable, who could leap only at Rhodes, that verse is almost impossible to me except at Weston. Tell my friend George that I am every day mindful of him, and always love him, and bid him by no means to vex himself about the tardiness of Andrews. Remember me affectionately to William and to Pitcairn, whom I shall hope to find with you at my return, and should you see Mr. Buchanan, to him also. I have now charged you with commissions enow, and having added Mrs. Unwin's best compliments, and told you that I long to see you again, will conclude myself, my dear Catharina, most truly yours,

WM. COWPER.

# LETTERS FROM WESTON UNDERWOOD.

### TO WILLIAM HAYLEY, ESQ.

WESTON, *September* 21, 1792.

MY DEAR HAYLEY—Chaos himself, even the chaos of Milton, is not surrounded with more confusion, nor has a mind more completely in a hubbub, than I experience at the present moment. At our first arrival, after long absence, we find a hundred orders to servants necessary, a thousand things to be restored to their proper places, and an endless variety of minutiæ to be adjusted, which, though individually of little importance, are most momentous in the aggregate. In these circumstances I find myself so indisposed to writing, that, save to yourself, I would on no account attempt it; but to you I will give such a recital as I can of all that has passed since I sent you that short note from Kingston, knowing that if it be a perplexed recital, you will consider the cause, and pardon it. I will begin with a remark in which I am inclined to think you will agree with me, that there is sometimes more true heroism passing in a corner, and on occasions that make no noise in the world, than has often been exercised by those whom that world esteems her greatest heroes, and on occasions the most illustrious: I hope so at least; for all the heroism I have to boast, and all the opportunities I have of displaying any, are of a private nature. After writing the note, I immediately began to prepare for my appointed visit to Ham; but the struggles that I had with my own spirit, labouring as I did under the most dreadful dejection, are never to be told. I would have given the world to have been excused. I went, however, and carried my point against myself with a heart riven asunder: I have reasons for all this anxiety, which I cannot relate now. The visit, however, passed off well, and we returned in the dark to Kingston;—I, with a lighter heart than I had known since my departure from Eartham, and Mary too, for she had suffered hardly less than myself, and chiefly on my account. That night we rested well in our inn, and at twenty minutes after eight next morning set off for London; exactly at ten we reached Mr. Rose's door; we drank a dish of chocolate with him, and proceeded, Mr. Rose riding with us as far as St. Alban's. From this time we met with no impediment. In the dark, and in a storm, at eight at night, we found ourselves at our own back door. Mrs. Unwin was very near slipping out of the chair in which she was taken from the chaise, but at last was landed safe. We all have had a good night, and are all well this morning. God bless you, my dearest brother. W. C.

TO THE SAME.

WESTON, *October* 2, 1792.

MY DEAR HAYLEY—A bad night, succeeded by an east wind, and a sky all in sables, have such an effect on my spirits, that if I did not consult my own comfort more than yours, I should not write to-day, for I shall not entertain you much; yet your letter, though containing no very pleasant tidings, has afforded me some relief. It tells me, indeed, that you have been dispirited yourself, and that poor little Tom, the faithful squire of my Mary, has been seriously indisposed; all this grieves me, but then there is a warmth of heart, and a kindness in it, that do me good. I will endeavour not to repay you in notes of sorrow and despondence, though all my sprightly chords seem broken. In truth, one day excepted, I have not seen the day when I have been cheerful since I left you. My spirits, I think, are almost constantly lower than they were; the approach of winter is perhaps the cause; and if it is, I have nothing better to expect for a long time to come.

Yesterday was a day of assignation with myself, the day of which I said some days before it came, When that day comes I will begin my dissertations. Accordingly, when it came I prepared to do so; filled a letter-case with fresh paper, furnished myself with a pretty good pen, and replenished my ink-bottle; but partly from one cause, and partly from another, chiefly, however, from distress and dejection, after writing and obliterating about six lines, in the composition of which I spent near an hour, I was obliged to relinquish the attempt. An attempt so unsuccessful could have no other effect than to dishearten me, and it has had that effect to such a degree that I know not when I shall find courage to make another. At present I shall certainly abstain, since at present I cannot well afford to expose myself to the danger of a fresh mortification.

Your kind postscript is just arrived, and gives me great pleasure. When I cannot see you myself it seems some comfort, however, that you have been seen by another known to me, and who will tell me in a few days that he has seen you. Your wishes to disperse my melancholy would, I am sure, prevail, did that event depend on the warmth and sincerity with which you frame them;

but it has baffled both wishes and prayers, and those the most fervent that could be made, so many years, that the case seems hopeless. But no more of this at present.

Your verses to Austen are as sweet as the honey that they accompany,—kind, friendly, witty, and elegant. When shall I be able to do the like? Perhaps when my Mary, like your Tom, shall cease to be an invalid, I may recover a power at least to do something. I sincerely rejoice in the dear little man's restoration. My Mary continues, I hope, to mend a little. W. C.

TO JOHN JOHNSON, ESQ.

*November* 5, 1792.

MY DEAREST JOHNNY—I have done nothing since you went except that I have finished the sonnet which I told you I had begun, and sent it Hayley, who is well pleased *therewith*, and has by this time transmitted it to whom it most concerns.

I would not give the algebraist sixpence for his encomiums on my *Task*, if he condemns my Homer, which, I know, in point of language is equal to it, and in variety of numbers superior. But the character of the former having been some years established, he follows the general cry; and should Homer establish himself as well, and I trust he will hereafter, I shall have his warm suffrage for that also. But if not it is no matter. Swift says somewhere—"There are a few good judges of poetry in the world, who lend their taste to those who have none," and your man of figures is probably one of the borrowers.

Adieu—in great haste. Our united love attends yourself and yours, whose I am most truly and affectionately
WM. COWPER.

TO SAMUEL ROSE, ESQ.

WESTON, *November* 9, 1792.

MY DEAR FRIEND—I wish that I were as industrious and as much occupied as you, though in a different way; but it is not so with me. Mrs. Unwin's great debility (who is not yet able to move without assistance) is of itself a hinderance such as would effectually disable me. Till she can work and read, and fill up her time as usual (all which is at present entirely out of her power), I may now and then find time to write a letter, but I shall write nothing more. I cannot sit with my pen in my hand and my books before me, while she is in effect in solitude, silent, and looking at the fire. To this hinderance that other has been added, of which you are already aware, a want of spirits, such as I have never known, when I was not absolutely laid by, since I commenced an author. How long I shall be continued in these uncomfortable circumstances is known only to Him who, as He will, disposes of us all. I may be yet able, perhaps, to prepare the first book of the *Paradise Lost* for the press before it will be wanted; and Johnson himself seems to think there will be no haste for the second. But poetry is my favourite employment, and all my poetical operations are, in the meantime, suspended, for while a work to which I have bound myself remains unaccomplished I can do nothing else.

Johnson's plan of prefixing my phiz to the new edition of my Poems is by no means a pleasant one to me, and so I told him in a letter I sent him from Eartham, in which I assured him that my objections to it would not be easily surmounted. But if you judge that it may really have an effect in advancing the sale, I would not be so squeamish as to suffer the spirit of prudery to prevail in me to his disadvantage. Somebody told an author, I forget whom, that there was more vanity in refusing his picture than in granting it, on which he instantly complied. I do not perfectly feel all the force of the argument, but it shall content me that he did.

I do most sincerely rejoice in the success of your publication, and have no doubt that my prophecy concerning your success in greater matters will be fulfilled.[1] We are naturally pleased when our friends approve what we approve ourselves; how much, then, must I be pleased when you speak so kindly of Johnny! I know him to be all that you think him, and love him entirely.

Adieu! We expect you at Christmas, and shall, therefore, rejoice when Christmas comes. Let nothing interfere. Ever yours, W. C.

TO THE REV. JOHN NEWTON.

*November* 11, 1792.

MY DEAR FRIEND—I am not so insensible of your kindness in making me an exception from the number of your correspondents to whom you forbid the hope of hearing from you till your present labours are ended, as to make you wait longer for an answer to your last; which indeed would have had its answer before this time had it been possible for me to write. But so many have demands upon me of a similar kind, and while Mrs. Unwin continues an invalid my opportunities of writing are so few, that I am constrained to incur a long arrear to some with whom I would wish to be punctual. She can at present neither work nor read; and till she can do both, and

---

[1] This alludes to Mr. Rose's edition of *Decisions of the English Courts*.

amuse herself as usual, my own amusements of the pen must be suspended.

I, like you, have a work before me, and a work to which I should be glad to address myself in earnest, but cannot do it at present. When the opportunity comes I shall, like you, be under a necessity of interdicting some of my usual correspondents, and of shortening my letters to the excepted few. Many letters and much company are incompatible with authorship, and the one as much as the other. It will be long, I hope, before the world is put in possession of a publication which you design should be posthumous.

Oh for the day when your expectation of my complete deliverance shall be verified! At present it seems very remote; so distant indeed that hardly the faintest streak of it is visible in my horizon. The glimpse with which I was favoured about a month ago has never been repeated, and the depression of my spirits has. The future appears gloomy as ever; and I seem to myself to be scrambling always in the dark, among rocks and precipices, without a guide, but with an enemy ever at my heels prepared to push me headlong. Thus I have spent twenty years, but thus I shall not spend twenty years more. Long ere that period arrives, the grand question concerning my everlasting weal or woe will be decided. A question that seems to have interested the enemy of mankind peculiarly, for against none, so far as I have learned by reading or otherwise, has he ever manifested such fury as I have experienced at his hands; yet all that I have felt is little in comparison with what he often threatens me, so that even God's omnipotence to save is a consideration that affords me no comfort while I seem to have a foe omnipotent to destroy. This may appear to you strange language, yet is it not altogether unwarranted by Scripture. Tell me who are the Principalities and Powers in heavenly places spoken of by Saint Paul? Against them we have to war; and they cannot be the angels who have fallen from their first estate, for they are said to have been long since thrust down in perdition, and to be bound in chains of darkness until the judgment of the great day. I recollect, and so do you perhaps, what was the opinion of Dr. Conyers on this subject, and it will be a pleasure to me to know yours. If my enemy's testimony could weigh with you as much as it does sometimes with me, you would not hesitate long in your answer, for he has a thousand times in my hearing boasted himself supreme.

Adieu! my dear friend. I have exhausted my time though not filled my paper. Our united thanks are due for some excellent skate, and with our united affectionate remembrances to yourself and Miss Catlett, I remain truly yours, WM. COWPER.

I enclose Nat's receipt. The fourpence purchased a loaf for a hungry pauper.

TO JOHN JOHNSON, ESQ.

WESTON, *November* 20, 1792.

MY DEAREST JOHNNY—I give you many thanks for your rhymes, and your verses without rhyme; for your poetical dialogue between wood and stone; between Homer's head and the head of Samuel; kindly intended, I know well, for my amusement, and that amused me much.

The successor of the clerk defunct, for whom I used to write mortuary verses, arrived here this morning with a recommendatory letter from Joe Rye and a humble petition of his own, entreating me to assist him as I had assisted his predecessor. I have undertaken the service, although with no little reluctance, being involved in many arrears on other subjects, and having very little dependence at present on my ability to write at all. I proceed exactly as when you were here,—a letter now and then before breakfast, and the rest of my time all holiday; if holiday it may be called, that is spent chiefly in moping and musing and "*forecasting the fashion of uncertain evils.*"

The fever on my spirits has harassed me much, and I have never had so good a night nor so quiet a rising since you went as on this very morning, a relief that I account particularly seasonable and propitious, because I had, in my intentions, devoted this morning to you, and could not have fulfilled those intentions had I been as spiritless as I generally am.

I am glad that Johnson is in no haste for Milton, for I seem myself not likely to address myself presently to that concern with any prospect of success; yet something, now and then, like a secret whisper, assures and encourages me that it will yet be done.           W. C.

TO LADY HESKETH.

*December* 1, 1792.

I AM truly glad, my dearest Coz, that the waters of Cheltenham have done thee good, and wish ardently that those of Bath may establish thy health, and prove the means of prolonging it many years, even till thou shalt become what thou wast called at a very early age, an old wench indeed. I have been a *pauvre misérable* ever since I came from Eartham, and was little better while there, so that whatever motive may incline me to travel again hereafter, it will not be the hope that my spirits will be much the better for it. Neither was Mrs.

Unwin's health so much improved by that frisk of ours into Sussex as I had hoped and expected. She is, however, tolerably well, but very far indeed from having recovered the effects of her last disorder.

My birthday (the sixty-first that I have numbered) has proved for once a propitious day to me, for on that day my spirits began to amend, my nights became less hideous, and my days have been such of course.

I have heard nothing from Joseph, and having been always used to hear from him in November, am reduced to the dire necessity of supposing with you that he is heinously offended. Being in want of money, however, I wrote to him yesterday, and a letter which ought to produce a friendly answer; but whether it will or not is an affair at present of great uncertainty. Walter Bagot is offended too, and wonders that I would have any connexion with so bad a man as the author of the Essay on Old Maids must necessarily be! Poor man! he has five sisters, I think, in that predicament, which makes *his* resentment rather excusable. Joseph, by the way, has two, and perhaps may be proportionally influenced by that consideration. Should that be the case, I have nothing left to do but to wish them all good husbands, since the reconciliation of my two friends seems closely connected with that contingency.

In making the first advances to your sister, you have acted like yourself, that is to say, like a good and affectionate sister, and will not, I hope, lose your reward. Rewarded in another world you will be no doubt; but I should hope that you will not be altogether unrecompensed in this. Thou hast a heart, I know, that cannot endure to be long at enmity with any one, and were I capable of using thee never so ill, I am sure that in time you would sue to me for a pardon. Thou dost not want fire, but meekness is predominant in thee.

I was never so idle in my life, and never had so much to do. God knows when this will end; but I think of bestirring myself soon, and of putting on my Miltonic trammels once again. That once done, I shall not, I hope, put them off till the work is finished. I have written nothing lately but a sonnet to Romney, and a mortuary copy of verses for the town of Northampton, having been applied to by the new clerk for that purpose.

Johnson designs handsomely; you must pardon Johnson and receive him into your best graces. He purposes to publish, together with my Homer, a new edition of my two volumes of Poems, and to make me a present of the entire profits. They are to be handsome quartos, with an engraving of Abbot's picture of me prefixed. I have left myself neither time nor room for politics.

The French are a vain and childish people, and conduct themselves on this grand occasion with a levity and extravagance nearly akin to madness; but it would have been better for Austria and Prussia to let them alone. All nations have a right to choose their own mode of government, and the sovereignty of the people is a doctrine that evinces itself; for whenever the people choose to be masters they always are so, and none can hinder them. God grant that we may have no revolution here; but unless we have a reform we certainly shall. Depend upon it, my dear, the hour is come when power founded in patronage and corrupt majorities must govern this land no longer. Concession too must be made to dissenters of every denomination. They have a right to them, a right to all the privileges of Englishmen, and sooner or later, by fair means or by force, they will have them.

Adieu! my dearest Coz. I have only time to add Mrs. U.'s most affectionate remembrances, and to conclude myself ever thine,              WM. COWPER.

Mr. and Mrs. Rose came on the twenty-second, and Johnny with them; the former to stay ten days. It is strange that anybody should suspect Mr. Smith of having been assisted by me. None writes more rapidly or more correctly—twenty pages in a morning, which I have often read and heard read at night, and found not a word to alter. This moment comes a very kind letter from Joseph. Sephus tells me I may expect to see very soon the strongest assurances from the people of property of every description to support the king and present constitution. In this I do most sincerely rejoice, as you will. He wishes to know my political opinions, and he shall most truly.

TO JOHN JOHNSON, ESQ.

*January* 31, 1793.

*Io Pæan!*

MY DEAREST JOHNNY—Even as you foretold, so it came to pass. On Tuesday I received your letter, and on Tuesday came the pheasants; for which I am indebted in many thanks, as well as Mrs. Unwin, both to your kindness and to your kind friend, Mr. Copeman.

> In Copeman's ear this truth let Echo tell,
> 'Immortal bards like mortal pheasants well.
> And when his clerkship's out I wish him herds
> Of golden clients for his golden birds.'

Our friends the Courtenays have never dined with us since their marriage, *because* we have never asked them; and we have never asked them *because* poor Mrs. Unwin is not so equal to the task of providing for and entertaining company as before this last illness. But this is no objection to the arrival here of a bustard; rather it is a cause for which we shall be particularly glad to see the monster. It will be a handsome present to them. So let the bustard come, as the Lord Mayor of London said to the hare when he was hunting, "Let her come, a' God's name; I am not afraid of her."

Adieu! my dear cousin and caterer. My eyes are terribly bad, else I had much more to say to you.—Ever affectionately yours, WM. COWPER.

TO LADY HESKETH.

*February* 10, 1793.

My pens are all split, and my ink-glass is dry,
Neither wit, common-sense, nor ideas have I.

IN vain has it been that I have made several attempts to write since I came from Sussex; unless more comfortable days arrive than I have confidence to look for, there is an end of all writing with me. I have no spirits; when the Rose came I was obliged to prepare for his coming by a nightly dose of laudanum—twelve drops suffice; but without them I am devoured by melancholy.

Apropos of the Rose! His wife, in her political notions, is the exact counterpart of yourself—loyal in the extreme. Therefore, if you find her thus inclined when you become acquainted with her, you must not place her resemblance of yourself to the account of her admiration of you, for she is your likeness ready made. In fact, we are all of one mind about government matters; and, notwithstanding your opinion, the Rose is himself a Whig, and I am a Whig, and you, my dear, are a Tory, and all the Tories now-a-days call all the Whigs Republicans. How the deuce you came to be a Tory is best known to yourself; you have to answer for this novelty to the shades of your ancestors, who were always Whigs ever since we had any. Adieu! W. C.

## TO THE REV. MR. HURDIS.

WESTON, *February* 23, 1793.

MY DEAR SIR—My eyes, which have long been inflamed, will hardly serve me for Homer, and oblige me to make all my letters short. You have obliged me much by sending me so speedily the remainder of your notes. I have begun with them again, and find them, as before, very much to the purpose. More to the purpose they could not have been, had you been poetry professor already. I rejoice sincerely in the prospect you have of that office, which, whatever may be your own thoughts of the matter, I am sure you will fill with great sufficiency. Would that my interest and power to serve you were greater! One string to my bow I have, and one only, which shall not be idle for want of my exertions. I thank you likewise for your very entertaining notices and remarks in the natural way. The hurry in which I write would not suffer me to send you many in return, had I many to send, but only two or three present themselves.

Frogs will feed on worms. I saw a frog gathering into his gullet an earth-worm as long as himself; it cost him time and labour, but at last he succeeded.

Mrs. Unwin and I, crossing a brook, saw from the foot-bridge somewhat at the bottom of the water which had the appearance of a flower. Observing it attentively, we found that it consisted of a circular assemblage of minnows; their heads all met in a centre, and their tails diverging at equal distances, and being elevated above their heads, gave them the appearance of a flower half blown. One was longer than the rest; and as often as a straggler came in sight, he quitted his place to pursue him, and having driven him away, he returned to it again, no other minnow offering to take it in his absence.

This we saw him do several times. The object that had attached them all was a dead minnow, which they seemed to be devouring.

After a very rainy day, I saw on one of the flower-borders what seemed a long hair, but it had a waving, twining motion. Considering more nearly, I found it alive, and endued with spontaneity, but could not discover at the ends of it either head or tail, or any distinction of parts. I carried it into the house, when the air of a warm room dried and killed it presently.

W. C.

TO THE REV. JOHN JOHNSON.

WESTON, April 11, 1793.

MY DEAREST JOHNNY—To do a kind thing, and in a kind manner, is a double kindness, and no man is more addicted to both than you, or more skilful in contriving them. Your plan to surprise me agreeably succeeded to admiration. It was only the day before yesterday that, while we walked after dinner in the orchard, Mrs. Unwin between Sam and me, hearing the hall clock, I observed a great difference between that and ours, and began immediately to lament, as I had often done, that there was not a sun-dial in all Weston to ascertain the true time for us. My complaint was long, and lasted till, having turned into the grass walk, we reached the new building at the end of it, where we sat awhile and reposed ourselves. In a few minutes we returned by the way we came, when what think you was my astonishment to see what I had not seen before, though I had passed close by it, a smart sun-dial mounted on a smart stone pedestal! I assure you it seemed the effect of conjuration. I stopped short and exclaimed—"Why, here is a sun-dial, and upon our ground! How is this? Tell me, Sam, how it came here! Do you know anything about it?" At first I really thought (that is to say, as soon as I could think at all) that this factotum of mine, Sam Roberts, having often heard me deplore the want of one, had given orders for the supply of that want himself, without my knowledge, and was half pleased and half offended. But he soon exculpated himself by imputing the fact to you. It was brought up to Weston, it seems, about noon; but Andrews stopped the cart at the blacksmith's, whence he sent to inquire if I was gone for my walk. As it happened I walked not till two o'clock. So there it stood waiting till I should go forth, and was introduced before my return. Fortunately, too, I went out at the church end of the village, and consequently saw nothing of it. How I could possibly pass it without seeing it, when it stood in the walk, I know not, but certain it is that I did. And where I shall fix it now I know as little. It cannot stand between the two gates, the place of your choice, as I understand from Samuel, because the hay-cart must pass that way in the season. But we are now busy in winding the walk all round the orchard, and in doing so shall doubtless stumble at last upon some open spot that will suit it.

There it shall stand, while I live, a constant monument of your kindness.

I have this moment finished the twelfth book of the *Odyssey;* and I read the *Iliad* to Mrs. Unwin every evening.

The effect of this reading is, that I still spy blemishes, something at least that I can mend; so that, after all, the transcript of alterations, which you and George have made, will not be a perfect one. It would be foolish to forego an opportunity of improvement for such a reason: neither will I. It is ten o'clock, and I must breakfast. Adieu, therefore, my dear Johnny! Remember your appointment to see us in October.—Ever yours, W.C.

### TO THE REV. WALTER BAGOT.

*Weston, May* 4, 1793.

MY DEAR FRIEND—While your sorrow for our common loss was fresh in your mind I would not write, lest a letter on so distressing a subject should be too painful both to you and me; and now that I seem to have reached a proper time for doing it, the multiplicity of my literary business will hardly afford me leisure. Both you and I have this comfort when deprived of those we love: at our time of life we have every reason to believe that the deprivation cannot be long. Our sun is setting too; and when the hour of rest arrives we shall rejoin your brother, and many whom we have tenderly loved, our forerunners into a better country.

I will say no more on a theme which it will be better perhaps to treat with brevity; and because the introduction of any other might seem a transition too violent, I will only add, that Mrs. Unwin and I are about as well as we at any time have been within the last year.—Truly yours, W. C.

### TO THOMAS PARK, ESQ.

*May* 17, 1793.

DEAR SIR—It has not been without frequent self-reproach that I have so long omitted to answer your last very kind and most obliging letter. I am by habit and inclination extremely punctual in the discharge of such arrears, and it is only through necessity, and under constraint of various indispensable engagements of a different kind, that I am become of late much otherwise.

I have never seen Chapman's translation of Homer,

and will not refuse your offer of it, unless by accepting it I shall deprive you of a curiosity that you cannot easily replace. The line or two which you quote from him, except that the expression "a well written soul" has the quaintness of his times in it, do him credit. He cannot surely be the same Chapman who wrote a poem, I think, on the battle of Hochstadt, in which, when I was a very young man, I remember to have seen the following lines:

> "Think of two thousand gentlemen at least,
> And each man mounted on his capering beast,
> Into the Danube they were pushed by shoals," etc. etc.

These are lines that could not fail to impress the memory, though not altogether in the Homerican style of battle.

I am, as you say, a hermit, and probably an irreclaimable one, having a horror of London that I cannot express, nor indeed very easily account for. Neither am I much less disinclined to migration in general. I did no little violence to my love of home last summer when I paid Mr. Hayley a visit, and in truth was principally induced to the journey by a hope that it might be useful to Mrs. Unwin; who, however, derived so little benefit from it that I purpose for the future to avail myself of the privilege my years may reasonably claim, by compelling my younger friends to visit *me*. But even this is a point which I cannot well compass at present, both because I am too busy, and because poor Mrs. Unwin is not able to bear the fatigue of company. Should better days arrive, days of more leisure to me, and of some health to her, I shall not fail to give you notice of the change, and shall then hope for the pleasure of seeing you at Weston.

The epitaph you saw is on the tomb of the same Mr. Unwin to whom the *Tirocinium* is inscribed, the son of the lady above mentioned. By the desire of his executors I wrote a Latin one, which they approved, but it was not approved by a relation of the deceased, and therefore was not used. He objected to the mention I had made in it of his mother having devoted him to the service of God in his infancy. She did it, however, and not in vain, as I wrote my epitaph. Who wrote the English one I know not.

The poem called the "Slave" is not mine, nor have I ever seen it. I wrote two on the subject—one entitled "The Negro's Complaint," and the other "The Morning Dream." With thanks for all your kindness, and the patience you have with me, I remain, dear sir, sincerely yours, W. C.

TO THE REV. JOHN NEWTON.

*June* 12, 1793.

MY DEAR FRIEND—You promise to be contented with a short line, and a short one you must have, hurried over in the little interval I have happened to find between the conclusion of my morning task and breakfast. Study has this good effect at least; it makes me an early riser, who might otherwise, perhaps, be as much given to dozing as my readers.

The scanty opportunity I have, I shall employ in telling you what you principally wish to be told—the present state of mine and Mrs. Unwin's health. In her I cannot perceive any alteration for the better; and must be satisfied, I believe, as indeed I have great reason to be, if she does not alter for the worse. She uses the orchard walk daily, but always supported between two, and is still unable to employ herself as formerly. But she is cheerful, seldom in much pain, and has always strong confidence in the mercy and faithfulness of God

As to myself, I have always the same song to sing—well in body, but sick in spirit: sick, nigh unto death.

> "Seasons return, but not to me returns
> God, or the sweet approach of heavenly day,
> Or sight of cheering truth, or pardon seal'd,
> Or joy, or hope, or Jesus' face divine;
> But cloud," etc.

I could easily set my complaint to Milton's tune, and accompany him through the whole passage, on the subject of a blindness more deplorable than his; but time fails me.

I feel great desire to see your intended publication; a desire which the manner in which Mr. Bull speaks of it, who called here lately, has no tendency to allay. I believe I forgot to thank you for your last poetical present: not because I was not much pleased with it, but I write always in a hurry, and in a hurry must now conclude myself, with our united love, yours, my dear friend, most sincerely, WM. COWPER.

TO THOMAS PARK, ESQ.

W. U., *July* 15, 1793.

DEAR SIR—Within these few days I have received, by favour of Miss Knapps, your acceptable present of Chapman's translation of the *Iliad*. I know not whether the book be a rarity, but a curiosity it certainly is. I have as yet seen but little of it,—enough, however, to make me wonder that any man, with so little taste for Homer or apprehension of his manner, should think it worth while to undertake the laborious task of translating him; the hope of pecuniary advantage may perhaps account for it. His information, I fear, was not much better than his verse, for I have consulted him in one passage of some difficulty, and find him giving sense of his own not at all warranted by the words of Homer. Pope sometimes does this, and sometimes omits the difficult part entirely. I can boast of having done neither, though it has cost me infinite pains to exempt myself from the necessity.

I have seen a translation by Hobbes, which I prefer for its greater clumsiness. Many years have passed since I saw it, but it made me laugh immoderately. Poetry that is not good can only make amends for that deficiency by being ridiculous; and because the translation of Hobbes has at least this recommendation, I shall be obliged to you, should it happen to fall in your way, if you would be so kind as to procure it for me. The only edition of it I ever saw (and perhaps there never was another) was a very thick 12mo., both print and paper bad, a sort of book that would be sought in vain, perhaps, anywhere but on a stall.

When you saw Lady Hesketh you saw the relation of mine with whom I have been more intimate, even from childhood, than any other. She has seen much of the world, understands it well, and, having great natural vivacity, is of course one of the most agreeable of companions.

I have now arrived almost at a close of my labours on the *Iliad*, and have left nothing behind me, I believe, which I shall wish to alter on any future occasion. In about a fortnight or three weeks I shall begin to do the same for the *Odyssey*, and hope to be able to perform it while the *Iliad* is in printing. Then Milton will demand all my attention, and when I shall find opportunity either to revise your MSS. or to write a poem of my own, which I have in contemplation, I can hardly say. Certainly not till both these tasks are accomplished.—I remain, dear sir, with many thanks for your kind present, sincerely yours, W. C.

## TO MRS. CHARLOTTE SMITH.

WESTON, *July* 25, 1793.

MY DEAR MADAM—Many reasons concurred to make me impatient for the arrival of your most acceptable present, and among them was the fear lest you should, perhaps, suspect me of tardiness in acknowledging so great a favour,—a fear that, as often as it prevailed, distressed me exceedingly. At length I have received it, and my little bookseller assures me that he sent it the very day he got it; by some mistake, however, the waggon brought it instead of the coach, which occasioned a delay that I could ill afford.

It came this morning about an hour ago; consequently I have not had time to peruse the poem, though you may be sure I have found enough for the perusal of the Dedication. I have in fact given it three readings, and in each have found increasing pleasure.

I am a whimsical creature; when I write for the public, I write, of course, with a desire to please—in other words, to acquire fame, and I labour accordingly; but when I find that I have succeeded, feel myself alarmed, and ready to shrink from the acquisition.

This I have felt more than once, and when I saw my name at the head of your Dedication I felt it again; but the consummate delicacy of your praise soon convinced me that I might spare my blushes, and that the demand was less upon my modesty than my gratitude. Of that be assured, dear madam, and of the truest esteem and respect of your most obliged and affectionate humble servant, W. C.

*P.S.*—I should have been much grieved to have let slip this opportunity of thanking you for your charming sonnets, and my two most agreeable old friends Monimia and Orlando.

TO THE REV. JOHN JOHNSON.

*August* 2, 1793.

MY DEAREST JOHNNY—The Bishop of Norwich has won my heart by his kind and liberal behaviour to you, and if I knew him, I would tell him so.

I am glad that your auditors find your voice strong, and your utterance distinct; glad, too, that your doctrine has hitherto made you no enemies. You have a gracious Master, who, it seems, will not suffer you to see war in the beginning. It will be a wonder, however, if you do not, sooner or later, find out that sore place in every heart which can ill endure the touch of apostolic doctrine. Somebody will smart in his conscience, and you will hear of it. I say not this, my dear Johnny, to terrify, but to prepare you for that which is likely to happen, and which, troublesome as it may prove, is yet devoutly to be wished; for in general, there is little good done by preachers till the world begins to abuse them. But understand me aright,—I do not mean that you should give them unnecessary provocation by scolding and railing at them, as some, more zealous than wise, are apt to do. That were to deserve their anger. No; there is no need of it. The self-abasing doctrines of the gospel will of themselves create you enemies: but remember this for your comfort, they will also, in due time, transform them into friends, and make them love you as if they were your own children. God give you many such; as, if you are faithful to His cause, I trust He will!

Sir John and Lady Throckmorton have lately arrived in England, and are now at the Hall. They have brought me from Rome several engravings on *Odyssey* subjects by Flaxman, whom you have heard Hayley celebrate. They are very fine, very much in the antique style, and a present from the Dowager Lady Spencer. Ever yours,

W. C.


TO MRS. COURTENAY.

WESTON, *August* 20, 1793.

My dearest Catharina is too reasonable, I know, to expect news from me, who live on the outside of the world, and know nothing that passes within it. The best news is, that though you are gone, you are not gone for ever, as once I supposed you were, and said that we should probably meet no more. Some news, however, we have; but then I conclude that you have already received it from the Doctor, and that thought almost deprives me of all courage to relate it. On the evening of the feast, Bob Archer's house affording, I suppose, the best room for the purpose, all the lads and lasses who felt themselves disposed to dance assembled there. Long time they danced, at least long time they did something a little like it; when at last the company having retired, the fiddler asked Bob for a lodging. Bob replied "that his beds were all full of his own family; but, if he chose it, he would show him a haycock, where he might sleep as sound as in any bed whatever." So forth they went together, and when they reached the place the fiddler knocked down Bob, and demanded his money. But, happily for Bob, though he might be knocked down, and actually was so, yet he could not possibly be robbed, having nothing. The fiddler, therefore, having amused himself with kicking him and beating him as he lay, as long as he saw good, left him, and has never been heard of since, nor inquired after indeed, being, no doubt, the last man in the world whom Bob wishes to see again.

By a letter from Hayley to-day I learn that Flaxman,

to whom we are indebted for those *Odyssey* figures which Lady Frog brought over, has almost finished a set for the *Iliad* also. I should be glad to embellish my Homer with them, but neither my bookseller nor I shall probably choose to risk so expensive an ornament on a work whose reception with the public is at present doubtful.

Adieu, my dearest Catharina. Give my best love to your husband. Come home as soon as you can, and accept our united very best wishes. W. C.

#### TO WILLIAM HAYLEY, ESQ.

WESTON, *October* 5, 1793.

MY good intentions towards you, my dearest brother, are continually frustrated; and, which is most provoking, not by such engagements and avocations as have a right to my attention, such as those to my Mary, and to the old bard of Greece, but by mere impertinences, such as calls of civility from persons not very interesting to me, and letters from a distance still less interesting, because the writers of them are strangers. A man sent me a long copy of verses, which I could do no less than acknowledge. They were silly enough, and cost me eighteenpence, which was seventeenpence halfpenny farthing more than they were worth. Another sent me at the same time a plan, requesting my opinion of it, and that I would lend him my name as editor; a request with which I shall not comply, but I am obliged to tell him so, and one letter is all that I have time to despatch in a day, sometimes half a one, and sometimes I am not able to write at all. Thus it is that my time perishes, and I can neither give so much of it as I would to you or to any other valuable purpose.

On Tuesday we expect company—Mr. Rose and Lawrence the painter. Yet once more is my patience to be exercised, and once more I am made to wish that my face had been movable, to put on and take off at pleasure, so as to be portable in a bandbox, and sent to the artist. These, however, will be gone, as I believe I told you, before you arrive, at which time I know not that anybody will be here, except my Johnny, whose presence will not at all interfere with our readings. You will not, I believe, find me a very slashing critic: I hardly indeed expect to find anything in your *Life of Milton* that I shall sentence to amputation. How should it be too long? A well-written work, sensible and spirited, such as yours was, when I saw it, is never so. But, however, we shall see. I promise to spare nothing that I think may be lopped off with advantage.

I began this letter yesterday, but could not finish it till now. I have risen this morning, like an infernal frog out of Acheron, covered with the ooze and mud of melancholy. For this reason I am not sorry to find myself at the bottom of my paper, for had I more room, perhaps I might fill it all with croaking, and make an heartache at Eartham, which I wish to be always cheerful. Adieu. My poor sympathising Mary is of course sad, but always mindful of you. W. C.


TO MRS. COURTENAY.

WESTON, *November* 4, 1793.

I SELDOM rejoice in a day of soaking rain like this; but in this, my dearest Catharina, I do rejoice sincerely, because it affords me an opportunity of writing to you, which, if fair weather had invited us into the orchard walk at the usual hour, I should not easily have found. I am a most busy man—busy to a degree that sometimes half distracts me; but if complete distraction be occasioned by having the thoughts too much and too long attached to a single point, I am in no danger of it, with such a perpetual whirl are mine whisked about from one subject to another. When two poets meet, there are fine doings I can assure you. My Homer finds work for Hayley, and his *Life of Milton* work for me, so that we are neither of us one moment idle. Poor Mrs. Unwin in the meantime sits quiet in her corner, occasionally laughing at us both, and not seldom interrupting us with some question or remark, for which she is constantly rewarded by me with a "Hush—hold your peace!" Bless yourself, my dear Catharina, that you are not connected with a poet, especially that you have not two to deal with; ladies who have, may be bidden indeed to hold their peace, but very little peace have they. How should they in fact have any, continually enjoined as they are to be silent?

\* \* \* \* \* \*

The same fever that has been so epidemic there, has been severely felt here likewise; some have died, and a multitude have been in danger. Two under our own roof have been infected with it, and I am not sure that I have perfectly escaped myself, but I am now well again.

I have persuaded Hayley to stay a week longer, and again my hopes revive that he may yet have an opportunity to know my friends before he returns into Sussex. I write amidst a chaos of interruptions: Hayley, on the one hand, spouts Greek, and, on the other hand, Mrs. Unwin continues talking, sometimes to us, and sometimes, because we are both too busy to attend to her, she holds a dialogue with herself. Query, is not this a bull? and ought I not instead of dialogue to have said soliloquy?

Adieu! With our united love to all your party, and with ardent wishes soon to see you all at Weston, I remain, my dearest Catharina, ever yours, W. C.

TO SAMUEL ROSE, ESQ.

WESTON, *December* 8, 1793.

MY DEAR FRIEND—In my last I forgot to thank you for the box of books, containing also the pamphlets. We have read—that is to say, my cousin has, who reads to us in an evening—*The History of Jonathan Wild*, and found it highly entertaining. The satire on great men is witty, and I believe perfectly just ; we have no censure to pass on it, unless that we think the character of Mrs. Heartfree not well sustained—not quite delicate in the latter part of it—and that the constant effect of her charms upon every man who sees her has a sameness in it that is tiresome, and betrays either much carelessness, or idleness, or lack of invention. It is possible, indeed, that the author might intend by this circumstance a satirical glance at novelists, whose heroines are generally all bewitching ; but it is a fault that he had better have noticed in another manner, and not have exemplified in his own.

The first volume of *Man as he is* has lain unread in my study window this twelvemonth, and would have been returned unread to its owner had not my cousin come in good time to save it from that disgrace. We are now reading it, and find it excellent, abounding with wit and just sentiment, and knowledge both of books and men. Adieu !                                                             W. C

# LETTERS FROM NORFOLK.
## 1795-1799.

TO THE REV. MR. BUCHANAN.

MUNDSLEY, *September* 5, 1795.

" ———to interpose a little ease,
Let my frail thoughts dally with false surmise!"

I WILL forget for a moment that to whomsoever I may address myself, a letter from me can no otherwise be welcome than as a curiosity. To you, sir, I address this; urged to it by extreme penury of employment, and the desire I feel to learn something of what is doing, and has been done, at Weston (my beloved Weston!) since I left it.

The coldness of these blasts, even in the hottest days, has been such that, added to the irritation of the salt spray with which they are always charged, they have occasioned me an inflammation in the eyelids, which threatened a few days since to confine me entirely; but by absenting myself as much as possible from the beach, and guarding my face with an umbrella, that inconvenience is in some degree abated. My chamber commands a very near view of the ocean, and the ships at high water approach the coast so closely that a man furnished with better eyes than mine might, I doubt not, discern the sailors from the window. No situation—at least when the weather is clear and bright—can be pleasanter; which you will easily credit when I add that it imparts something a little resembling pleasure even to me. Gratify me with news of Weston! If Mr. Gregson and your neighbours the Courtenays are there, mention me to them in such terms as you see good. Tell me if my poor birds are living! I never see the herbs I used to give them without a recollection of them, and sometimes am ready to gather them, forgetting that I am not at home. Pardon this intrusion.

Mrs. Unwin continues much as usual.

### TO LADY HESKETH, CHELTENHAM.

Mr. Johnson is again absent—gone to Mattishall—a circumstance to which I am indebted for an opportunity to answer your letter as soon almost as I have received it. Were he present, I feel that I could not do it. You say it gives you pleasure to hear from me, and I resolve to forget for a moment my conviction that it is impossible for me to give pleasure to anybody. You have heard much from my lips that I am sure has given you none; if what comes from my pen be less unpalatable, none has therefore so strong a claim to it as yourself.

My walks on the sea-shore have been paid for by swelled and inflamed eyelids, and I now recollect that such was always the condition of mine in the same situation,—a natural effect, I suppose, at least upon eyelids so subject to disorder as mine, of the salt spray and cold winds, which on the coast are hardly ever less than violent. I now therefore abandon my favourite walk, and wander in lanes and under hedges. As heavy a price I have paid for a long journey performed on foot to a place called Hazeborough. That day was indeed a day spent in walking. I was much averse to the journey, both on account of the distance and the uncertainty of what I should find there; but Mr. Johnson insisted. We set out accordingly, and I was almost ready to sink with fatigue long before we reached the place of our destination. The only inn was full of company; but my companion, having an opportunity to borrow a lodging for an hour or two, he did so, and thither we retired. We learned on inquiry that the place is eight miles distant from this, and though by the help of a guide we shortened it about a mile on our return, the length of the way occasioned me a fever, which I have had now these four days, and perhaps shall not be rid of in four more; perhaps never. Mr. J. and Samuel, after dinner, visited the lighthouse; a gratification which would have been none to me for several reasons, but especially because I found no need to add to the number of steps I had to take before I should find myself at home again. I learned, however, from them that it is a curious structure. The building is circular, but the stairs are not so, flight above flight, with a commodious landing at every twentieth stair, they ascend to the height of four stories; and there is a spacious and handsome apartment at every landing. The light is given by a patent lamp, of which there are two ranges; six lamps in the upper range, and five in the lower; both ranges, as you may suppose, at the top of the house. Each lamp has a broad silver reflector behind it. The present occupant was once commander of a large merchantman, but, having chastised a boy of his crew with too much severity, was displaced, and consequently ruined. He had, however, a friend in the Trinity House, who, soon after this was built, asked him if he would accept the charge of it; and the cashiered captain, judging it better to be such a lamplighter than to starve, very readily and very wisely closed with the offer. He has only the trouble of scouring the silver plates every day, and of rising every night at twelve to trim the lamps, for which he has a competent salary (Samuel forgets the amount of it), and he and his family a pleasant and comfortable abode.

I have said as little of myself as I could, that my letter might be more worth the postage. My next will perhaps be less worth it, should any next ensue, for I meet with little variety, and shall not be very willing to travel fifteen miles on foot again to find it. I have seen no fish since I came here, except a dead sprat upon the sands, and one piece of cod from Norwich, too stale to be eaten. Adieu! W. C.

### TO THE SAME, CHELTENHAM.

MUNDSLEY, *September* 26, 1795.

MR. JOHNSON is gone forth again, and again, for the last time I suppose that I shall ever do it, I address a line to you. I knew not of his intentions to leave me till the day before he did so. Like everything else that constitutes my wretched lot, this departure of his was sudden, and shocked me accordingly. He enjoined me before he went, if I wrote at all in his absence, to write to Mr. Newton. But I cannot, and so I told him. Whither he is gone I know not; at least I know not by information from himself. Samuel tells me that he thinks his destination is Weston. But why to Weston is unimaginable to me. I shall never see Weston more. I have been tossed like a ball into a far country, from which there is no rebound for me. There indeed I lived a life of infinite despair, and such is my life in Norfolk. Such indeed it would be in any given spot upon the face of the globe; but to have passed the little time that remained to me there, was the desire of my heart. My heart's desire, however, has been always frustrated in everything that it ever settled on, and by means that have made my disappointments inevitable. When I left Weston I despaired of reaching Norfolk, and now that I have reached Norfolk, I am equally hopeless of ever reaching Weston more. What a lot is mine! Why was existence given to a creature that might possibly and would probably become wretched in the degree that I have been so? and whom misery, such as mine, was almost sure to overwhelm in a moment. But the question is vain. I existed by a decree from which there was no appeal, and on terms the most tremendous because unknown to, and even unsuspected by me; difficult to be complied with had they been foreknown, and, unforeknown, impracticable. Of this truth I have no witness but my own experience—a witness whose testimony will not be admitted. But farewell to a subject with which I can only weary you, and blot the paper to no purpose. You assure me that I shall see you again; tell me when and where I shall see you, and I will believe you if it be possible.

Samuel desires me to present his duty to you. His wife is gone to Weston, and he wishes me to say that if Mrs. Herbert has any concerns there that Nanny can settle for her and will give her the necessary directions, she may depend upon their being exactly attended to. With Mrs. Unwin's respects, I remain the forlorn and miserable being I was when I wrote last.     W. C.

### TO THE SAME, AT BATH.

*January* 22, 1796.

I LITTLE thought ever to have addressed you by letter more. I have become daily and hourly worse, ever since I left Mundsley: there I had something like a gleam of hope allowed me, that possibly my life might be granted me for a longer time than I had been used to suppose, though only on the dreadful terms of accumulating future misery on myself, and for no other reason; but even that hope has long since forsaken me, and I now consider this letter as a warrant of my own dreadful end: as the fulfilment of a word heard in better days, at least six and twenty years ago,—a word which, to have understood at the time when it reached me, would have been, at least might have been, a happiness indeed to me; but my cruel destiny denied me the privilege of understanding anything that, in the horrible moment that came winged with my immediate destruction, might have served to aid me. You know my story far better than I am able to relate it. Infinite despair is a sad prompter. I expect that in six days time, at the latest, I shall no longer foresee, but feel the accomplishment of all my fears. Oh, lot of unexampled misery incurred in a moment! Oh wretch! to whom life and death are alike impossible! Most miserable at present in this, that being thus miserable I have my senses continued to me only that I may look forward to the worst. It is certain at least, that I have them for no other purpose, and but very imperfectly even for this. My thoughts are like loose dry sand, which the closer it is grasped slips the sooner away. Mr. Johnson reads to me, but I lose every other sentence through the inevitable wanderings of my mind, and experience, as I have these two years, the same shattered mode of thinking on every subject and on all occasions. If I seem to write with more connexion, it is only because the gaps do not appear. Adieu.—I shall not be here to receive your answer, neither shall I ever see you more. Such is the expectation of the most desperate and most miserable of all beings. W. C.

TO THE SAME.

*February* 19, 1796.

COULD I address you as I used to do, with what delight should I begin this letter! But that delight, and every other sensation of the kind, has long since forsaken me for ever. The consequence is, that I neither know for what cause I write, nor of what materials to compose what shall be written; my groans, could they be expressed here, would presently fill the paper. I write, however, at the instance of Mr. Johnson, and, as I always think so, always on the last occasion, more assuredly than on any of the former, for the very last time. He, I know, inquired in a letter he lately sent you, when we might expect you here. Whatever day you name in your reply will be a day that I shall never see; nor have I even the hope, unless it come to-morrow, that your reply itself will reach this place before I am taken from it. The uncertainty is dreadful, and all remedy for it impracticable. But why tell you what I think of myself, of my present condition, and of the means employed to reduce me to it? My thoughts on all these subjects are too well known to you to need any recital here. All my themes of misery may be summed up in one word,—He who made me, regrets that ever He did. Many years have passed since I heard this terrible truth from Himself, and the interval has been spent accordingly. Adieu.—I shall write to you no more. I am promised months of continuance here, and should be somewhat less a wretch in my present feelings, could I credit the promise, but effectual care is taken that I shall not. The night contradicts the day, and I go down the torrent of time into the gulf that I have expected to plunge into so long. A few hours remain, but among those few, not one is found a part of which I shall ever employ in writing to you again. Once more, therefore—adieu—and adieu to the pen for ever. I suppress a thousand agonies to add only      W. C.

Mr. Johnson says he shall expect me to resume the pen and my former employments on Tuesday se'ennight. But what I have written here on my reperusal of it convinces me, as it may him, that it will be in vain. Some other dreadful thing will happen to me, and not the desirable one announced.

### TO THE SAME.

*May* 15, 1797.

To you once more, and too well I know why, I am under cruel necessity of writing. Every line that I have ever; sent you I have believed, under the influence of infinite despair, the last that I should send. This I know to be so. Whatever be your condition either now or hereafter, it is heavenly compared with mine even at this moment. It is unnecessary to add that this comes from the most miserable of human beings, whom a terrible moment made such.

### TO THE SAME.

*June* 1, 1798.

UNDER the necessity of addressing you, as I have done in other days, though these are such as seem to myself absolutely to forbid it,—I say as usual, my dear cousin; and having said it, am utterly at a loss to proceed. Mr. Johnson says that we are going on Monday to Mundsley, and bids me to tell you so; but at present he acknowledges himself that it is uncertain whether we go or not, since we cannot know till to-morrow whether there is a place for us there, or the lodgings be already full.

Whether the journey be practicable or otherwise, and wherever I am, my distress is infinite; for I see no possible way of escape, in my circumstances, from miseries such as I doubt not will far exceed my most terrible expectations. To wish, therefore, that I had never existed, which has been my only reasonable wish for many years, seems all that remains to one who once dreamed of happiness, but awoke never to dream of it again, and who, under the necessity of concluding as he began, subscribes himself your affectionate   WM. COWPER.

### ·TO THE REV. JOHN NEWTON.

*July* 29, 1798.

DEAR SIR—Few letters have passed between us, and I was never so incapable of writing as now, nor ever so destitute of a subject. It is long since I received your last, to which I have as yet returned no answer; nor is it possible that though I write I should even now reply to it. It contained, I remember, many kind expressions, which would have encouraged, perhaps, and consoled any other than myself; but I was, even then, out of the reach of all such favourable impressions, and am at present less susceptible of them than at any time since I saw you last. I once little thought to see such days as these, for almost in the moment when they found me there was not a man in the world who seemed to himself to have less reason to expect them. This you know; and what can I say of myself that you do not know?

I will only add, therefore, that we are going to the sea-side to-morrow, where we are to stay a fortnight; at the end of which time may I expect to find a letter from you directed to me at Dereham?—I remain, in the meantime, yours as usual, WM. COWPER.

Mr. Johnson is well, and desires to be kindly remembered to you.


TO LADY HESKETH.

MUNDSLEY, *Oct.* 13, 1798.

DEAR COUSIN,—You describe delightful scenes, but you describe them to one who, if he even saw them, could receive no delight from them; who has a faint recollection, and so faint as to be like an almost forgotten dream, that once he was susceptible of pleasure from such causes. The country that you have had in prospect has been always famed for its beauties; but the wretch who can derive no gratification from a view of Nature, even under the disadvantage of her most ordinary dress, will have no eyes to admire her in any.

In one day—in one minute, I should rather have said—she became an universal blank to me; and, though from a different cause, yet with an effect as difficult to remove as blindness itself. In this country, if there are not mountains there are hills; if not broad and deep rivers, yet such as are sufficient to embellish a prospect; and an object still more magnificent than any river, the ocean itself, is almost immediately under the window. Why is scenery like this, I had almost said, why is the very scene which many years since I could not contemplate without rapture, now become, at the best, an insipid wilderness? It neighbours nearly, and as nearly resembles, the scenery of Catfield; but with what different perceptions does it present me! The reason is obvious. My state of mind is a medium through which the beauties of Paradise itself could not be communicated with any effect but a painful one.

There is a wide interval between us, which it would be far easier for you than for me to pass. Yet I should in vain invite you. We shall meet no more. I know not what Mr. Johnson said of me in the long letter he addressed to you yesterday, but nothing, I am sure, that could make such an event seem probable.—I remain, as usual, dear cousin, yours, WM. COWPER.


TO THE REV. JOHN NEWTON.

DEREHAM, *April* 11, 1799.

DEAR SIR—Your last letter so long unanswered may, and indeed must, have proved sufficiently that my state of mind is not now more favourable to the purpose of writing than it was when I received it; for had any alteration in that respect taken place, I should certainly have acknowledged it long since, or at whatsoever time the change had happened, and should not have waited for the present call upon me to return you my thanks at the same time for the letter and for the book which you have been so kind as to send me. Mr. Johnson has read it to me. If it afforded me any amusement, or suggested to me any reflections, they were only such as served to embitter, if possible, still more the present moment by a sad retrospect to those days when I thought myself secure of an eternity to be spent with the spirits of such men as He whose life afforded the subject of it. But I was little aware of what I had to expect, and that a storm was at hand which in one terrible moment would darken, and in another still more terrible blot out, that prospect for ever.

Adieu! dear sir, whom in those days I called dear friend with feelings that justified the appellation.—I remain, yours, WM. COWPER.

THE END.

*Printed by* R. & R. CLARK, *Edinburgh.*

www.ingramcontent.com/pod-product-compliance
Lightning Source LLC
Chambersburg PA
CBHW031858220426
43663CB00006B/676